# TELL THEM WHAT YOU KNOW

## Katy's Story

by Patty Reel

*For Amy and Lenny*
"My greatest allies in life"

ISBN: 9798443925448
Library of Congress Control Number 2022907869

First paperback edition printed April, 2022

Edited by: Rachel Lam, Ph.D
Book Layout and Design: Dallas Ryan
Cover Design: Bob Ryan
All photographs used by permission

# Contents

# Forward

Many voices were brought together in this book to tell Katy's story, including her own. Katy had found her heart's home among distressed children and families in a Phoenix barrio. Her loving care graced everyone she encountered, her smile infectious. A few days before her 26th birthday she was suddenly faced with her own battle. The following nine months and two days were arduous and intense, but Katy's steadfast trust in God's love helped carry her family and friends through those terribly difficult days.

This telling explores what led to her remarkable attitude during that difficult time. How did a child who liked climbing trees, roller skating, making gingerbread houses, and reading new books become someone who "made a huge impact" on a community 1800 miles from home, and whose face "radiates the love of Jesus"? The amazing journey that Katy traveled after leaving home for college would not have been possible without the journey of her earlier years. The question became, "What happened in her youth that formed that attitude?"

Katy pursued the path offered to her by the God she loved from an early age, one step at a time. She persevered through many challenges, always trying to find God's best for her life. She felt that the only way she could repay how extraordinarily she had been blessed was to joyfully offer herself to His service. In doing that she touched a multitude of lives.

In short, this narrative seeks to highlight the transforming love of God. It shows how the response of someone who understood how much He loved her, and wanted to share that knowledge, could impact the world around her.

—Patty Reel, Katy's mother

# Part One

*The Promise Was:*
*When Everything Fell We'd Be Held*

## 2005

# Chapter 1
## *A Frightening Phone Call*

We rushed into the hospital room, frantic to see her. Katy spied us as we squeezed our way through the crowd of friends surrounding her bed. She looked right at me and said, "I'm so sorry you're going to have to go through this." Typical of Katy, concerned about other people and not herself.

A phone call the night before, sometime after midnight, had brought the news all parents dread: our 25 year old daughter, living in Phoenix 1800 miles from home, had been taken to the ER with a terrible, unrelenting headache and numbness on her right side. I tried to make sense of what I was hearing while I scribbled notes on the pages of a book and beat my fist on Rick with my other hand. "Abnormality on brain… tumor… bleeding a little… MRI tomorrow… neurosurgeon… numbness on right arm comes and goes… room 723."

Kit Danley, who was not only Katy's boss but her best friend Heather's mother, had called with the devastating news. Trying to comprehend the incomprehensible I sputtered, "We should come?"

"Yes."

"Right away?"

"Yes."

Kit gave us her phone numbers and assured us that Heather would stay with Katy all night, and that Katy was getting some relief from pain.

I told Rick, Katy's dad, what Kit had said. Then I called Lenny, our son and Katy's younger brother, and asked him to come home right away. Of course, he asked why I needed him in the middle of the night. I didn't want to say those words over the phone, but he insisted. I told him what I had just heard about Katy, and he was there in a few minutes. As he hugged me, I started to cry. Then I caught myself, took a deep breath and resolved to get to Phoenix as fast as possible. Lenny got us the last two seats on the earliest possible flight while we threw things into suitcases. He found another ticket for himself that would get him to Phoenix a little later that morning.

I dreaded calling our other daughter, Amy, our youngest, who was studying art in Rome, Italy. This was such devastating news to share on a long-distance phone call. But I knew I had to. Amy was shocked and wanted to come right away. I tried to get her to wait until we knew more details about Katy's condition, but she determinedly started searching for flights to Phoenix.

Wanting prayer, I called Dot, a friend who lived nearby. She called back 15 minutes later and said, "I'm in your driveway." The first glimpse of God's grace in this.

As soon as we were packed, Lenny drove us to the airport. We were sitting on the floor in front of the ticket counter at 5:00 a.m., when it opened. I called people I thought would be up that early to pray for Katy. Everyone was shocked. I heard, "Not our Katy!" over and over.

As we waited anxiously for our plane, I started thinking about Kit's phone call. A brain tumor? How can that possibly be true? We were just there with Katy three weeks ago. We had visited her classroom and watched her with the sweet little Head Start preschool children.[1] She had taken us to a concert for my birthday. I didn't notice anything wrong then. Although when I looked back, I did remember a few things she had done that were odd. When she was driving, she would wait much longer than necessary at a stop sign before entering an intersection. I wondered why. I also noticed she had a lot of trouble finding an address. She had never had a good sense of direction, so I wasn't too concerned. Also, Katy should have renewed her passport several weeks before to visit Amy, but she hadn't done it. That was unlike her; usually she was very responsible and efficient. Each of these instances were a little unusual for Katy, but surely they were not symptoms of something as serious as a brain tumor.

Katy and I had always had a close connection. We could somehow sense when the other one was troubled, even if we were far apart. Katy once wrote on a birthday card she sent me, "What do you say to someone anyway, who can read your mind and shares your heart?" The week before that fateful phone call, I had a gnawing feeling that something was wrong. I called her several times. There was no answer. She didn't return my messages for several days. When she did, she sounded so weak I thought about going to Phoenix. The only reason I didn't was that Kit was coming over to help her with what we all thought were migraines. Katy had had a couple of migraines when she was in middle school, so that seemed the likely culprit for the awful pain in her head. Kit deals with her own migraines, so she would know better what to do. No one suspected anything this drastic.

It's difficult to express the urgency I felt to get to Katy. The flight seemed interminable. The line to get the rental car moved in slow motion. Trying to find Good Samaritan Hospital, in a city we didn't know, was so frustrating.[2] Where do you park? Where is an elevator? Where is the neuro unit? Where is Katy? "I have to get to her..." was racing through my mind.

At last, we were in her room. There were so many people around her bed, people I recognized and had been with just a few weeks ago. Her friends had gathered the night before for a surprise birthday party that obviously didn't happen. Katy's "I'm so sorry," her apology for what we would have to go through, nearly broke my heart.

Katy was moved to a private room and attended to by nurses, neurosurgeons, oncologists, radiation oncologists, physical and occupational therapists, anesthesiologists and other medical personnel. The neurosurgeon, Dr. Byron H. Willis, kindly, but honestly reported on the MRI taken that morning: the mass was probably brain cancer. They would need to do a resection and open biopsy at the same time under general anesthetic using computer guidance. They were going to take out as much as they safely could and treat the rest. The mass was one inch deep in her brain and about six centimeters long. It was in the left parietal lobe affecting coordination and sensation on the right side of her body. It was pushing against the motor strip, not necessarily invading it. Surgery was scheduled for three days later on Katy's 26th birthday. Katy listened carefully to Dr. Willis. Then she said, "You have a horrible job. I'm so sorry you had to tell me that." He started to reply, "Well, I…" then caught himself. "I'm so sorry you had to hear that news."

Surgery in three days? I was numb but trying desperately to grasp what was happening. My knowledge of medical terminology, much less of the implications of a diagnosis of brain cancer, was negligible. I tried to comprehend it, but this was my daughter, my first-born. Katy was the one who took care of everyone God put in her path: school children, friends, siblings and other family members, even strangers she happened across. I tried to process everything, but it was difficult to accept how critical her situation was. It had happened so suddenly and was so traumatic that it was hard to believe.

A friend of Kit's, who was the Director of ICU, came into Katy's room to offer to care for her after surgery, and also to affirm the giftedness of her neurosurgeon. "If my brother or sister were here,

I would call Dr. Willis." The Chief Medical Officer of the hospital echoed the same opinion when he came by to offer his support. In such overwhelming and terrifying circumstances, these felt like miraculous confirmations.

Katy's journey to Phoenix had been unique. After she graduated from Biola University in Los Angeles, she taught first grade in Whittier, California for two years.[3] She then moved to Arizona in 2002 to join Neighborhood Ministries (NM) and help launch their Head Start classroom.[4] NM was the organization founded and run by Kit. It was a holistic ministry that served urban families in poverty. Katy had interned at NM the summer after her freshman year in college and felt God's call to return to the families and children she had grown so close to there. Neighborhood Ministries fit well with Katy's passionate desire to serve God by working with children in need, especially those of a different culture. In addition to working with Head Start, she also became involved with and co-led *Moms Place*, NM's program that supported young mothers.

Phoenix was a long way from Indiana, but Biola University in Los Angeles was even farther. It had been hard to have Katy be that far away, but I had always encouraged her to follow where God led her; to become who He was making her to be. I met Kit Danley and her husband, Wayne, when they moved their daughter, Heather, into the same dorm room with Katy the girls' freshman year. Katy raved about the work NM was doing after her summer in Phoenix as an intern, so I was comfortable having her move there. She became part of a close group of friends and built enduring relationships with Kit and Wayne and many of her colleagues.

Like us, everyone there was terribly shocked at what was happening to Katy. Chris Sommers, the Information Technology Specialist at NM, initiated a blog for Katy, www.katyreel.blogspot.com. Kit wrote the first entry the day after Katy was admitted to the hospital to provide information about Katy's illness and to ask for prayer. Soon the blog was being read by people around the world, and they were responding with prayers, love, and encouragement. As she was able, Katy wrote entries herself praising God for His faithfulness, thanking everyone for their prayers and support, and describing her experiences. It was the perfect way for her to connect with friends, family and other supporters in her community and beyond. The blog gave all of us a glimpse of her trusting, loving and joyful attitude, even when she was tired or in pain. Kit wrote most of the blogs, and I added a few here and there.

April 1, 2005 was the day Katy was taken to the ER at Good Samaritan hospital. April 6 was the day she was scheduled to have a large mass surgically removed from her brain. Kit wrote the first entry in the blog:

> *I have one request, dear friends: Pray for Katy. Pray strenuously with and for her—to God the Father, through the power of our Master Jesus, through the love of the Spirit.*
>
> • *Please pray about this tumor, that it would be demolished, destroyed, completely removed.*
>
> • *Pray for Katy, that her journey through this terrible disturbance would be one where Jesus is alive in every dimension giving her peace.*
>
> • *Pray for all the medical personnel, particularly her neurosurgeons, that they would be beyond their best for her in giving care.*
>
> • *Pray for the work she has so much responsibility for.*
>
> *And would you pray for us.*
>
> • *For our fragile "family", the body of Christ here at the Neighborhood Center and Neighborhood Ministries who love Katy dearly and carry this suffering in its fragility.*

*For rest, for love exchanged everywhere, for faith, for conviction that Jesus can be glorified in these troubles!*

*Will you let me know that you are praying so that I can tell her?*

*We love you and treasure your bearing us up.*

*—Kit Danley*

One of the first responses on the blog told me how God was caring for Katy in the midst of her pain:

*Dr. Willis has exceptional skill, rare talent. Before this month his practice wasn't on call for Good Sam on the first weekend of each month and the surgeons in his practice had switched calls with each other only last month. I do not believe that this was mere coincidence. I don't believe your care is in the hands of any doctor, but in His. I will pray that His hands guide Dr. Willis and bring you a speedy recovery. Much love,*

*—Alma Alonzo*

The next day, Dr. Barry Kriegseld, an associate of Dr. Willis, gave his assessment. "We're going to make this better. The lesion could be an abscess or growing tumor. On the MRI it looks like a tumor." That statement gave me the tiniest hope that this wasn't a horrific crisis. Maybe it was just an abscess. I saw Dr. Willis in the hall and asked him. "You're sure of what she has, aren't you?"

"Yes."

"How long do we have?"

"Maybe 18 months."

"How can I tell her father that?" I asked as the feeling of devastation gripped me again.

"Maybe you don't have to, yet. Let him have this time before the surgery."

I decided that was what I would do. I called Scott Reitano, a friend of Rick's who had offered to come, and asked him to be here with Rick.

The nurses brought in a cot for me. When everyone else had left, a tear ran down Katy's cheek. After scolding me for not crying enough (I was desperately trying not to let her see how scared I was) she said, "I'm just processing. I don't know what is going to happen to my body, but I know God and I trust His character and I'm at peace." That attitude never changed throughout her illness. Katy's steadfast love for Jesus and belief that He wanted only His best for her set the tone for those next nine months. Whatever medical news came to light, no matter how discouraging, was "just another piece of the puzzle."

Katy's room soon filled with balloons, flowers, banners, get-well cards, and visitors from Phoenix, LA, and Indianapolis. Amy was still trying to get a flight out of Rome, but Lenny was there, always keeping watch by her side, protecting, listening. Three close siblings that shared an exceptional bond and were always looking out for each other.

Word of Katy's brain tumor spread like wildfire, and people responded with encouraging messages on the blog:

> *...despite the tragedy and shock of the news we've all been dealing with since Sunday, God has used this; your situation and you, Katy, are causing this immeasurable explosion of love and prayer, spreading at a furious rate throughout our community. It's insane. It's beautiful. God's will and His reasons may often be difficult to understand, but the results are always the same: Love.*
>
> *If the spirit of love and prayer were physically visible, there would be a fantastic, radiant glow over Phoenix right now.*
>
> *We love you Katy.*
>
> *—Mike Plaster*

Katy was part of a remarkable community in inner city Phoenix at NM, made of a close-knit group of young adults who worked and

*Amy, Lenny & Katy*

worshiped there in the barrio, living among the people they loved, served, learned from, and generally "did life with." God had woven a rich tapestry from the divergent cultures and economic classes that were found there. Katy had intentionally immersed herself in this community. She moved into the barrio, where she could get to know the little preschoolers and their families. She wanted to shop at the same grocery store and run into them in the vegetable aisle, to worship in the same space, to experience their difficulties and challenges of living in the inner city.

That was why she had moved into the neighborhood—to be a part of it. She became friends with her neighbors; she openly shared her life with them because that was who she was. If a parent needed a place for their child to go before school, she could take him to Katy's. Katy's Head Start co-teacher, Ericka, shared this years later:

*She put in all the hard work. She showed up at parties, took kids for haircuts, let them sleep at her house if needed, and took them to school. She was even the contact person on kids' emergency cards. Once she went to a restaurant to buy dinner for a family when she found out their money had been stolen. She worked hard to write a reference letter for a man who was marginalized, unseen. This was the community she came to be a part of. There was something important in how she related to the community as a whole. There was a sense of the way that Katy communally lived; she also allowed others to impact her. That example changed people.*

Heather also confirmed Katy's insistence in joining this community, building relationships and loving the people that were a part of it. She wasn't merely "helping" it; she was a member.

*She was loved from the minute she got there. Her innate ability to make people feel seen and loved by her won people's hearts. She had a unique ability to enter into people's lives, even people who didn't usually trust anyone because of the hard life they had led. People just knew they could trust her right away. She was always so full of grace for everyone, even difficult people, no matter where they were at.*

*She also showed up in the community in practical ways for people; some of that started the summer we did our internships together, but it was more about who she was than what she did that made her so special. She had a grace about her. It shouldn't be that hard, but it is really unique to find somebody who can make others feel loved and seen for who they are without having expectations for them.*

*Our community doesn't trust easily, but they had only open arms for her. It was like she had always been there. She just became a part of so many families. That's why there are so many Katys.[5]*

*That's who God made her to be and she was faithful to His plan.*
*She didn't ever fight Him and she had a lot of hard things. Her*
*first year of teaching in California was so, so hard, with many*
*extremely challenging children.[6] I've never seen any teacher*
*work so hard. She took that same 'give it 200%' mentality to*
*Neighborhood Ministries. There was no precedent for waking kids*
*up, getting them to the bus, which was what Ericka and Katy often*
*did, especially at the beginning. They didn't do it in a shaming way.*
*They were so impactful with the kids and knew they also had to*
*care for the parents, not in a "look at me, I have so much to teach*
*you" way, but by coming alongside, doing life with you because I*
*love you and your life has value.*

Now, these same people were there for Katy, giving back. Decorating her hospital room with crepe-paper flowers and posters, writing messages in her guest book and on the blog; helping and loving. So many of them came faithfully to the hospital to comfort, encourage and support Katy and us.

The word quickly went out from Phoenix. Soon people were traveling there to be with Katy. Two close high school friends, Katie and Anne, flew in from Indiana. Kristen Kinard, who had taught with Katy in California, took time off from work and hurried to Phoenix. Katy's youth director, Dan Rexroth, now director of a neuropsychology clinic, came armed with information about parietal lobe functions and our tax papers that needed to be mailed soon. Support was coming from near and far.

As the news spread, Katy heard from a former student in California, who knew Katy when she was only a first grader:

*When I heard you had a brain tumor I was very sad. I still*
*remember how nice you were to me. You are a very special teacher.*
*May God's love always be with you.*

A teacher colleague that she had spent those two years with wrote in:

21

*In the midst of hard times (whether it is Sam[7] putting glue in his nose or a brain tumor) God wants us to come to Him. Katy, I admire you in so many ways… your heart for people, your passion for the Lord, your calm spirit, your wisdom, and your desire to share Christ.*

Many notes on the blog were anonymous:

*It sure doesn't seem fair that such a wonderful, good person like you would have this tumor, BUT—you are spreading God's love in an incredible way and are such an inspiration to me! You have that special something—I know now that it's God's love shining through you in all you do in your life.*

There was encouragement from her preschoolers' moms:

*There is not a moment that my kids and I don't think and pray for you. Never forget you are a major part in our lives. You're in our prayers.*

The team of professionals she worked with shared:

*… your spirit speaks of strength, courage and grace under fire…*

◆

*… your heart speaks of care and sacrifice for others and joy for what God is doing through you and around you.*

◆

*…You are a very bright light … your connection to God inspires me.*

At the time, the concept of a blog was new to me, and I was amazed by the effect it had. Kit captured these wondrous results in one of her posts:

*We have all had the privilege to be used by God to honor Katy for her service once she became sick. The blog is filled with her testimony and it has gone out throughout the world. If we knew everything that has been said about her, everything that has been testified about her, and the fruit it is all bearing, we would be overwhelmed with it. And yet, all we wanted to tell her was how we loved her and cherished her in our midst and suffered with her in this sickness. And true to her nature, she encouraged us, comforted us, instructed us.*

Katy, being Katy, used the blog to help her family, friends and community process her tragedy. The entries she wrote radiated with her trust in God's plan for her, her resolute faith in His goodness and love, and the peace and wisdom she exemplified throughout her sickness. And she was only 25.

For me, the blog brought comfort when nothing else could. When I didn't know what else to do to get relief from the ever-present tension, I would read those loving messages and could sense my stress easing a bit. Their caring seemed like God's comforting touch.

In addition to the blog, Kit brought a guest book to the hospital for visitors to write messages to Katy. These visitors who had gathered from many pages of her life shared what she meant to them. The notes they wrote affirmed that God loved her, their certainty that He would heal her and how much they loved her.

As the surgery date approached, Kit questioned Dr. Willis, "We're praying people. What specifically should we pray for?" He paused thoughtfully, then responded, "that we don't touch the Corpus Callosum," and other specifics. I doubt that he was often asked that question. Just before surgery, Kit entered the following post:

*I want to pray with all of you for a minute. I am hearing us cry out to God for our dear friend and loved one, Katy.*

*Lord, I have been so surprised by the capacity you have given Katy to not only give love but to receive it. You would think that people who are really good at loving others might not be used to being the one being loved. Well, today was a love firehose and Katy attempted to drink from it. And did a pretty good job.*

That sentiment was echoed in a note written by Dianne Johnson, one of Katy's roommates:

*Since I lived with Katy, I've seen many presents that people have given her, and in all the time that I've known her, I've never seen her scoff at a gift. If anyone ever brought her something that was not quite her style, not quite something she would have gotten herself, she graciously received the gift. She'd wear it, display it, or use it, whatever it was. This might seem like a small thing in the face of all her other qualities, but I feel like it's such a profound gesture, she really saw a person's heart in the gifts they gave her, and she accepted our love by taking our gifts. She accepted what we gave her because she knew we desperately wanted to give her our hearts, even if we could only fumble forward with yet another stuffed animal. I really appreciate how she accepted my love and made me feel good about how I loved her.*

Continuing Kit's post…

*Lord, when that Head Start mom came in today, to Katy's room it almost took my breath away. I know this mom. Her hard, rocky life has kept her from being able to take care of those You have placed in her hands. She is a broken lady, desperate, poor and most of the time emotionless. Yet today, she stood outside that door. Who knows how she got to the hospital as she rarely had transportation. Who knows how she knew which hospital. Did she know Katy's last name? Somehow, she found Katy's room and peered in past the layers of people who had come to visit and stood shaking. Shaking not for the nervousness of the crowd, but for sadness for Katy. She shook because she hates that Katy has a tumor and somehow the terribleness of this injustice rose above all her own injustices and out of sheer love found a way to get to the hospital to say, "the angels will be there protecting you," in Spanish. And that was it. She shook and tears came out and she reached out and it felt like love, God's love, to anyone observing it. Katy's face was radiant. She didn't miss it; she didn't miss the love God had sent in the form of this woman.*

My memories of those first days in the hospital are blurred with scenes of a multitude of visitors including the City of Phoenix Head Start officials sitting quietly talking to each other while the moms of her preschoolers decorated the room for Katy's birthday; her friends coming from Phoenix, California and Indianapolis, so anxious to see her.

I remember the NM elders praying around her bed and Lenny and Rick watching each therapist, doctor and nurse carefully as they evaluated Katy's condition, trying to grasp how this tumor had affected her. Heather, Dallas (Heather's husband), Kit and Wayne, as well as other NM colleagues and friends, came almost every day. Dianne and Jana, Katy's roommates, brought her toothbrush, other toiletries and changes of clothes when they could sneak away from their jobs. It was heartening to watch Katy's friends entertain her with old jokes and funny stories. I watched Turtle, the uncle of some of her preschoolers, walk down the hall to Katy's room carrying a large stuffed animal and an armful of flowers. The word that kept coming to my mind to describe what was happening was "outrageous." A healthy 25-year-old with a brain tumor is outrageous. But the outpouring of love I was witnessing was astonishing.

The afternoon before her scheduled surgery, Katy asked to have legal papers drawn up to appoint a Health Care Power of Attorney and donate her organs, just in case. That request caught me off guard. It was so sobering. And scary. Of course, Katy wanted to donate her organs. Again, Katy being Katy. But it was late in the day and we had to wait while hospital personnel found someone who was qualified to do that.

What she didn't know was that NM was throwing her a birthday party downstairs in the healing garden. Finally, the hospital attorney came with the appropriate papers; they were signed and witnessed and we whisked Katy downstairs in a wheelchair to "get some air." Was she surprised! Kit's blog entry described it well:

> And then the party. Wow, what a birthday! The flood gates opened and there it was: this huge birthday party, outside in a lovely garden, which could have been, for one night, mistaken for a restaurant or resort crowded for a wedding reception. We were a hundred people or so, all with our sticky white hole reinforcements to match the fiducials, those small round electronic components that have been glued to her face, that somehow will tell the computer tomorrow how to locate the parts of the brain that matter. A friend arranged for a mariachi band. The children of the ministry made cards to give her, hundreds of expressions of love. There were sodas and food and the birthday cakes baked by the kids at Kids Life and presents and more flowers and balloons. So much love! She received it and looked into the face of everyone loving her and loved them back. It was her birthday party, but it was also her "we love you" party because of tomorrow's surgery. Lord, you were present in all of this. It was obvious, she didn't miss it.

> Right in the middle of this beauty, you brought Amy to Katy all the way from Rome. Thank you for the speedy trip, the escort through customs by airport security in Newark that was only and just for her, and her safe landing. Thank you for this family who finally get to be together in this!

The nurses brought in another cot for Amy. Getting out of Rome,

clogged with mourners for the Pope who had just died, must have been harrowing for a sister who was in shock and desperately trying to get to Katy. She had rolled up her canvases and tied them to her carry-on luggage and dragged her suitcase to the train that took her to the airport. Thankful for the escort in Newark arranged by her friend's dad with the Port Authority, she arrived in Phoenix without any American money or working cell phone. She finally saw Lenny who had left the party to pick her up and take her to her big sister. From that moment on, she was rarely away from Katy's side.

Kit's blog post ended with this prayer:

> *Lord, rescue Katy tomorrow. For you O Lord are good. We know you are hearing us, hearing her. We know Lord you are near. This brain tumor is a terrible thing, please deliver Katy from it. Lord, redeem everything awful in this situation, we run to you for refuge.*

April 6—her birthday: As Katy was wheeled out of her room to surgery, I overheard one of her nurses lamenting, "It's not fair," through her tears. Another rock thrown at the armor I had put on to protect myself from this reality. During the surgery I purposefully didn't think about what the neurosurgeon was doing to my daughter, I just prayed that God would heal her. The waiting room was crowded with friends and family. Rick's cousin Frank from Indianapolis appeared saying, "I was just in the neighborhood." No one noticed the sign that stated visitors were limited to six people per patient.

During the surgery, Rick and I went to the chapel to pray and found some of the paper hole reinforcements everyone had worn at the party scattered on the floor. People had been praying there last night. An affirmation of God's care. Waiting for the elevator to return to the surgery floor, Scott Reitano stepped behind Rick and said, "This is the first time I've seen Rick Reel in anything other than a three-piece suit or running shorts." Totally surprised, Rick whirled around and hugged Scott, relieved to have such a close friend there with him.

Years later, I looked back at the blog and the notes that were written to Katy during these tumultuous few days. Some of the messages showed such unequivocal evidence of God's work in Katy and in the circumstances surrounding her:

> *I know this is scary and hard but you have so many friends, family, and loved ones here for you. Lean on us when things get scary and of course lean on God, He loves you so much and He will keep you safe. I trust that.*

◆

> *I see God in your face—God is with you through it all.*

◆

> *I pray for you to rest in the love and care of our Father as He takes care of everything.*

◆

> *Heal her body and give her your strength and peace. You are a good God… make that real for us. Thank you Jesus.*

◆

> *I now have more faith and trust in Him than ever and I have no fear at all and pray all the time that you won't either!*

An elder from NM named Isaiah Oakes shared a particularly poignant message. To this day he and his family remain our dear friends:

> *Sometimes it's not easy to understand why such things happen in our lives, especially at such a young age. But it's in these hard times and times of wonder when God reveals to us His power and strength and His "I AMness." The Lord will show you, Katy, His greatness and wonderfulness and His special special special love for you. The Lord has "chosen you" for a special journey that only He and you will walk in the very deep and close times of intimacy. We will walk with you in our prayers and love. Remember Katy, He has a wonderful plan for you and it is through these times that He reveals this to you, His loving and precious child. Katy, we love you and Jesus will hold you tight.*

Katy's demeanor in this precarious situation was a testament to her faith, and it affected the faith of others. During those pre-surgery days people wrote messages of hope and victory, love and compassion, and belief in God's power to heal:

> *You are an incredible woman and I am so absolutely serious when I say your face radiates with the love of Jesus. It glows and shines. It's incredible and a gift of God. You are a gift of God, your life a gift to Him.*

◆

> *I really feel a peace about you in this because God is using you to change our community and teaching us so much.*

◆

> *You've made a huge impact on us all. This is where your faith and Love for The LORD and Trust will really come into play. God will take care of you in his loving, comforting hands throughout*

*this whole ordeal.*

As we were waiting, a nurse from the neuro floor came to ask us to remove Katy's things from her room because they needed it for another patient and Katy would go to ICU from surgery. I looked around at the crowd and asked Kristen, her teacher friend from LA, to handle that. I knew she was resourceful. It wasn't long before Kristen returned with a wheelchair loaded with the flowers, posters, signs, boxes of chocolates and books that had been given to Katy.

In time, Dr. Willis came out to report on the surgery. "It went well. We got all of the tumor out that was grossly evident, about 95%, and didn't hit any scary parts. She is moving everything okay. Right side movements are okay. It did not invade the part of her brain that controls motor functions, so she will probably not require a great deal of rehabilitation." Such a beautiful answer to prayer!

But there was hard news. It was a very malignant tumor, called a high-grade glioma.[8] The final biopsy results would be back in a few days to a week. Katy would need further treatment: chemotherapy and radiation. This kind of tumor sends microscopic tendrils into the brain, cell-like structures that always cause the tumor to regrow. This kind of tumor was not curable. His words confirmed my worst fears. Not curable. The pad I was scribbling notes on slipped from my hand and fell to the floor. I was devastated.

When Rick, Amy, Lenny and I were allowed to see her in the recovery room, her head was wrapped, but she was smiling. She looked me in the eye and said, "Mom, God is good!" I replied, "You're right," and patted her arm. Katy grabbed me and repeated insistently, "Are you listening to me? God is good!" Katy's first words after surgery.

The nurse returned to the waiting room. "Who's here to see Katy?" About 35 people stood up expectantly. She warned, "No crying, it will give her a headache," and let everyone who had been waiting file past Katy's bed to say, "Happy Birthday."

Katy was moved to an ICU room. Heather stayed with her overnight so Amy and I could get some rest. When they were alone, she told Katy what Dr. Willis had said. They cried together.

Part One's title comes from a song called "Held" by Christa Wells.

1. Head Start is a program of the United States Department of Health and Human Services that provides comprehensive early childhood education, health, nutrition and parent involvement services for low-income children and families. The program services and resources are designed to foster stable family relationships, enhance children's physical and emotional well being, and establish an environment to develop strong cognitive skills.

2. Good Samaritan Hospital became University Medical Center of Phoenix.

3. Biola University is a private Christian college in La Mirada, California. Over 6000 students are enrolled in the 150 academic programs in nine schools at bachelor's through doctoral levels. Their mission is biblically-centered education, scholarship and service—equipping men and women in mind and character to impact the world for the Lord Jesus Christ.

4. Neighborhood Ministries (NM) began in 1982 as a small, church-based food and clothing bank trying to reach urban distressed families stuck in the cycle of poverty. Starting with building relationships with kids in a park, it has grown to become a comprehensive, holistic ministry that combines community development with church planting targeting vulnerable, at-risk children, youth and families. NM now serves about 1000 people (young and old) weekly, on their eight-acre campus with 29 various programs.

5. I know of five babies that have been named after Katy.

6. When I visited Katy's classroom in her first year of teaching in California, her principal apologized to me for the exceptionally difficult class Katy had been assigned.

7. Name changed.

8. Gliomas are tumors that arise from the supportive tissue of the brain and spinal cord and are often malignant.

# Chapter 2
## *Moving Life to Arizona*

*All the "blow-me-away" one-liners belong to Katy today! I'll try and help you picture it... do your best, because it is a little unusual!*

*She is in her intensive care bed with her head wrapped in gauze. She is fully alert, arms and legs working well, with the right side maybe even a little stronger than before her dad said. And talking with so much energy that once we said she might be too loud for the other intensive care patients!* "Oh, these past few days have been the best days of my life!" *What in the world... you have to know that what she is talking about are the miracles. The miracles of the outpouring of love from everywhere.* "I don't deserve this," *she says with a winsome smile. The miracles of people from her many stages and seasons of life coming, calling, sending messages (these blogs), visiting, traveling to Phoenix from here and there. The miracles of the message of her situation being told to strangers and those strangers sending her a message of their commitment to pray. "We were forwarded the email about you and we do not know you personally, but know you are in our prayers in Tashkent, Uzbekistan and we have passed this on to our friends here and elsewhere around the world." The miracles of the changes that are happening to people because of her brain tumor. "I thought this would make me angry and separate me from God, but instead—it has brought me closer and now I love and trust Him—and just wait for his plan for you."*

"It takes a brain tumor, sometimes," *she will often be quoted from now on. The miracles unseen, for we know that there are all kinds of things that haven't been exposed yet. The miracles of the message that is going out from her life, to... well, just about everywhere.*

*(blog entry from Kit)*

Where should Katy do her treatments? In Indianapolis or in Phoenix? While Katy recuperated, Rick, Lenny, Amy and I regrouped in the hospital cafeteria to figure it out. We invited Scott Reitano to facilitate as an impartial voice. He affirmed Amy's statement, "She *is* home." So it was decided. She would have her treatments in Phoenix. We would all stay there to help, the five of us together for the first time in eight years. It felt like a good solution. Phoenix was Katy's home. She was happy there with her group of friends and work that gave her purpose. Besides, we were beginning to become familiar with the physicians who specialized in neuro-oncology. We didn't know any specialists in that field in Indianapolis. Next, we needed to find a place to live, close to Katy and close to the hospital. Kit sent the word out: who could help us find a place to stay? Before we even started to look, Katy's roommates, Dianne and Jana, came up with their own solution. They offered to move out so we could live with Katy in the house they all rented. Such a generous, loving act. They relocated not far away to a tiny apartment that didn't seem at all safe to us. I worried about them but was so touched by their sacrifice. For the time being, our life moved to Phoenix.

Katy was released from the hospital and went home on April 8th, two days after surgery. The next day Katy had a headache that Percocet couldn't touch. I was terribly concerned about what was causing this dreadful headache and felt at a loss about how to treat the pain. I converted to problem-solving mode and remained there for the duration of Katy's illness. Problem solving, not processing, became my principle task and took most of my time and most of my energy. I contacted her doctor who reasoned, "We reduced the Decadron (a steroid) too quickly and that caused her brain to swell." He then outlined a dosage timetable to control the swelling until her treatment started. So I began what became the complicated task of managing Katy's many medications. During her illness Katy took four different anticonvulsants, steroids to reduce swelling in her brain, ulcer preventatives, five different pain medications, pills to control her nausea, two different chemotherapy medicines, two different sleep aides, an antibiotic and more, most of which I administered. Something else to distract me from our reality.

The medical parts of her illness (surgeries, radiation, chemotherapy, multiple allergic reactions, contradictory prognoses, treatment plans, etc.) were so difficult and would have been impossible to bear if it weren't for God's comfort-giving presence in those times of unknowing. His faithful followers in Phoenix, Indianapolis, California, and indeed, it seemed the whole world, sustained us. Heather, who worked as an oncology nurse at Good Samaritan Hospital, was Katy's devoted advocate. We relied on her medical knowledge and nursing experience. She would often accompany us to doctor's appointments and help explain what was said. So many friends persistently stuck by Katy. And of course, Amy and Lenny had rushed to be by her side. They relocated their lives (Amy from Rome and Lenny from Indianapolis) to become her constant caretakers and companions. This,

and Katy's steadfast love for Jesus and belief that He wanted only His best for her, set the tone for those months.

People we barely knew donated mattresses and other furniture, repaired the air conditioner, replaced broken plumbing, brought meals and stopped by to visit with Rick's favorite frozen fruit popsicles (they appeared in the fridge almost weekly). The mom of one of Katy's students who lived nearby walked around the corner to deliver tamales she had made just for Katy. Kathleen and Tom Boltz, the parents of Katy's Head Start co-teacher, Ericka, delivered meals every week for months, bringing so much food that I would invite the neighbors to "come on over and bring a fork, Kathleen has been here." Dianne, Katy's roommate, bought hooks and blinds to create a studio in the back of the kitchen where Amy could paint. A friend hosted a lovely afternoon tea for Katy and her friends. Another invited us to his private box at the Diamondback's baseball stadium to watch a game.

I was numb and trying to figure out how to navigate all this. But I was also getting to know Katy's friends and getting a greater glimpse of her Phoenix world. I had missed Katy so much in the eight years she had been gone: four years as a student at Biola University, two years teaching first grade in Whittier, California, then two years at Neighborhood Ministries. Several times during those years I had suddenly been overcome with an intense longing for Katy, seemingly out of the blue. Amy had had similar experiences; we called them "Katy moments." Now, being there with her helped fill the void I had felt for those years. I felt blessed to be able to see Katy in the community she loved deeply and who loved her. I was so impressed by her network of peers who continually encouraged her.

Katy's initial recovery from surgery was amazing. It seemed to me that the only challenge for her at first was difficulty typing. Lenny helped her write her first blog entry on April 11th:

Dear Friends and Family,

> I will extol the Lord at all times;
> His praise will always be on my lips.
> My soul will boast in the Lord;
> Let the afflicted hear and rejoice.
> Glorify the LORD with me;
> Let us exalt his name together.
> I sought the LORD and he answered me;
> He delivered me from all my fears.
> —Psalm 34:1-4

I cannot even count the miracles I have seen in these amazing days that have blessed me beyond anything that I could ever have imagined. It was just a few weeks ago at our board and staff retreat as we were casually talking about our biggest dreams in life, that I mentioned without hesitation my biggest wish would be to have all of my friends and family in one place, to have everyone that I loved to know each other. Miraculously in the last few days friends and family have flown in from all over the country and I have received countless phone calls, emails and blogs. The people that I love dearly are knowing and loving one another.

I received phenomenal care from everyone I encountered at Good Samaritan Hospital (it helps to have a nurse for a best friend). I will look back on my time in the hospital as knowing the presence of God in a more intimate way than I ever have. He gave me such an incredible sense of peace.

I am so thankful to be in my own home in the care of my friends and family.

Thank you so much for your thoughts, prayers, hugs, meals, phone calls, cards, balloons, flowers, and visits. This outpouring of love is incomprehensible. May you know this day how great your Father's love is for you. I will continue to thank God and pray that you know His goodness each day.

I will keep you posted as I begin chemo and radiation late this week or early next week.

All my love!

Katy

When the final pathology report came in, it offered a ray of hope: Anaplastic Oligodendroglioma, Grade III.[1] Still a high grade glioma, but one that responds differently to treatment. This type of tumor was considered rare. Because it was so uncommon, we sought a second opinion from Dr. William Shapiro, a neuro-oncologist at Barrow Neurological Institute. He requested all Katy's medical information for his neuropathologist to make his assessment. Dr. Shapiro agreed that

Katy could have her radiation treatment at Good Sam, if the radiation oncologist used IMRT (Intensity Modulated Radiation Technique). I was encouraged when I discovered that Barrow was a world renowned neurological institute. Katy should get the best care there.

Two days after getting that new diagnosis Katy returned to Good Sam for preliminary work to prepare for her radiation treatments, a process that exhausted Katy, who was just a week past surgery. The radiation oncologist hadn't seen the final pathology. After he read it he announced, "AO is actually curable. There's a 60% chance it wouldn't come back at all. It responds better to treatment. The tendrils of this kind of tumor don't go out as far and therefore are easier to kill with the chemo and radiation. Radiation for it isn't much different. It's usually in children. Pretty rare…" What good news! Maybe there was a chance this would all be behind us someday. I felt relief for the first time since April 1st. Katy immediately sent word through her blog about the good news she had just been told.

Still, his comments conflicted with what Dr. Willis had told us. Is her tumor 60% curable or is it not curable? I didn't know what to think about this striking discrepancy, so I started carefully researching. The information I discovered was discouraging. Survival rates were measured in months. I didn't say anything to Katy or anyone, but somehow Katy always knew. "Have you been on the computer again, Mom?" she would ask me knowingly. I would just smile. We would find out later that the radiation oncologist's remarks unfortunately were inaccurate and misleading. The July 2008 publication of "Current Treatment Options in Neurology" stated that Anaplastic Oligodendroglioma (AO) "is a terminal brain cancer even with maximal therapies." It occurs most often in older men. He was correct in saying that it's rare; only 3% of all brain tumors are AO. His misinformation cruelly gave us false hope.

• • •

It wasn't long before support started arriving from out of town.

Our wonderful friends, Joe and Julie Kukolla, loaded our van with our clothes, Rick's bike and household things we might need and drove it to Phoenix—an 1800 mile trek. My sister Nancy and her husband Don went to Indianapolis to care for my father who had Alzheimer's disease so my mother and sister Judy could come to Phoenix. They were all very concerned about Katy, so sick and living so far from home, but were reassured when they witnessed all the people who were helping. Judy wrote in Katy's guest book before she left, "Now that I've seen your house with the revolving door, I feel more at ease knowing how many loving, caring friends you have." My mom sketched a picture of Katy and explained, "Here's the way I picture you: with an aura of prayers, good thoughts, good wishes and good friends surrounding you, keeping you in their care, and I know you are safe."

Two of Katy's cousins, Ashleigh and Holly, came with similar concerns and left a week later with the same impressions.

> *Hey Katy. It's hard to believe you're not doing well when you look so great. The strength and courage that you show is amazing! Before coming out to visit I found myself often wishing you were back in Indy, but I now see this is home. You have so many great friends here taking care of you and supporting you every step of the way. God has put you in the right place. I love you very much. You will remain in my prayers.*
>
> *Love, Holly*

Another cousin Libet, who was working in South Korea, resigned from her job and came to Phoenix to see Katy soon after. Her upbeat spirit was infectious and cheered all of us while she was visiting.

Those dear friends and relatives were among the first to come to love and support Katy and us. In the time that we stayed there we had 61 out of town visitors that brought homemade soup, encouragement, massages, medical information, a week at a timeshare at a Scottsdale resort, goods to restock the food pantry at NM, and lots of hugs. Often

41

they were housed, fed and transported by people from Neighborhood Ministries. We were so grateful for this outpouring of love. A particularly meaningful visit happened when Rick's Aunt Sue and Uncle Chuck traveled from Los Angeles to see Katy. Aunt Sue was a survivor of Stage IV ovarian cancer. She assured Katy she had inherited "good genes."

We never had to ask for help. Our amazing friends and family even took over our responsibilities at home. Our grass was mowed all summer. Our house was cleaned. Julie helped my parents downsize and organized volunteers to move them into their new home next to our house. Our cars were kept in working order. A neighbor took in our mail until we could get it forwarded to Phoenix. I had been calling on the homebound members of our church, Tabernacle Presbyterian (Tab), as a parish visitor for several years.[2] Now other Tab staff members called on those precious folks for me. Rick's work was covered at his office. Spring flowers were planted along a path in our woods. It would take pages and pages to list everything that was done for us, much of it anonymously. I was deeply moved every time I heard about another kind deed.

Kit shared the support that was gathering worldwide for Katy in the April 15th blog:

> Katy came into the offices of the Neighborhood Center yesterday for what she must have thought would be just a short visit. She came through the downstairs into the area where The Lost Boys of Sudan have their Community Center.[3] They surprised her with their delight; they were seeing her for the first time since hearing of her brain tumor. Oh, she was greeted as if this sister belonged just to them, their sweet loved one who they have been crying out to the Lord for.
>
> What is going on here is more than compassion and concern. It is the Spirit of God knitting hearts together across all sorts of

*boundaries for His purposes. We prayed together, this supernatural gathering of saints. These "lost boys" who have lived through barbarous human indecency now part of this "Katy" rescue operation. This gathering includes a Native American daughter dancing in a jingle dress dance lifting Katy to her Creator for healing, the 350 kids at Monday Nights, a Christian group at ASU, Sandy and Gary from Bosnia, a brother from Scotland, a prayer group in Washington, people in Texas, children who were in Katy's classes in Los Angeles, a fellow worker in inner-city missions with a heart for injustice and the poor, ...deployed overseas... on and on, people interceding for Katy.*

I was there when the Lost Boys of Sudan prayed with Katy. I had goosebumps observing this astounding sight. I will never forget what a privilege it was to see God blessing Katy with this incredible touch of His hand through those young men. I have met people, some years later, who have asked if I am Katy Reel's mother. They wanted to know because they had prayed for her without ever meeting her. God's network.

One Sunday, barely two weeks after Katy's surgery, we went to Church at the Neighborhood Center, NM's Sunday church service. I was worried; it was so soon after the operation that I was afraid the children might unintentionally hurt Katy in their enthusiasm. Evelyn Oakes, wife of Isaiah Oakes, shared a conversation she had with Katy that day. She was also concerned, but Katy told her, "Don't worry. God is protecting me."

On April 18th, Katy found herself at St. Joseph's Hospital for her first appointment with Dr. William Shapiro at Barrows Neurological Institute. This was the second hospital she had been to in two weeks. The neuropathologist there had examined Katy's MRI's and agreed with the pathology report. The fact that it was already anaplastic (fast growing) was significant. Dr. Shapiro marveled that Katy had been walking around with such a large tumor. Radiation would be the first line of defense. The rest of her treatment was discussed but not decided for several months.

Katy asked him about her prognosis. He said, "You're fine. You're going to be fine for a long time. Patients have five to 12 years, some to 18. I'm not saying don't live your life. Get married. Have children." I took Dr. Shapiro's prediction to heart. 18 years! By then there would be a cure. I was counting on that.

However, I didn't know what to think when I talked to two physician friends from home later on. Both of them were fathers of friends of Katy and knew her well. Both of them were very fond of Katy. They had called to ask about her treatments, her progress. Both of them were crying when they spoke to me on the phone. I was confused, but deliberately chose to hang on to Dr. Shapiro's prognosis, 18 years and my plan, by then a cure. I chose to have hope. But still all these differing predictions were unsettling. Not being able to sort out all these conflicts intensified my numbness.

Still, Katy seemed to be doing well. I shared on the blog on April 24th:

> *I wish you could see her. She looks just like herself. Only when she lifts up her hair to show the incision site can you see anything different. She's feeling well; no more headaches! Every once in a while she'll take a short nap, but not every day. She goes for walks, laughs with her friends, greets Head Start friends and their families with hugs and smiles.*
>
> *You should have been here Friday. The Head Start class took a field trip to Teacher Katy's backyard! They have been learning about insects and here they came with little nets and tiny plastic containers with holes punched in the top picking up ladybugs that the teacher was shaking out of a plastic bag when they weren't looking. Katy was happily in the middle of them admiring every discovery.*

*But there's more. She's peaceful and even happy. Katy is thrilled to see friends and family from other pages of her life come here to love her in her Phoenix home.* "It just keeps getting better and better." *We suspect that her peace in the midst of such trying times helps to sustain us all.*

*That and your wonderful, faithful prayers. It seems that God has knit an army together to support Katy and us in prayer. Please know that we can sense your prayers. We are so grateful for them and ask that you would continue to remember us to the Father.*

*What can we say except, "Thank you, thank you."*

*This blog has been a lifeline connecting us to you and allowing us to witness some of the prayers being offered for Katy. When we couldn't do anything else, we would read your responses and were comforted. Thank you Kit, Chris, and each of you who respond and each of you who read about Katy and pray.*

*We are resting in God's sovereignty and grace. We are sustained by His love.*

*Are not two sparrows sold for a penny?*
*Yet not one of them will fall to the ground*
*apart from the will of Your Father.*
*And even the very hairs of your head are all numbered.*
*So don't be afraid;*
*You are worth more than many sparrows.*
*—Matthew 10:29-31*

*There's so much more we want to share. As we are able to find the words, we will. Thank you for loving Katy and lifting her up. You are precious to us.*

*Love,*

*Rick, Patty, Amy and Lenny*

1. Anaplastic Oligodendroglioma is a fast growing, malignant tumor that arises from oligodendrocytes, a type of supportive brain tissue.

2. Tabernacle Presbyterian Church was founded in 1851 in Indianapolis, Indiana. Intentionally located in the center-city, it has always been committed to a balance of evangelical witness from the pulpit and social involvement in the community. Tab's outreach includes many community ministries (a year round recreation program, after school tutoring, serving meals and fellowship to neighbors). Tab also partners with several other local ministries and supports multiple global missions. Tab is the church where Katy was baptized, attended Sunday School, and took part in youth group (including mission trips).

3. The Lost Boys were survivors of the second Sudanese Civil War who were orphaned or separated from their families and trekked enormous distances over unforgiving wilderness seeking refuge from the fighting. They experienced mind-numbing horrors and intense hardship with many dying along the way. In 2001, 550 of the Lost Boys were resettled in Arizona and a community center for them was opened in the same building as the Neighborhood Ministries offices.

# Chapter 3
## *Living with Cancer*

We sought nutritional counseling and discovered Virginia G. Piper Cancer Center. Their oncology dietician was very helpful. She commented on all the support that Katy had; all five of us had gone to the appointment. After the consultation, she handed us a CD with her recommendations. The service was free of charge. I found their first-class library full of resources on cancer. Again, with helpful staff. Again, free of charge. I have used their library on other occasions and gotten the same valuable service.

Katy's radiation treatments began on April 25th and continued for five weeks, every morning at 8:30, Monday through Friday. She wrote a blog entry on May 5th that described those appointments.

Dear Loved Ones,

I wanted you to hear from me directly what this last week and a half has been like. As your prayers have asked, I continued to see many miracles.

Every day my parents escort me to my radiation appointment at 8:30. I sign in and wait for the nurse to call my name. They know me. There are several of us in the waiting room. We all know each other at this point or feel like we do. We are all in various stages of treatment but we share the same appointment time and the same disease. There is a strange camaraderie among us. When they call my name I walk back to a room with a door worthy of being a vault in a different lifetime. I then lay on a narrow table in the middle of this room. It has a clear plastic piece that is rounded to comfortably hold my head and secure my mask. They rubber band my feet together, I suppose to keep me from escaping, and then they attach my mask to the plastic piece. The placement of the mask is the most complicated part of the whole procedure. The nurse and the technician both lean over my head and move the mask this way and that until it is just right (I almost have to laugh as I watch through the tiny holes because often what does the trick is me wiggling my nose or some other such complicated motion.) Once all is set they take refuge behind the door of the "vault" and leave me laying strapped to the table staring up at an illuminated coral reef photograph. For the first week they kept checking to make sure that I was OK, which made me wonder if I should be panicking, but I decided against that because the whole procedure seemed more intriguing than frightening. The machine itself reminds me of those robots from the movie "Batteries Not Included" that went around fixing broken buildings and appliances. It seems to sneak up from the side and think carefully before it makes each move. It makes a loud hum, but it does not hurt as it moves around my head. Before I know it the whole thing is over and I am in the waiting room saying my good-byes.

I don't know what the rest of my treatment will be like, but right now I feel great. I have had a few headaches but they have been treatable with Tylenol.

I still have all of my hair! I sometimes have to remind myself that I just had brain surgery. Thank you for all of your prayers and support. May God continue to bless you, as he is me, thru this experience.

I love you, Katy.

Katy planned to work out at the gym after her treatments, so we all joined LA Fitness and would head there when she was finished. Katy did the elliptical; I tried water aerobics. However, her energy waned after a few days, so that plan was abandoned.

When Katy heard her grandfather, "Frenchy," who was struggling with his own cancer, was scheduled to have an MRI, she called him. He had avoided the medical world for most of his life and was especially concerned about having diagnostic tests, so she knew it would be difficult for him. I overheard their conversation on the phone. "I've had lots of MRI's. You don't need to worry, they don't hurt. The only thing that will be hard for you is that you have to hold perfectly still, but I know you can do it. Just try to hold still. You'll be fine." Such sweet encouragement from a granddaughter. Katy being Katy.

At about this time, Rick and Lenny returned to Indianapolis to be with Frenchy. After several days, Lenny was back in Phoenix, but Rick stayed with his father. It was so difficult for him to divide his time between these very ill loved ones.

It was challenging to navigate those days. Trying to figure out the next step, the next appointment, the next medication or the next meal, while trying to problem-solve the next dilemma—a new symptom or a questionable prescription—left no time or energy to process what was happening. But the nights were even harder, especially when Rick was not there. I was so tired and alone with the thoughts that I was trying to avoid. To be able to relax, I played a CD of familiar hymns and was usually asleep before it finished. One night, I remember waking up suddenly. My arms and legs were stinging. I was covered with tiny biting ants. This was before we had much furniture and I was sleeping on a mattress on the floor. I jumped up flailing my arms and ran into the living room. The exterminator was there the next day. After he sprayed outside, he warned that there were enormous numbers of those ants living underground in the yard. He suggested that I could spray the baseboards with Windex to keep them from coming into my room; they wouldn't go past that. From then on, every night, I painted the baseboards blue with Windex.

Katy had incredible help from her friends, but Rick and I were also supported by our own "angels," both new acquaintances and people we'd known a long time. One of my friends had also walked this path with her daughter who had a difficult cancer diagnosis. Maureen's advice was, "As her mother you always have to believe she's going to be all right. You cannot accept anything else. Your job is to have hope." That mantra helped to guide me in difficult times, but the underlying wariness was always there, weighing me down.

Leigh, a friend I've had since 4th grade, and her husband flew in from Sugar Land, Texas, bike in tow. As John and Rick raced down South Mountain, Leigh and I talked for hours at a coffee shop. Her son had had a medical emergency as a toddler when they were living in Saudi Arabia, his life spared when Dr. Michael DeBakey performed heart surgery. Leigh understood my state of mind. It was comforting to talk with someone I knew so well. I didn't have to pretend that everything was fine with her.

At the end of the first week of radiation, Katy and Heather drove to a Mom's Place retreat. I was uncomfortable about Katy going, even though Heather was an oncology nurse. My mother's protective instincts had been triggered on April 1st and were set on high alert ever since. Dallas' parents, Bob and Helen, invited Rick and me to dinner that evening. Budding friendships gave me a brief respite from worry. I was relieved to be able to lay aside my vigil and relax for an evening.

Unfortunately, it wasn't long before Katy began to experience complications and life got bumpy again. Her blog informed readers of the side-effects she experienced. She asked for prayer for God's intervention and protection. Medical misinformation, pharmacy mistakes and dangerous prescriptions had to be carefully monitored. Katy shared in her blog entry from May 24th.

Dear Loved Ones,

I apologize that it has been so long since I have updated you on the happenings here in Phoenix. Our time apart has been quite eventful due to an allergic reaction to my medicine, the onset of the fatigue that I have been warned about, and the loss of hair in a patch on the back of my head the size of my hand. (Those of you that know me know that I had a few strands to spare, so I am able to cover up easily.) If you ask me those seem like such small side effects for having had BRAIN SURGERY! Thank you for your prayers; they are carrying me through this. Each day is precious to me.

I also had an appointment with my oncologist to discuss the timing and procedures surrounding my chemotherapy. He told me that I would have two weeks off between radiation and chemo to rest and take some tests. As some of you know my grandfather, Frenchy, has cancer as well. Unfortunately his prognosis is that he will only live for a few more months. I have been praying for an opportunity to visit him in Indianapolis, so I am thankful to be able to use this small break to see him. My dad and brother have gone back to Indiana to be with him. Please pray for my extended family as you pray for my immediate family during this difficult time.

All my love, Katy

One of Katy's doctors concluded that at least one pre-surgery episode had been a seizure. Since surgery she had been on anti-convulsants because she was at risk for more, but it began to get complicated finding one she could tolerate. She was experiencing symptoms that could have been a partial focal seizure. Then suddenly her headaches were back, severe enough to warrant a trip to the ER and a resulting increase in steroids.

Katy continued to be blessed with phone calls, flowers, movies, treats, books, and visits. She was delighted when Justin, a close friend from Indianapolis, came for a short visit during a break in his studies at medical school. They had attended different high schools, but got to know each other in the youth group at Tab. While he was in Phoenix, he went to church with us and out to lunch with Katy and her friends. He also went to Katy's radiation treatment and observed the specific technique that was being used. He tasted Katy's world of baby showers and birthday parties for six-year-olds. Later Katy told me that she really enjoyed having Justin there, especially when they walked around the neighborhood and she had a chance to share what she had experienced working and living within the NM community.

And then, her 30 radiation treatments were finished. The June 6th blog stated:

> *Your love O LORD, reaches to the heavens,*
> *Your faithfulness to the skies.*
> *Your righteousness is like the mighty mountains,*
> *Your justice like the great deep.*
> *O LORD, you preserve both man and beast.*
> *How priceless is your unfailing love!*
> *Both high and low among men find refuge*
> *In the shadow of your wings.*
> *They feast on the abundance of your house;*
> *You gave them drink from your river of delights.*
> *For with you is the fountain of life;*
> *In your light we see light.*
> *—Psalm 36:5-9*

Today I received my last radiation treatment! I am so thankful to complete this portion of my treatment feeling very well, having some of my hair, and they let me keep my mask. I will find out how the remnant of the tumor has responded to this treatment when I have my MRI read on June 16. Thank you for taking this journey with me. Thank you for all of the many ways that you have loved my family and helped carry some of the burden at this time.

I will be in Indy for a short time to visit my grandfather and attend my family reunion. When I return I will see my doctors and get the final word on the rest of my treatment.

—Katy.

Our trip to Indianapolis was the first time Katy, Amy and I had been home since this unexpected detour began so abruptly in April. We found our house cleaned, grass mowed, flowers planted, and cars washed and gassed. What extraordinary friends and family God had blessed us with. Many came by to visit, some of whom had traveled to Phoenix to see us. I witnessed an incredibly poignant moment when a friend of Lenny's who had recently survived harsh treatments for testicular cancer came over. The hug between Mike and Katy seemed almost sacred. It was as if they understood what no one else could: what each other had gone through and the uncertainty they still faced. Amy's friends rallied to her side. She hadn't seen most of them since she left for her spring semester in Italy.

Almost all of the Reel clan (over 80 people) gathered for the family reunion. People who had been faithfully following Katy's journey on the blog came with hugs, kisses and encouragement. Distance didn't seem to be a deterrent; they came from all over to love and support Katy and Frenchy. Such a blessing. Then it was time to go back to Phoenix, back to our daunting reality.

So much had happened in so little time. How do you deal with such unexpected and drastic changes in your life? An entry Katy wrote in her journal in June shares how she was processing all that was happening to her.

> How strange a time of life is this. Even as I write this tears are welling up in my eyes, which in and of itself is a rarity for me that has now become somewhat of a normal affair. "26 and a brain tumor" even as I hear another express their shock over and over, I can almost step outside of myself and experience my own sense of shock and confusion

while listening to my own story. How do you comprehend having such an extreme diagnosis when your health history contains wisdom teeth extraction as its most severe entry?

Dealing with the health/physical aspects of this have been one thing. Understanding and knowing what to do with the individual responses of everyone else is another. People have been amazing. I cannot begin to absorb even half of the love that has been shown to me. I am absolutely blown away by the literally hundreds of acts of kindness and cards and letters and flowers and they keep coming. I feel so undeserving. And the calls. I have heard from people that I haven't heard from in years.

I have been blessed beyond all that I could have imagined through this experience.

On June 16th, Katy had her first MRI since the radiation treatments. According to her neuro-oncologist, "It looks great! Nice and clean, no swelling, nothing going on. There's barely anything there!" Along with that information, we were anticipating the schedule for chemotherapy that he had previously indicated Katy would be using for a year. But things were not as clear as we had thought. He continued, "Katy has three choices: Temodar (a chemotherapy drug) now; do nothing until the tumor recurs, then treat; take part in a study using Temodar and Motexafin Gadolinium together." Dr. Shapiro explained his reasoning, "Anaplastic Oligodendroglioma tumors are rather rare and treatment options are few. It is known that they respond to radiation, but chemotherapy results are unsure." He told Katy to take three weeks off treatment to recover, return to work and weigh her options. He was going to consult the Tumor Board for their recommendations.[1] Katy reported what they suggested on the blog on June 22nd.

A quick update:

Dr. Shapiro reported that the Tumor Board approved my enrollment in the Clinical Trial using Temador (a chemotherapy drug) and Motexafin Gadolimium if I choose. If not, they recommended that I have no further treatment at this time, but be closely monitored. So, essentially one of the options has been eliminated: Temador for a year (which is what he has been talking about for a month.)

Answers to prayer:

1.  The Tumor Board information is another piece in the puzzle toward making the larger decision about treatment.

2. I am close to being off the steroids.

3. I have had several opportunities to be in the Head Start classroom this week and will get to see nine of my favorite little ones graduate on Thursday.

4. I am having a reaction to my medication, so tomorrow I will try a new one (but hey, third time is the charm, right?). I am just thankful they have so many types for me to try.

Praise God for all of these blessings!

:) Katy

I wasn't expecting the doctor's change in the course of her treatments. I had mentally prepared for Katy to take chemotherapy for a year to fight her brain cancer. I remembered when my sister

Nancy finished the chemotherapy for her cancer. She said she felt vulnerable, almost helpless without that weapon. When Katy's doctor proposed doing nothing except wait and watch as one of her options, I understood what Nancy meant. I felt powerless.

Graciously, Katy held a family discussion on her treatment options. Lenny and Rick were in Indianapolis visiting Rick's father, so Katy initiated a conference call. She was always careful to include every member of the family in these conversations and listen to our opinions. She shared her decision in a blog entry on July 10th.

> Friday morning before heading off to the famous "Lake Day" with busloads of my favorite kids, I took the last available spot on the Temador/Motexafin study. I was able to see the room where I will do my infusion five days out of every month and met a woman just finishing her first week of the trial. Each day that I have treatment I will take Zofran (to help with nausea) and will go to the clinic for my IV of Motexafin (which is dark green and may temporarily turn my skin and the whites of my eyes green. Eat your heart out Hulk!). Then later that same day I will take my Temador and more Zofran. I will do that five days in a row and then have the rest of the month to recover. The study lasts for three months. If I like the Motexafin I can continue, and my doctor is going to decide whether I need six or 12 months of chemo once he sees how I am responding. I feel a great sense of peace about this decision. I am trusting God for this next phase of my treatment and what He has in store for me.
>
> Huge answers to prayer:
>
> 1. I am completely off of steroids and headache free!

59

2. My Dad is back in Phoenix for a visit and Lenny will be here next week.

3. I have been given the ok to drive.

Love, Katy.

We were graced with several visitors in the few weeks we had before the clinical trial began. My sister Nancy, her husband Don and daughter Libet rented a timeshare in South Phoenix and invited us to come enjoy their pool. This was Nancy and Don's first chance to be with us in Phoenix. They had stayed with our Alzheimer's afflicted father in April so our mom could come be with Katy then. Nancy, a Spanish teacher, bought a press in a Mexican grocery store and taught us how to make tortillas. Before they went home, Nancy offhandedly mentioned that she was having trouble with one of her eyes. Her comments reminded me of the time twenty years before when she had mentioned symptoms that were later diagnosed as breast cancer. This time the doctor thought her eye problem was due to allergies. Unfortunately, a few weeks later she called with bad news. "I don't want to have to tell you this now of all times, but I've been diagnosed with ocular melanoma." How do you process yet another dire diagnosis for someone you love?

Katy's participation in the clinical trial began on July 11th. She recounted that experience in her blog.

From Princess Fiona/Katy

It is hard to know where to begin. There are so many potential punch lines when you find yourself green (which consequently makes blonde hair look pink.) Several nicknames have already been suggested—Princess Fiona, Emerald Princess, Jolly Green Giant, and many more. Needless to say, this week has been quite eventful. I began my IV and

60

chemo treatments on Monday feeling well, but finished looking slightly yellow and feeling sick. Tuesday I felt much better, turned green faster, and then got a rash which is probably a reaction to one of the many medicines I am on. Wednesday and Thursday I continued to have a rash so I earned Friday off from the IV and Chemo and will return on Monday to do my last treatment for this round. Most of Thursday and Friday I spent resting due to my large consumption of Benadryl. I am feeling much better today and am almost back to my normal color, so hopefully I will be able to finish this round and determine what I am allergic to.

Thanks for praying!

All my love, Katy

Katy had the last treatment of the first round without incident, then four days later had an allergic reaction. An ER doctor decided it was caused by her anti-convulsant medication, so she switched to anti-convulsant number four. The next round of treatment was scheduled four weeks later, on August 8th.

The next two weeks were filled with work—preparing for the new Head Start class and planning the Mom's Place calendar. Amy painted a wonderful mural on the wall of the Head Start classroom. There were four trees, one for each of the seasons—complete with snow, tender grass, birds, butterflies, ants and colorful autumn leaves. The children came, precious 3- and 4-year-olds, and Katy figured how much time she could spend there. Lenny immersed himself in the children's activities, stacking blocks, reading books, passing the corn at the lunch table. I was thrilled to see Katy with the little ones. She thrived there; she was in her element.

Lucia Oerter, pastor of Central Presbyterian Church in Lafayette,

Indiana, still uses Katy's journey as an example. To encourage others to "let their light shine," she has shared the following message in sermons and youth retreats:

> *Even with a cancer diagnosis, Katy was fully focused on serving Jesus. She pressed on to fill her life with even more goodness and service. Her life was lived as a mission to serve Jesus. Katy lived her life in service with authenticity, compassion and connection especially with the little ones in need.*

One morning in the middle of the week, Katy woke up very tired. She came home early from work and slept four hours, got up to eat, then went back to bed and slept 11 more hours. The next day, she moved from her bed to the couch and, again, went back to sleep. In the following days, her fatigue wasn't as severe, but she was still tired. The doctor said it was probably due to the new anti-convulsant. Hopefully her body would adjust soon. The good news was that her blood work "looks great! Perfect!" And when the doctor examined her, he pronounced Katy was "remarkably healthy."

One certain Sunday morning, Amy and Rick were back in Indianapolis; Amy to be in a wedding, Rick to visit his father. Lenny was at Kids Camp near Payson, AZ, helping with the 60 kids at NM's weeklong Bible camp for junior high-schoolers. Katy and I were going to church at the Neighborhood Center and she had arranged to take one of her preschool students with us. This child had known much hardship in his short life. His attendance in school had been erratic, but he still called her "Teacher." He didn't realize she was ill. We all sat together on the folding chairs. As the worship music began, tears welled up in Katy's eyes and slid down her cheeks. Church is a place for deep contemplation; I've been there, exactly where Katy was. Her little friend, not knowing what was wrong, reached over and silently put his arm around her. God's comfort through a little child.

A few days later Rick called, "What's our insurance agent's phone number?" When I asked him why he needed it, he told me that he was driving Lenny's Jeep when a truck had crashed into him. I slid down to the ground. I couldn't take in this new trouble, and then I heard my mom saying, "Hold still while I get this glass out of your hair." Thankfully, Rick wasn't injured, but the Jeep was totaled. We were afraid that Lenny would be upset. It was his first car. So we decided to have Katy tell him what had happened when he got back from Camp. Who could get angry at anything Katy said? To his credit Lenny quickly replied, "It's only a car. Is Dad ok?"

Then it was time for her second week of chemo. And time for her next rash, this time along with swollen eyes. By Tuesday the doctor decided it was too risky for Katy to continue in the study. She was obviously allergic to something she was taking and each reaction was more pronounced than the last. He gave her the day off treatment, hoping the rash would disappear. She could try the Temador alone on Wednesday. If a rash or any other allergic symptoms appeared, she would have to stop taking the Temador too.

Fortunately, she was able to take Temador the rest of the week without incident. Evidently Motexafin was the culprit. Since Katy didn't have to go to the clinic for infusions, she flew to San Diego that weekend to join Heather, Kit and many other friends for a few days on the Beach. I didn't worry—there were three nurses in the group. Her fatigue seemed to have lessened. Thank you, Lord, for refreshing sunshine, ocean breezes and sandy beaches. As I stood in the airport watching her walk to her gate, a passerby commented, "It's hard to see them go, isn't it?" I must have looked stricken standing there. "If you only knew," I thought.

I shared these events in a blog on August 10th.

> Another change in the journey. It's too new to process yet, but in a way it's a relief. The Motexafin made her feel terrible Monday. So we continue, but not alone. We are so thankful for your prayers lifting Katy.

*Praise be to the Lord, to God our Savior,*
*Who daily bears our burdens.*
*—Psalm 68:19*

*I want you to know that Katy continues to feel peace. That's not*
*to say that there have not been very hard days, but she knows she*
*is loved and trusts in God's goodness. Thank you for walking along*
*with us. It means more than we can say.*

*Love,*

*Patty and Rick*

When Katy got back from San Diego, she encouraged Amy to return
to school; insisted is more accurate. Somehow Amy had finished her
interrupted spring semester online and by mail, an almost impossible
task when your major is painting and your professors are in Italy. Now
it was time for her senior year. She arranged for classes and housing
in Philadelphia, where she was attending Tyler School of Art, a part
of Temple University. Amy and I flew to Indianapolis, then drove to
Philadelphia in a car packed with her belongings. We both were terribly
reluctant to leave Katy. The only reason we did was because she would
have been too upset if we didn't. As we wrestled a sofa up the stairs to
her second floor apartment, I muttered, "Whose plan was this? Why
isn't Rick or Lenny here?"

After helping Amy get settled in the apartment she was sharing
with a friend, I flew back to Indianapolis. It felt so strange to be back
in our house, just Rick and I, with no one to care for. I was at a loss not
knowing exactly what was going on with Katy each day. What is it I do
here? I had resigned my position as parish visitor to the homebound
members of our church, amid protests that the job would be held for
me when I returned. I had insisted that it was important for those dear
people to have a consistent contact they could rely on. I was planning
to resign anyway; I had lost too many people the year before and gone

on too many hospital visits. I needed a change, especially now.

My car had died and wasn't worth repairing, so I needed to buy a replacement. I had no interest in looking at cars. I asked Rick if he would take care of that for me. I didn't care what car he got. Who cares about cars when their daughter is so ill?

Two weeks later, Rick and I returned to Phoenix to see Katy and Lenny and hear the doctor's plan for Katy's treatment now that she was no longer participating in the clinical trial. She explained in her September 8th blog.

Dear Ones,

I had an appointment with my neuro-oncologist today to review the results of Monday's MRI. Praise God there has been no new growth! The doctor said, "This scan looks so good we might not put you on Temodar. We do not routinely do this unless there's a recurrence. Your allergies make it a little tougher." Based on this and the fact that there is no research that indicates chemotherapy is effective at treating an initial brain tumor of this type, I am going to follow the advice of my doctor and discontinue the chemotherapy treatment. The plan as it stands now is to have an MRI every two months unless something shows up or I begin having symptoms. If new growth is observed my doctor will take into consideration location, size, etc., to create a new plan. Until then, no more turning green or being a human pin cushion.

For now things are beginning to feel strangely normal. My hair is growing back, I am enjoying being back at work full time with the kids and families that I love, my best friends, Heather and

Dallas, have moved in across the street (along with several others), Dianne (my former roommate) along with Lenny (my brother) have moved into my house (making three pairs of siblings between the two houses), Amy (my sister) is back at school in Philadelphia, and my parents are just finishing a week-long visit with me before heading back to Indy.

I praise God for all He has done and continues to teach me through this experience. The blessings continue to astound me. I thank you for your faithfulness in prayer and support of myself and my family.

Love, Katy

I too was praising God, but at the same time it was unsettling to hear that Katy would not have further treatment for an illness that was going to recur. It felt like she was left defenseless, but we were relying on the doctor's expertise, even though he kept changing his treatment plan. I'm not a neurological oncologist; I'm not a doctor or even a scientist. Obviously there was no known miracle cure or everyone would be aware of it. I searched through lists of clinical trials online and by phone, but there were none at that time that Katy qualified for. The doctors had said that Anaplastic Oligodendrogliomas respond better to treatment than other high grade gliomas, but Katy's sensitivity to medicine complicated planning for her care.

Katy seemed to be happy with this suspension of treatments and who could blame her? I had told her that I would always be there when she needed me, but if she didn't, I would go home and let her live her life. She was always the one everyone turned to for help and advice, so it must have felt strange for her to be living with her parents. But Katy was amazingly gracious about having us there. I hated the thought of leaving her, but I knew it was time to go. After all, Lenny was staying. He could take her to her medical appointments. He was already driving her to Head Start and had fallen in love with the kids himself. Katy's friends soon became his friends... those faithful, supportive friends. They made sure that Katy's life went on as normally as it could.

Kristen, Katy's friend who taught in the same California school, described this part of Katy's journey well.

> *The Lord spared her life and she continued to touch many lives throughout her recovery process. Katy was never scared or questioned God. She knew that He was not finished with her yet. Katy went back to work and remained dedicated to the Lord's calling in her life.*

Billy Thrall, a pastor at Neighborhood Ministries, shared a conversation he had with Katy.

> *I asked her, "What big dream do you have that hasn't come true?" I was going to make it happen, no matter the cost. Katy told me she loved her life and her work. She wouldn't change a thing. She looked at me and said,* "You don't get it Billy. I'm living my dream."

Even though everyone tried to return to normal, it was difficult to pretend, even to ourselves, that all was well. We were aware that the future was uncertain. Each day that passed without bad news was a gift. I held tightly to God's comfort holding my breath, still hoping that the doctor's prediction of 18 more years would be true and that by then a cure would have been found.

I had assumed that Katy was doing alright when we left. She had the support of Lenny, her bodyguard and chauffeur; Heather, her personal nurse; Ericka, her co-teacher; Selina and many other friends who were eager to help her with whatever she needed. What I didn't realize was that Katy was increasingly having difficulties. I had given Ericka Dr.

Shapiro's contact card, asking her to call him if Katy had a problem. Ericka dutifully placed it in the pocket of her Head Start apron so she always had it with her. Katy wanted to do life again. She was ready to figure out how to do that. I learned later, after years had passed, that she had struggled.

In remembering the circumstances around Katy during this time, Ericka admitted that she had a sense that Katy had a brain tumor even before her diagnosis. She recalled from March of 2005…

> *Katy was transitioning into a new staff position as director of all the education pieces at Neighborhood Ministries. She was working part time in this new role and part time for Head Start. She started having terrible headaches. Katy, who used to play along with the children, running up the slide after them, etc. was sitting on the step of the jungle gym with the preschoolers rubbing her head. Katy, who had always been so quick intellectually now couldn't figure out how to say what she wanted to say. Katy, who had always been so decisive, had trouble making decisions. One day we made plans to watch a movie at my apartment. Katy had such a bad headache she didn't want to drive, so I came to pick her up. We stopped by the grocery store for ice cream, but Katy just couldn't decide which kind she wanted, so we ended up with three different flavors, three gallons of ice cream! When we got to my apartment building Katy couldn't figure out how to climb the stairs, so I put my hands under her arms and helped her up the three flights. I had a sense that Katy wasn't going to be the same again.*

She reminisced about how it was after Katy's diagnosis, as she tried to resume as normal a life as she could.

> *Katy being in the classroom was a joy for her and the children. But, as her disease progressed she no longer led at circle time or introduced new activities; she mostly played with the kids. In*

October we took them to the grocery store to buy little pumpkins, then to the park to carve them. Katy, who loved doing crafts and was so good at them, almost decapitated her pumpkin when she tried to carve it. Still, it was better to have her there than not, although she wasn't playing the role she had before.

Lenny was with Katy all the time in the classroom. He followed her around, watching carefully, ready to help if need be. Once when he had to step out of the room, Katy climbed on a table to fix something on the wall, even though she was unsteady. "Don't tell Lenny I'm up here or he will call Mom."

I remember a field trip to the Railroad Park in Scottsdale. There were other kids there with their parents. The cab our class climbed into was full, so Katy got into the next one. After the train ride we all waited for Katy's cab to empty. When she got out she said, "I just realized that when I have kids, they won't look like our kids; they'll look like these blonde Scottsdale kids."

As teachers of our new preschool, we were in the trenches together. We did so much collaboration that we used to say we shared a brain. "Did I think of that or did you?" After Katy got sick, we didn't say that anymore.

Katy, who used to be the leader in planning lessons, no longer had the capacity to do that. Instead, I took the lead. We had had a rhythm of how we worked together and then that rhythm became too much for Katy. Nothing was ever said; it was only intuitive. It was difficult for me when people, mostly our students' moms and Neighborhood Ministries staff, looked to me to be prayerful and hopeful. That wasn't what I was feeling. For me this was about reckoning on letting Katy go.

Heather also confessed that she was aware of the inevitable outcome of Katy's illness early on. As a nurse at Good Samaritan hospital in the oncology unit, Heather had access to more accurate medical information than we were privy to, but it was difficult for her to face what she knew would happen. She confirmed that Katy continued to struggle after our return to Indiana.

> *I didn't know how to check on her when she got sick; there was no space to do that, no alone space. It was just a surreal way of doing life. We had our rhythm and it was thrown into chaos. Like a lot of things, Katy just took it in stride. She put on such a brave, strong face and had such pain tolerance that people often didn't realize how much she was suffering.*

> *As Katy began to have trouble with her equilibrium, she would sometimes need help getting around her house. At night she would call Lenny who was sleeping in the bedroom next to hers to help her into the bathroom, but when she fell in the shower she called me. Fortunately I lived across the street and could be there quickly. The last time that happened, after I got Katy settled in bed, out of the blue Katy said,* "I'm not afraid. I just had another MRI and it was negative. I'm not afraid of this one."

> *She had a lot of peace. We prayed together. She trusted God and that gave her such a capacity to withstand what she was experiencing.*

When we left in early September, I don't remember being aware of her dizziness or difficulty figuring out how to say what she wanted to communicate. She certainly wasn't falling and she wasn't in constant pain. If I had known, I doubt I would have left. But it was time to let her resume her life as well as she could. That was what she seemed to need. I regret that I never talked to Katy about how she felt about her prognosis. I asked Heather if she and Katy ever had that conversation.

> *Once, when we were talking about having kids and our future*

I said, "There's an elephant in the room." But it was her nature to always be more concerned about others than herself.

Katy had another good friend, Selina, who experienced Katy's continued difficulties. She was a case worker at NM but had actually met Katy years before, when Katy was studying elementary education at Biola. "I was just entering college with the hope of becoming an educator too, and so the connection we shared in those initial moments stemmed from the call we felt to ministry—and the desire in our hearts for changing lives through educating children."

Selina told me...

> Many of Katy's friends wanted to have hope too much to take in the reality of her illness, but I couldn't do that. This group of young adults that we were all a part of was a close community. We used to hang out together regularly and did a lot together, even more intensely when she got sick. We wanted to be with Katy, but were reluctant to crowd her space. We continued to go to lunch together on Sundays as usual. Afterwards, the boys would watch football at Katy's and fall asleep on the worn green couch that had been donated to the ministry.
>
> When Katy was sick, everyone tried to be on their best behavior. They made promises to God. If He healed Katy they would... fill in the blank. Her healing was supposed to be a modern miracle, proving that Jesus was who He said He was and show today's world His power. They argued with God and each other. But when Katy was with them, everyone tried to be happy and talk about regular things because if they were sad, she would have tried to take care of them. When she was in the hospital these friends would visit faithfully and, just as faithfully, pray. A few didn't go inside but parked on the grass behind Good Sam and prayed.
>
> Katy was never not Katy. She was always concerned about

*everyone else. She never stopped wanting to engage with the people she loved and who loved her. She didn't stop living. Katy never stopped thinking and talking about the kids and families in the community and what was happening to them.*

Selina also remembered incidents as Katy's disease was progressing.

*I would go to Katy's so she wouldn't be by herself. If I called to tell her I was coming Katy would say, "Good. I really need to hear that funny story about Jose[2] today." She would have forgotten some of the details. That story would always crack her up. I read Katy's emails and get well cards to her. I never understood whether Katy was just giving me things to do because I always have to have something to do, or if she really needed my help. Katy told me that focusing on reading made her dizzy and gave her headaches. She would lie down and put her hands over her eyes or on the side of her head. When our girlfriends went roller blading, I didn't want to go and Katy couldn't. We waited for a while, then got in the car and drove to Starbucks to meet them.*

It was troubling to hear these stories that confirmed I was wrong to think that Katy was doing just fine during that time. At the same time I was so touched by the love and assistance she constantly received from her friends. Because of that support Katy was able to continue living her life as normally as she could.

1. A Tumor Board is a meeting made up of specialized doctors and other healthcare providers to discuss cancer cases that are unusual and/or challenging. The goal is to decide on the best possible treatment for a patient as a group.

2. Name changed.

# Chapter 4
## *"This is the End"*

Early in October my phone rang. It was Katy. She had started feeling strange, not like herself and she was dizzy. I said that I'd be right there, but she responded, "You can't come every time I feel funny." Her MRI that was scheduled for November 3rd was moved up to that Saturday, October 9th. Lenny was going to take her.

The blog entry Katy wrote on October 19th only hints of some of the problems she was having.

> Last week I found myself back in the hallways of Good Samaritan Hospital visiting a friend who had just given birth to her fourth daughter. As I held her precious baby who was just hours old, I couldn't help but remember how she visited me in the same hospital just six months earlier. In many ways it feels that this journey began a short time ago, but in many other ways it feels as though I have lived a lifetime since April.

You have been on this journey with me.

From the beginning, my prayer and the prayer of many of you has been that God would meet me, meet us, in all of this. We know that He has answered our prayers in some mighty ways. He has carried me through surgery, radiation, chemotherapy, green skin, multiple allergic reactions, and now the latest MRI that shows "No new growth!" I believe that we have truly seen a miracle.

I am incredibly grateful, as I have already outlived my life expectancy. However, I feel as though my greatest challenge is ahead of me. How do I live my life knowing that my tumor could return at anytime and that I will spend the rest of my life without all of the innocent assumptions that I once had about my future? I have been thinking about this question for days now and I have to return to what I know and have seen to be true: Our God is faithful and loving. In the midst of the most difficult time of my life, He has made himself the most evident to me.

In response to the question of how to live my life now, the only answer that I know is to return to the people and places and activities that God has gifted to me. I go to Head Start and play with the kids and visit with the families that I have done so much life with. I take kids to the library to discover new books. I call friends and family to stay connected. I go to birthday parties and baby showers and eat pozole. I feed the ducks at the park, because that is all four year old boys' favorite part. I hang out with moms who are much younger than I am and they tease me about being so old and not having any kids. I make plans for the holidays, and plant fall flowers because it is finally cooling off. I take moms and kids to doctors for appointments. I cry when I feel sad and I see many people with so much pain of their own. I sit on my friends' front porch and talk about our dreams for the future. I go for walks in the evening. I look at pictures of my party the night before the surgery and I wonder if I will ever be able to take it all in.

Thank you dear friends for your prayers and support; they help sustain me. I would like to give you a quick medical update. A short time ago I began experiencing some symptoms that led to the date of my latest MRI being moved up. As you might imagine, the days before the scan were very difficult and took my mind back to a place that felt all too familiar. I was not sure how to share this with all of you, so I am sorry that this is the first that many of you are hearing of this. I am thankful that there was no new growth found on the scan, however I continue to experience dizziness that cannot be explained. I was in bed a few days last week due to nausea caused by this dizziness. Thankfully these last few days have been better. I would be very grateful for your prayers on this matter.

Love, Katy

Her symptoms worsened, and because the MRI showed no new growth, her doctors started searching for other explanations. I was getting very frustrated, "Really? She has a brain tumor. Why are you looking anywhere else?" I desperately wanted to go back to Phoenix, but against my better judgment, I honored Katy's request.

The dizziness and nausea continued despite various medications prescribed by her doctors. The Mom's Place newsletter reported:

> *The hardness of our journey began in early October as Katy began having difficulty with her balance, eyes and nausea. Katy valiantly continued to work with us; teaching, visiting, loving until mid-November.*

The Christian Community Development Association (CCDA) was holding its national convention in Indianapolis in November that year.[1] Several staff members from Neighborhood Ministries, including Katy and Lenny, were attending. I was very concerned about Katy traveling that distance, but having Lenny and Kit with her eased my fears a little.

I hadn't realized how sick Katy had become until I saw her. She was exhausted, yet unable to sleep. Walking up stairs was challenging. She used to be quick-thinking and fluent, now it was difficult for her to express herself easily. She seemed so fragile.

We had planned a "Thank You Dessert" at Tab to give Katy a chance to thank the people who had been praying for her and explain what she had been doing in Phoenix. I sought out Dave Streit, Tab's Director of Media Ministries, and asked him to arrange for someone to record Katy's remarks. I remember telling him that we just didn't know how much time we had left, verbalizing for the first time, my fear that Katy's illness was progressing. The Unleavened Bread Café, one of the ministries Tab had helped establish in the neighborhood, provided delicious deserts. Friends, family, and even the youth group gathered in our church dining room. Kit, Lenny and the other Neighborhood Ministries staff who had flown to Indianapolis for the CCDA joined us that evening. Katy told about her work in Phoenix and thanked everyone for their support.

It is so overwhelming to know you're

representative of virtually hundreds of people that have been praying for me and have done so many things for me and my family. I just want to thank you personally for what you've meant to my life and the lives of my family, friends, and extended family.

When I start to talk about the journey of this year I really think of two different parts that have come together. I can't share the journey of my tumor without sharing the journey of my life, especially my last two years of my life when I moved to Phoenix and began my internship. I want to read one of my favorite passages to you out of a book called *Compassion* by Henri Nouwen. "God is a compassionate God. This means, first of all, that He is a God who has chosen to be God-with-us... What really counts is that in moments of pain and suffering someone stays with us. More important than any particular action or word of advice is the simple presence of someone who cares."

When I started my internship this is one of the first things that I began to learn as I began building relationships with our families. Their problems and the things that they're faced with, even the children, is overwhelming to me as an adult. I can't even imagine, can't even begin to fathom having to deal with or sort through the problems they have. Coming into this you feel so vulnerable and helpless, so I felt a lot of comfort in this passage knowing that this was the role that I could play in these people's lives.

But as I myself came to a place of suffering

through my tumor and through the helplessness that I felt, I experienced this from other people, the very people that I thought I was there to comfort, in turn, comforted me.

One example of this is one of the families that I became really close with, the family of a little girl named Rosa[2]. I'd pick her up for school every day in our 15-passenger van. We'd talk about her day during our long drive. I got to know her really well, then I got to know her mom, then I got to know her mom's sister, and her other sister and all the family. Now they call me family. They came to visit me at the hospital and they call me sister. It's been an incredible experience to see how that changes from me thinking I had something to give them when it's really them giving back so much to me.

Again, I just want to thank you so much for all your prayers and support. So many of you passed this prayer request on to people in other countries that have been praying. Thank you so much.

I want you to know through this experience I've known God in a way that I never would have and it's an incredible blessing. I tell people that and I say, "You might think I'm crazy, but in your pain God will meet you in a way that you could never imagine." I know that many of you in this room know that, but until you experience it for yourself it's hard to understand. But I definitely have experienced that.

I just want to thank you for being in this journey with me and I thank you for your continued prayers.

Lenny was asked to give a medical report as Katy's caretaker. He shared that other than her equilibrium problems and her reactions to the medicine to help with that (hallucinating that there was a giant ant on the wall), she was "fine." The other NM staff members answered questions from the audience and even asked Katy a few of their own. Richard Speck, Neighborhood Ministries CEO posed, "Katy, what is the hardest thing you have ever had to do in preschool?" She thought, then answered, "Comb the lice out of a three-year-old's hair while they are screaming." (I am so thankful to have the tape that Dave Streit recorded that night. It is precious to me.)

Katy's Guest Book was brought to the Thank You Dessert, and several comments were written in it:

> You do not know me, but your trial and faith has brought hope to me as I go through my own trials. God bless.

♦

> It is such a privilege to keep you in our prayers! Your story has truly brought glory to God and He will continue to be glorified through your life!

♦

> Thanks for the wonderful witness to God's amazing grace.

♦

> You are a wonderful example to everyone around you. You truly live your life as a testimony.

What might not have been obvious was how frail and unsteady Katy had become, and that she was so very tired because she had trouble sleeping.

Due to their grandfather's declining health, Katy and Lenny extended their time in Indianapolis. Then, as Katy explained in her November 28th blog...

I hope that you all had a wonderful Thanksgiving holiday. I had a blessed day with my family, but also lost my grandfather that morning. As many of you may know, Frenchy has been battling cancer for over a year, so in some ways we are thankful his suffering is over. Your continued prayers for my family are greatly appreciated.

Love, Katy

My heart sank as I became more aware of her increasing weakness. Without expressing that terrible thought, even to myself, I was oppressed by what I couldn't name until later: dread. Dread for what was going to happen.

Katy needed something to wear to Frenchy's funeral, but she was too unsteady to shop. So I drove to the mall and wandered through a couple of stores. Weighed down by despair, I could hardly look through the clothing racks, until a sympathetic sales clerk approached me. I managed to explain what I needed and she sensed I couldn't do it myself; I was too overwhelmed with sadness. I'll be ever grateful for that kind person. She had me sit down and brought over a few things for me to chose from in Katy's size. Another blessing. Another angel.

All of Frenchy's grandchildren went forward together to support the ones who were going to speak at the funeral. A couple of them took Katy's arms and helped her up the steps. After the funeral, we drove to the site of Frenchy's Life Celebration. For some now forgotten reason, Katy and I ended up alone in my car. There was no place to park near the door. I couldn't let her out at the entrance without someone to help because she was so unsteady, so I steered to the closest parking space I could find. As I put the car into park, Joe Kukolla opened Katy's door and said, "May I escort you in?" A Godsend.

Indeed, it was a celebration as Frenchy had planned. Music,

delicious food, pictures of Frenchy enjoying his friends and family. Katy reveled in all of it. We sat at a table and friend after friend came by to greet her. At one point, her cousin, Brandon, came over, and Katy asked him to take her to see someone across the room. He took her arm and when they returned, Katy smiled and said, "I love you Brandon." A tear rolled down Brandon's cheek. That heartbreaking scene is forever imprinted on my mind.

I was so reluctant to watch Lenny and Katy leave when they returned to Phoenix on December 1st. Would Katy be alright on the four-hour plane ride? What was happening to her that was causing such dizziness, such weakness? I sensed we'd be going to Phoenix soon, so I delivered the few Christmas presents I'd already purchased in the now familiar daze.

Lenny took Katy to her next scheduled MRI a week later. The doctor was shocked to find three new tumors. He quickly checked the earlier MRI from October 9th to see if anything had been missed, but it did not show any new growth. Katy phoned me, "Not good. I have three new tumors. We're in the elevator on the way to the neurosurgeon. May operate tonight. I'm going to call Dad and Amy. What do I say to Amy? Heather is coming." I offered to call Amy for her, but Katy insisted she needed to do it.

I was stunned—the catastrophe I'd feared was here. Rick came home from work. It seemed to take him forever. It was starting to snow. I called my sister Judy and said, "I need you to come over." Then I called Julie and said the same thing to her. They walked in together, helped gather our things to pack and got airline tickets for a plane that was scheduled to leave at 5:50 p.m. Judy called her husband Boyd and told him to get his Christmas presents, new suitcases that were hidden in the trunk of their son's car, and bring them over. Boyd drove us to the airport. The usual 25 minute trip took two hours because of the deepening snow and snarled traffic. I phoned multiple people on the way, including Kit. They all prayed that we'd get to our flight in time. We rushed to the check-in counter and the attendants said not to worry; the crew was stuck somewhere on the interstate. Finally we boarded the plane, but then had to wait one-and-a-half hours while it was de-iced at least three times and an electrical malfunction was investigated. To make matters worse, when the plane was finally cleared to fly, we had to wait our turn to take off on one of the few runways that were still open. After we took off, the flight was uneventful except for the terrible thoughts racing through my mind, "This is the end…" Amy hurried to Phoenix from Philadelphia as Kit quickly wrote on Katy's blog.

> *Hello Dear Praying Friends,*
>
> *I wanted to hurry to the blog, to give you the best update we have to date regarding Katy's current and unexpected medical situation. It allows us to pray together and to be of one mind, for and with her.*
>
> *At this very minute, Katy is sitting in the waiting room of the emergency portion of St. Joseph's hospital where Barrow Neurological Center is located. Her treatment and care will be provided here at this renowned hospital. She will be moved as quickly as possible to an intensive care room.*
>
> *Currently there are three areas of Katy's brain where the cancer has returned. One of the areas is causing a build up of pressure in the brain. This increased pressure is causing Katy's symptoms.*
>
> *She is going to be admitted today (December 8th) into the hospital and will have surgery tomorrow (December 9th) morning at 9:30 to have a procedure to decrease the pressure and help her symptoms. The surgery will also be to remove parts of the cancer. She may also get chemotherapy to treat the other parts.*
>
> *Although all brain surgery has risks, it is necessary. Afterwards Katy may have some problems with her speech and her balance.*

*So, dear friends, I know this news is so difficult for you to bear, as you love our dear Katy so much. But it is of great comfort to her that you are praying and seeking God on her behalf. Know that she is surrounded by the love of God, this is evident.*

*Pray for Rick and Patty Reel, as they are coming from Indianapolis in a blinding snowstorm. As of this writing, their flight crew wasn't even at the airport yet, stuck somewhere because of the storm.*

*Amy has also gotten a flight out. Pray for her safe arrival.*

*Lenny remains here, so faithful to take care of Katy through all of this. It is off of his notes that this email blog comes to you.*

*We stand with Katy, in Jesus. In confidence that His love not only binds us together but gives us access to the throne of grace that we might boldly come. For He says I will never leave you nor forsake you so that we might boldly say, "The Lord is my helper." Please pray for Katy's healing.*

*Loving you, Kit*

*"I've told you all this so that trusting me, you will be unshakable and assured, deeply at peace. In this godless world you will continue to experience difficulties. But take heart! I've conquered the world."*

*—John 16:33*

When we finally arrived at the hospital, Heather and Lenny were sitting in the waiting room. Katy had just been taken to a room in the ICU. After she was settled, we were allowed to see her. As we walked into the room, she said, "I'm sorry." Still our amazing daughter, still selfless, even in the midst of this crisis.

According to the neurosurgeon, Dr. Kris A. Smith, he would "remove the largest spot on the fourth ventricle and count on chemo to treat the others." (That seemed to be the favored approach. That was the plan back in April.) "Don't worry about trouble expressing words, that will recover, but maybe not 100%; may radiate the other two spots... might need a shunt... spinal fluid not circulating... Risks: all of brain stem functions are on the floor of ventricle; balance may not get better."

The nurse let me spend the night in her room (this time in a chair—no cots for visitors in the ICU). The nurses working in the ICU were wonderfully kind and helpful.

I learned much later that the doctors did not expect Katy to live through that night.

Surgery was the next morning at 9:45. Several of Katy's close friends and Rick, Lenny, Amy and I staked out the small surgery waiting room. It was staffed by a volunteer "pink lady." Food and drinks were restricted; the guild had gotten tired of replacing the carpet. After four hours and 45 minutes, the surgery was over. Katy was returned to the ICU with a drain still in place.

Kit wrote an update for the blog.

> *First, your praying is felt here, as hearts are finding strength somehow, in the midst of it all. Katy made it through the surgery and the surgeon said he was very pleased with Katy's rapid recovery and how well it went.*
>
> *There was some removal of the designated tumor.*
>
> *The current tumors appear to be highly aggressive, however the final pathology is not in yet.*
>
> *Thank you for being led by the Spirit of God in your praying as you intercede for Katy...*

I heard the doctor's report. "The frozen section indicated the cancer was highly malignant, much more aggressive. The pathology is due Monday. The problems are: how soon new tumors formed; there are multiple tumors in the fourth ventricle, on the left occipital lobe, on the right frontal lobe; two rounds of Temodar and radiation were ineffective. The key is how the tumors respond to treatment." These words are from the notes I took. I couldn't process them then. Now, years later, his unstated prognosis seems clear. I was just not ready to hear it.

Joe Kukolla appeared that evening. He had flown out "to bring us coffee, whatever we needed." He didn't expect to see Katy, but when she heard he had come, she said she wanted to see him. With her eyes shut, she asked about his family. As Joe was leaving she said in a loud voice, "I love you, Joe."

This was all happening too soon. It was not expected for several years. This hospital experience was very different from the last one, much more difficult. Very few visitors were allowed to see Katy, but the ICU waiting room was always full of her friends and family. A vigil for Katy. Justin called asking if he could come see her. I asked Katy. She said, "Yes," but because she was heavily medicated I waited and asked her again later and again she said, "Yes." On the third "Yes," I told Justin that Katy wanted to see him.

The nurses allowed one person to spend each night with her, so she was never alone. One evening Katy said to Lenny, Amy and Rick, "Go home and get something to eat. We'll do this again tomorrow."

The Tumor Board was consulted again. They designed a treatment plan that included Gamma Knife Radiosurgery (minimally invasive radiation) and two chemotherapy drugs: Depo-Cyt every two weeks in combination with Temodar. The hope was that the chemo had a good chance of working because these three tumors grew after she had stopped taking Temador.

Katy was weak and challenged with vision problems, a lack of equilibrium, recurrent nausea, fatigue and fevers. She was not always aware of her body position. One night she even pulled some of her lines out in her sleep. But, as you can imagine, whenever asked by the medical staff if she would like this or that, she commonly responded, "Whatever works for you." She was asked for permission for the Barrow Neurological Institute Tumor Board to use the unneeded tissue of the tumors for research, and she consented.

A few days after surgery, Katy had Gamma Knife radiation on three areas of her brain. It was an extremely difficult day for Katy. She hadn't been out of bed since the operation, yet they transported her in a wheel chair. The procedure took eight hours. We were all exhausted and upset by what we had allowed the doctors to do, even though they were following the recommendations of the tumor board. Looking in the rearview mirror, I wonder if they were trying, almost desperately, to buy Katy more time.

The very next day, Katy had a one-hour surgery to implant an Ommaya Reservoir, a synthetic dome that was placed beneath her scalp and attached to a catheter that was inserted within her brain. The Depo-Cyt would be administered through the reservoir in an effort to bypass the blood-brain barrier. The other chemotherapy drug, Temodar, would be taken orally in the form of a pill. Dr. Smith reported that the procedure went well. "Her eyes are improving and should continue to improve. It will still be a few more days until they see if they can remove the drain. I'm still hopeful that she won't need a shunt." If she would need a shunt to divert the fluid, it would empty into her abdomen and negate any benefit from using the reservoir to give her chemo.

Katy had questions that she wanted me to ask the doctors, "What is the goal of treatment—just to feel better? What's my prognosis?" When I relayed her questions, Dr. Smith said the Final Pathology was "Anaplastic Oligodendroglioma, Grade III, same type, but bad enough. Her prognosis is dependent on how this does. It's not a good complication to have. I have a patient that is 18 months out." I refused to think about the implications of his answer then, but it is apparent to me now—she didn't have much time.

Dr. Smith had physical and occupational therapists come to evaluate Katy; they don't usually come to ICU, but made an exception for her. The physical therapist explained that her persistent nausea was related to the eye movement. Her eyes moved back and forth together like windshield wipers. A couple of solutions were suggested: cover one eye, maybe glasses with special tape would help. But we soon discovered that her eyes had more problems when one was covered. Next was an evaluation by the occupational therapist, who said she needed to be up in a chair three times a day. "She will need a hand held shower in her bathroom at home." Of course, Tom Boltz installed one right away. Such a busy day. Katy slept most of the afternoon, then had a good evening. "Quiet is better. Just too much stimulation during the day."

The nausea battle continued. We discovered that chocolate ice cream worked better than the scrambled eggs and orange juice Katy had asked for; ice chips worked better than apple juice.

The ICU nurses were wonderful to me as well as Katy. They found toiletries I could use to wash my face and brush my teeth. They listened to me with compassion and gave good counsel. I remember one middle-of-the-night conversation at the nurses' station when I asked, "When should we take Katy home (to Indiana)?" That kind nurse gently suggested that when Katy went into hospice would be a good time. A plan. Somehow that was comforting.

Katy's drain was finally removed and she went to a regular neurology room. The problem was that it was a double room, so none of us could spend the night with her, which made me very fearful. She was so unstable. How would she get to the restroom by herself? What if she fell? The nurses on that floor weren't nearly as helpful and didn't seem interested in coming up with solutions.

The occupational and physical therapists came into Katy's room to help her adjust to her current limitations. "She needs a walker. Check the thrift stores." The rehabilitation doctor said Katy could stay in the hospital for rehab or do it as an outpatient. She also will need to see a neuro-opthamologist to assess her eyes and a neuropsychologist to get a baseline on language. Katy insisted on outpatient treatments, so after 13 days in the hospital (10 in ICU), Katy went home.

I was terrified to take her home without doctors and nurses across the hall if she needed help. She seemed so fragile. She was so nauseous that she couldn't keep much food down and was losing weight. Her eyes weren't tracking. She couldn't even watch tv. We all sat on the couch and played funny movies on the VCR so she could listen. Her equilibrium was compromised; she couldn't walk by herself. We all huddled together on the green couch and tried to recuperate from the last two weeks.

Kit's December 20th blog explained...

*Katy came home today, about 1:00, along with all her helpers, Patty, Rick, Lenny, Amy and Heather. How strange that all these terrible difficult procedures and some recuperation have all been in just 12 days. The challenge is in understanding it, feeling it, living with it. These loved ones are very tired.*

*Katy is sleeping a little better right now than when she first came home. Yet, she is very glad to be home in her own bed, even though her bed feels weird for some reason. She is still exhausted and it isn't time for visitors yet. When she is feeling better the visits will be the best thing for her. But right now she needs to make the transition. She is so happy to be back in her own home.*

*On Tuesday she'll go to the neuro-oncologist's office to have chemo at his office, which will then happen every two weeks. The Temodar will be taken orally once a month.*

*Rehab will start in about two or three weeks and will probably include an ophthalmologist. Her eyes haven't settled down yet.*

*The pathology is in, and there is no change. It is the same type of*

90

*tumor, but has proven to be very aggressive.*

*Pray*

- *against this nausea, and for strength, that her eyes would settle down.*

- *For her physical and mental response to the chemo, as you know Katy is very sensitive to medications, for little to no reaction.*

- *For no more tumor growth, for complete healing.*

- *PRAY with us that this tumor would respond to Jesus and to His demands.*

- *PRAY that her strength would increase, that she would have a great appetite and regain some weight and that physically she would be ready for the chemo onslaught.*

*Your love and encouraging words mean so much to each reader of the blog. Thank you for your commitment to persevere in prayer. Keep trusting Katy into the arms of her Protector, in whom she has found shelter.*

*If the LORD had not been my help,*
*My soul would soon have dwelt in the abode of silence.*
*—Psalm 94:1*

Everyone made an effort to celebrate Christmas. Heather brought over a Christmas tree and decorated it in the living room. Katy asked us to get a present for her little friend Sughey, so Amy and I went to Target and bought markers and an art book for her. Many friends gathered at Heather and Dallas' house across the street for Christmas dinner. It was a potluck and it seemed that almost everyone had brought a meat dish to share. Fortunately, it was 80 degrees that day, perfect for grilling outside. Katy had practiced with a walker to go over there. She was able to stay a short while, smiling and visiting with some of her closest friends in the front room.

Katy's strength slowly improved over the next few days. She was able to walk a little more, but her equilibrium was still off so she needed help getting around the house. Her nausea lessened and she had a bit of an appetite, but her vision problems made reading impossible and even watching tv difficult. She was frustrated that she was tired all the time, not completely herself, lying on the couch so much. She began to lament, "What good am I?"

Two days after Christmas, she received Depo-Cyt chemotherapy through the Ommaya Reservoir, a simple procedure that was scheduled to be repeated every two weeks. In addition, she took Temodar orally, which was prescribed for five days each month in a pill form. Dr. Shapiro's nurse, Andrea, warned Katy that the worst thing she could do was to lose weight; she needed to regenerate the cells that the chemotherapy would take away. She needed fuel to fight it. "Try ginger ale to stop the nausea. Vomiting and gait problems are caused by the tumor. Take Zofran half an hour before taking Temodar."

Meanwhile, in Indianapolis, Tab was hosting "A Day of Prayer For Katy and All the Reels" from 8:30 a.m. to 5:00 p.m. that day. People were invited to drop in and pray in the Chapel any time during the day. At 3:30, Kirsten Guidero led a special time of prayer. I had sent Kirsten an updated prayer list. If they were not in the area, people were encouraged to pray wherever they were. Many who came to pray wrote loving notes of encouragement in a notebook. Especially dear to my heart are those from a couple of homebound members that I had visited.

*You are often in my thoughts and prayers and coming where we can give our full devotion and love is meaningful to us all.*

◆

*May God's grace continue to be upon you.*

◆

*Life, light and wholeness be in, through, and to you.*

Prayer shawls, lovingly knitted, were sent to Amy and me. A shawl had already been sent to Katy. Part of Katy's army doing battle for her.

Sleep eluded her; she was awake for two nights. I contacted the doctor, who prescribed a sedative to help her sleep. Justin came to visit and Katy was delighted, even motivated to try to go out to lunch. We all went: Amy, Rick, Justin, Heather, Lenny, Katy and I. Afterwards Amy and I went shopping while the others took Katy home to rest. She needed some clothes that would fit. She had lost so much weight that hers were way too large. A sad errand for two terribly sad people.

The next day, December 29th, I announced that I was going to Sam's Club and Katy chimed in saying that she wanted to go. I couldn't believe she had enough energy to do that, but Katy wanted to try, so she and Justin rode there with me. We parked, walked inside, wrestled a cart from the row and started down one of the long aisles. After a few steps, Katy said that she couldn't go on. She and Justin went back to the car while I grabbed a few necessities, paid quickly and hurried out to the parking lot. We were heading home when Katy suddenly said she felt weak and wanted to get something to eat right away. We stopped at a nearby restaurant. Eating a little helped her feel better and we were able to go the surgeon's office to have some sutures removed; they had been left in by mistake.

Katy kept trying. Rick and Justin adjusted her walker so it worked better for her. We continued to encourage Katy to eat more, but her nausea made it difficult. Rick would buy Katy energy and protein drinks, desperately trying to help her build up her strength. Not wanting to disappoint her dad, she would try to sip it, but just couldn't swallow any. When Rick walked out of the room, Justin quickly (and kindly) would empty the can. I think he knew we were feeling helpless and frustrated. We wanted to fix her and we couldn't.

Katy went to bed and woke four hours later crying, with pain in her legs. I gave her two Tylenol, but the pain got worse, so she took stronger pain medicine at 6:00 p.m. I phoned the Neurology Resident on call, who suggested that perhaps her electrolytes were off. "Try Gatorade," he said. That didn't help. Her pain was terrible, so I decided to contact Dr. Shapiro, who sent her to the ER. "It's not from Temodar." Katy and her caretakers, including Justin, went to the hospital emergency room. There she had an ultrasound, to check for blood clots, and blood work done. Both tests found nothing to explain the pain, so they treated her symptoms with stronger pain medicine administered through an IV, then sent her home with a prescription for more.

Katy was exhausted and only wanted to spend the evening quietly with Justin. He was such a comfort to her.

She woke the next morning with the same leg pain, but the prescribed pain medicine made it manageable. Then came a headache.

Katy's first radiation treatments had caused a bald spot the size of a palm on the back of her head. It wasn't noticeable at first because her long blond hair covered it, and then curly brown hair started peeking through. Looking in a mirror Katy said, "This isn't working for me," and asked Amy to cut her hair. She perched on a stool on the front porch while Amy carefully trimmed Katy's long blond hair to match the short dark curls. Amy made a salon appointment and had her own hair cut short in solidarity. Heather grabbed a pair of scissors and followed suit.

Justin had to return to Indianapolis the next day; his holiday break was over. It was sad to see him leave. He was such an encouragement to Katy. Heather brought pizza over, spent the evening, then left at 10:00 p.m. Having Heather and Dallas living just across the street felt like a safety net. Medical help wasn't far if we needed it.

Katy had another headache when she went to bed at 11:00.

Amy and I attempted to wake her around 3:00 a.m. to give her a pain pill. It was important to stay ahead of the leg pain. But it was hard to fully wake her up; she didn't really talk. Lenny came into her room to help. He was more successful at getting her to swallow the pill (or so we thought). We assumed she was just very tired. Except for her headache, she had seemed alright when she went to bed, about four hours earlier. Lenny had an early morning flight to go to a wedding in Indianapolis. As I drove him to the airport, I told him I was worried that Katy might be starting to develop the "altered state of consciousness" we had been warned about. We agreed that she was just very tired. By 8:00 a.m., we couldn't get any response from Katy; she wasn't talking at all. We found the pain pill still in her mouth; she hadn't swallowed it. I called Heather, thankful that she lived so close. As Rick, Amy and I huddled around Katy's bed, her beautiful bedspread covered with red satin patches, rumpled, Heather noted Katy was hot and discovered she had a fever of 102.5. I really started to worry. We decided to call an ambulance to take her to the hospital. The driver turned out to be a friend of Heather's and he informed us that St. Joseph's ER was closed due to overcrowding, so they rushed her to Good Samaritan Hospital instead. Heather wondered aloud why God had planned that change. I rode in the ambulance with Katy and watched with growing apprehension as the medics worked on her. That ER was jammed too, probably because it was the day after New Year's Eve, so we had to wait awhile before she was seen. It was exasperating; my underlying numbness turned to quiet desperation. Fever meant infection, didn't it? Identify the infection and treat it with the right antibiotic and Katy would be fine. But it didn't happen that way. The medical personnel tried to find the source of her symptoms with blood work (19,000 white count) and a CT scan (no obvious swelling). We watched as they administered an antibiotic and morphine to help block any pain, but Katy was still unresponsive.

She was transferred to the oncology floor where Heather worked. Spinal fluid from a lumbar puncture was cloudy, consistent with infection. Friends quickly gathered as word of the crisis spread. As Heather typed the admission information into her computer, Kit and

95

others from Neighborhood Ministries surrounded Katy's bed to pray. While someone was pleading with God to release Katy from her pain, Rick noticed a sudden, distinct change in her eyes. He recognized that change. It had happened to his father—was it only five weeks ago? A code was called and the nurses and doctors rushed to intubate Katy and hurry her to the ICU. I overheard a young nurse say, "We don't usually intubate terminal patients."

What on earth was she talking about? No one had used that word to describe Katy's condition. Admittedly, Katy was very ill, but she was going to get better. If they could just find out what the infection was and find the right antibiotic, she'd be fine for a long time. She was talking to me just last night, a few hours ago. That young nurse ripped away the last shred of hope I had. We all followed to the ICU on another floor. At some point, I called Lenny. He had just landed in Indianapolis. The ICU waiting room began to overflow. I called our phone tree contacts back home. Amazingly, a friend of Kit's, Dr. Julianne Thompson, somehow sensed she should go to Good Sam. She was a Godsend. Doctors, nurses and other medical personnel were rushing in and out of Katy's room. Julianne would talk to them then tell us what was happening in words we could understand. I called Justin, who had just gotten home, and handed the phone to Julianne so they could speak physician to physician.

At last we were allowed into her room. The scene seemed surreal. She was laying peacefully on the bed, not moving, a respirator pulsating as it pumped air in and out of her lungs. A monitor on the wall beeped loudly as it tracked her vital signs. One of the nurses came in wearing a mask. She apologized, "I'm sorry, but I have small children. I can't risk taking an infection home." I understand; I have children too. None of us worried that Katy had anything contagious. The hall was crowded with Katy's friends sitting on the floor.

Eventually the doctor explained that Katy's brain had had too much and herniated. There was no brain activity. If she were taken off the respirator she would not take a breath. She wasn't really alive; the machines were breathing for her, forcing air in and out of her lungs. She was gone. My darling, precious daughter, my firstborn, was no more. We couldn't disconnect her then because Lenny, her brother, "body guard, caretaker..." wasn't there. He needed to be there to say goodbye to her in person. I think perhaps that was God's gift to Lenny for his faithful care; he did not have to see her leave.

No one hurried us. The nurses turned off the irritating sound of the loud monitor. There was no pressure. Just gentle support. We let everyone who was waiting come into Katy's room to say goodbye. Imagine, just over nine months ago they were telling Katy, "Happy Birthday," in the same hospital.

Lenny was on his way back to Phoenix. I made a final call to Justin and told him we planned to have two services, one in Phoenix and one in Indianapolis. I heard, "Thank you, Mrs. Reel, but I have to go. They're calling my plane." He was in the Indianapolis airport, catching the first fight back to Phoenix.

As the hours passed, people drifted away. But we stayed. She was never alone. Who can say what a person in this state is aware of? I couldn't, so we kept talking to her, hugging her, singing to her. God sent two more angels that night. Kathleen and Tom Boltz came and stayed with us through the night, quietly stepping in whenever they were needed. The nurses made a room available where we could rest. Someone was always with Katy, talking to her, singing, reciting familiar scriptures, stroking her arm, just loving her.

At dawn her friends returned, drawn by their love for Katy. Justin and Lenny arrived. Each of them was able to be alone with Katy for a while, as long as they wanted. And then it was time. Time to let her go. In all honesty, I believe she had left us while the group around her bed was praying, before she was intubated. The machine was turned off and just as the nurse had warned, Katy didn't take a breath. She had already "flown to Jesus and lived" her heart's desire.

●●●

Katy had wanted to donate her organs, but having brain cancer disqualified her. The doctors asked about an autopsy, but I shook my head and said, "No. She's had enough."

Walking out of that room was the hardest thing I have ever had to do. Leaving Katy there all alone felt like I was abandoning her. I knew she had passed, but her body was still there. The body that had contained the soul of my beloved daughter. How precious it was, even lying there, lifeless. That was all I had left of her. I felt compelled to make certain she would be respectfully cared for. The nurses assured me that the funeral home staff would be sensitive as they attended to her.

When we finally forced ourselves to step into the hallway, a few friends were still lingering there; we weren't the only ones reluctant to leave. They respectfully moved aside to let us pass. Their faces sorrowful, eyes full of compassion and grief.

I was in a fog as we drove to the house we had shared with Katy for most of nine months. I remember wandering around from room to room, not knowing what to do when I had a distinct impression of Katy quietly whispering, "I'm ok. I'm ok." I wasn't seeking that reassurance; it just happened.

1. Christian Community Development Association (CCDA) is a network of Christians committed to seeing people and communities holistically restored. Their mission is to inspire, train and connect Christians who seek to bear witness to the Kingdom of God by reclaiming and restoring under-resourced communities.

2. Name changed.

# Chapter 5
## *Laid to Rest*

I was in shock, numb, exhausted, walking around in disbelief. What had just happened? Katy went to bed one evening—I hugged her and said good night—I never got to hear her voice again. I was grateful she didn't seem to be aware of what was happening, but it was such a shock to the rest of us.

I wandered into her bedroom, wanting to grasp a sense of her. My eyes swept the scene—rumpled sheets and covers on the bed where she so recently slept, exquisite pictures of African animals, lovingly painted by Amy, fastened on the wall above the headboard. I had slept there with her until Amy took my place. There was the closet and dresser that held her clothes, a tall covered bamboo basket full of notes, letters, emails and airline receipts—all mementos that she kept. They became our treasures, our pieces of her. Then my eyes rested on her bookcase. I walked over and sat down in front of it. I had never paid much attention to the books she had collected. Her library amazed me. The shelves were packed with such a variety of books: Christian books like

*My Dear Children* by Mother Teresa, *Beloved* by Henri Nouwen, *The Cost of Discipleship* by Dietrich Bonhoeffer, and many others; books on urban ministry, racial justice, and educating hurting children; books about different cultures and places; Bibles; children's books. I remember thinking that one could tell a lot about a person by the books they read. Her library revealed her heart.

I reached over to pull a book off the bottom shelf and noticed something wedged behind the bookcase. Wondering what had fallen, I pulled the unit out from the wall and grabbed hold of what was hidden there. It was a small notebook. Curious, I opened the cover. Inside there was a picture of six junior-high-aged children sitting on a low stone wall, four expressionless and two smiling shyly. On the next page was an inscription, "for Katy Reel, June 6, 1997, to record your dreams, your thoughts, your prayers. Mommy Nancy." Between those words Katy had written "Summer '98 Neighborhood Ministries Internship..." I couldn't believe it. I had found a journal of Katy's that I didn't know existed! I had lost her, but she left behind a piece of her heart written on these pages. I turned the page and found more pictures: Katy with a child on her shoulders; Katy with Kit, Heather and two other young adults; Katy with another young lady. She titled the page "Christopher Creek, AZ—Mountain Meadows" and wrote:

> This work is in no way complete; it is merely a glimpse into amazing memories, unrevised dreams, unpolished responses and amateur thoughts...

Intrigued, I turned another page and saw the word "POWER" cut out from a magazine and pasted diagonally across the page. Following was the first entry, January 18, 1998, a five-page account written at the end of her first semester at Biola.

I was overwhelmed and delighted; I felt like I had discovered a priceless treasure. Holding it close, I hurried into the living room where Amy, Lenny, Heather and Rick were sitting, still stunned by the trauma we had just experienced, and breathlessly told them what I had found. They were as surprised and curious as I was and wanted me to read what Katy had written. I started, but just then Lenny asked, "What are you doing? Aren't those private?" I stopped immediately. He was right, of course. I was caught up in the excitement of finding something of Katy's that I didn't know existed. I was a little embarrassed at what I had started to do, glad that Lenny had called the indiscretion. I returned to Katy's room and pondered the situation. What had she documented? How would we know if no one read it? I decided that I, as her mother, was uniquely qualified to do that. I resolved that I would read it and determine what should be shared, if anything.

Soon afterward, I recovered other journals, more to absorb and decipher. I raced through them, astonished at what she had written, at the experiences she recorded. She wrote of being blessed with a wonderful childhood, but also expressed (the usual teenage) distress at family interactions that made me squirm in my chair. She wrote of how it felt going to college so far away, making new friends and attending intriguing classes. However, most of her journals revealed her extraordinary relationship with God, and her intense desire to love and serve Him. Those enlightening entries gave details I hadn't known about Katy's determination to follow Jesus no matter the cost. When Kit called to gather information for the tribute she was writing for Katy's funerals, I shared a few of those paragraphs. But, I would have to get back to her journals later. There was a funeral to plan.

I had never planned a funeral before. How do you do that for your daughter? We leaned on others who gently guided us. Kit contacted a funeral home she had recently used; she and Heather accompanied the four of us to a meeting there. The four of us—for the last 22 years it was the five of us. There was a hole in our family. There was a hole in my heart. Such an abrupt loss of a fundamental anchor of my life.

Kit also wrote the obituary. We wanted a picture for it, but couldn't find one of Katy by herself. We had to crop one of her with a friend. Even in photos Katy was rarely by herself; she was always with other people. While Kit and I took the obituary to the newspaper I called Andrea, the kind infusion nurse at Barrows, to tell her that Katy had passed away. (We had just seen her a few days ago when she administered chemotherapy to Katy.) When Andrea stopped crying, I asked her how she was able to do her job. She must lose so many of her patients. She said, "I don't usually let my patients in, but Katy was different." She went on to say that losing Katy so quickly was actually the most merciful thing that could have happened to her. The suffering that was imminent would have meant very bleak days for her. I tucked those words deep in the back of my brain to mull over. Months, maybe years later when I dared to look more closely at what had happened, I realized that the events that had ended Katy's life so suddenly also mercifully shortened her suffering.

People gathered like they did when Katy first became ill. I was so relieved when my sisters came from Indiana to help. They hugged me. They cried with me. Then they pitched in to help. Judy paid the overdue bills; Nancy went with Dianne to shop for flowers. Even today, whenever I smell the lovely fragrance of stock (also known as Gillyflower, perfume plant, and Matthiola Incana), I remember the beautiful ones they found at Home Depot. Rick's sister and her family flew in. Two of Amy's best friends came to be with her. Julianne Thompson picked flowers and cut vines from her yard, bought candles and enlisted us to decorate the church at Neighborhood. I'm sure she didn't need our help, but was wisely giving us something to do. Lenny and Heather searched through pictures and Katy's favorite music to make a slideshow for her funerals. A picture of Katy appeared on the railing of her front porch surrounded by candles. Patrick, who lived next door, brought over a huge, lavish bouquet of white flowers. I marveled at his generosity and placed it at the front of the church. Others were mourning Katy.

On the day of Katy's funeral service in Phoenix I was still in a daze, thankful that others took the lead guiding us and asking for input at times (Katy's favorite hymn, which flowers for the casket, what clothes should Katy wear, etc.). I couldn't think or feel, unable to process what had happened so quickly. I learned how to say the words "Katy passed" without acknowledging what those words meant. The large worship room of the church at Neighborhood was already filling with mourners when we pulled up. Someone had arranged a table with pictures of Katy. Heather brought cards and pens so people could write their memories of Katy to be put into a book for us. There were other cards to write messages that would be tied to balloons and released to fly to Katy. The room seemed to be filled with snapshots of Katy's life--her preschool classroom, her friends, her family. There were photographs of the moms and kids she had done so much life with. Vases of colorful flowers were placed around the stage, the tables that held the pictures, and in front of her casket. The room was humming with the voices of children and adults as they searched through pictures, hugged each other for comfort, and strained to get a glimpse inside the casket. Others who were too upset to enter the room hesitated outside, perhaps wanting to be near Katy, but too overwhelmed with grief to come inside. Hundreds of people, mostly from the Neighborhood community, filed by Katy's open casket and hugged Rick and me. I was surprised I could recall each of their names. I usually have trouble remembering names in the best of circumstances, but during those moments it felt like the quiet voice of God was whispering each name into my ear. The crowd was not only from the NM community; friends and family came from California, Nevada and even all the way from Indiana. The grandmother of one of Katy's former Ocean View students in California brought her granddaughter to the funeral because she wouldn't stop crying. Even the doctor who had attended to Katy this last time in the hospital came to see what her life had been about.

The preschool children who knew and loved Katy looked at the pictures of her and their classroom over and over. Many of them put bracelets and flowers in her casket. At first this bothered me. I felt so protective of her and didn't want her disturbed. When someone gently explained this custom of placing favorite possessions in the casket with loved ones, I relaxed. Katy would love these gestures of affection. A few weeks later one of these children asked me, "Did you see Katy in the treasure box?" Out of the mouths of babes.

Katy's favorite praise music in English and Spanish filled the worship space. Bilingual prayers were offered by pastors Billy Thrall and Jorge Macias. The testimonies (some in Spanish, some in English) that were shared at that service remain cherished memories.

Pastor Jorge Macias shared stories of picking up the Head Start children in the Neighborhood van. Every day Katy rode with him and went into homes to collect the kids, often waking them up and getting them dressed for school. He began...

*These days I have been thinking about her a lot and the many experiences we had in the van driving the children. The first year was so hard. There are many stories I could share, but perhaps this is a time for teaching. We know from the heart that when angels come to earth, they are here for only a short time; they don't stay and they go again. This is what Katy meant. She was an angel that came to the earth, stayed awhile and then left. She had great love for the children.*

*One day I was driving and a child learned how to take off the safety belt. He got out of his seat and Katy said, "I think one of the children got out of his seat, because he is not there." When we realized this we discovered that he had gone to the back of the bus, opened the door and was waving to those following us. Katy said, "You have to stop! You have to stop!" And we stopped.*

*On another occasion I was driving and suddenly Katy began to smell smoke. One of the children was smoking. I took down the fire extinguisher and sprayed everything behind me. We finished that morning covered with dust from the extinguisher—the children and the seats.*

*Another time the school bus arrived at an apartment to pick up a child, and as Katy was accustomed to doing, she would carry the child in her arms because the child would run [away]. This time the child opened the door quickly and got himself out. Then we saw him behind the garbage, then on the roof of the car. Katy said, "Get down!" If it were me, I would strangle him, but Katy said, "Let's go and we'll take you to your house." And that is why I said that she loved the children. I believed that was one of Katy's qualities. Bring the children, love them, take care of them, protect them.*

*So many things happened, so many things.*

*The only explanation I have is that she is an angel. It is the only way we can continue forward. As I said, angels only come for a moment to the earth and they take care of us, love us, protect us and they are gone. This is what I think of Katy.*

◆

Daniel Arbizu, one of the most beloved young people at Neighborhood and one of the most troubled, asked to share his eulogy. He had come to NM so full of despair and anger from his abusive childhood that it was a battle for him to experience light. He bravely stood in front of the crowd supported by friends on each side of him and haltingly read what he had written.

*Katy was and still is a loving person. Her beauty just enlightened up the most darkest places, hearts like mine. You see her love was like a cage and her beautiful mind was like the key to putting my demons in my mind and heart away. And I would like to thank her for showing me how precious life not was but still is and that no one should take it for granted. And I would like to tell her thank you for showing us and I say us because she showed everyone not just me. She was and still is stronger that anyone I know. You see, as a Gangster I did not understand what pain and love meant. Now I know. It's painful to know she's gone but her love that she'd branded in my mind and heart is and always will stay with me. And I love her for putting up a good fight. But my prayer is now asking God to let Katy sit on the side of Your throne and let her watch the men and women she loves here. Don't let her forget us because even though it hurts that she's left, it will hurt more to know she's forgotten about us. This writing is dedicated to the beautiful and loving mind of Katy Reel. We love you and you will not be forgotten.*

Sadly, Danny slipped back into his old life and was killed a few months later during a robbery attempt.

◆

A volunteer from the Head Start class shared.

*I worked with her in the children's room. One time I told her that I regret that I don't know how to work with the children: they don't pay attention to me. I can't deal with them. She said, "Why not? You help us." I told her that I wanted her to teach me how to be with the children, how to take care of them. She said that I have the most important thing for working with children, patience.*

*She taught me that your color wasn't important or where you came from. I don't speak English and she only a little of Spanish, but we communicated. She made me begin to feel that I was important and capable and I now I have a been here a year. The angel that she had inside of her made me feel good and important. How could a woman so young be so?*

108

◆

Another witness was moved to give an "altar call."

*What can I say about Katy? Her actions spoke louder than all the words that we can say. Katy was a blessing in my life. I will not be able to pick up a child without saying "gracias" for Katy. She came to earth and now she is in Heaven and we are sad because she isn't with us. The important part is that she no longer is suffering because now she is in a better place, a place where there isn't pain or tears or illness. Although we are without her body to hug and kiss, she is with God in Heaven. We want to see her again and all we need to do is give our heart to the Savior. The ticket to see her again is free, it is to accept Jesus as your Savior. Katy now is with the children in heaven; she is the teacher of the children in heaven. That is what my companions, daughter and I all say. But we can't avoid being so sad.*

◆

Evelyn Oakes' special music, a soulful a cappella hymn, soothed my heart.

More than one person thanked us for encouraging Katy to stay in Phoenix after her surgery. They loved her that much. I knew then that had been the right decision. Their testimonies confirmed it.

*As one of Katy's Phoenix "family", I can only thank you for lending her to us for this short time. Her ministry here went far beyond the little walls of our church and the streets of our neighborhood community. She will be missed.*

◆

Kit posted her tribute to Katy on the blog and read it at the funeral. Part of it is shared here.

*I have been describing Katy in a lot of detail lately, since we* set up her blog and as I asked scores of people to pray for her. Sometimes I would be a little apologetic, saying I know that I sound like I am exaggerating, but usually I would say something like... but she really is that PURE. The purity was just the crystal clear way in which Katy lived. Her purity was seen in the way she trusted God, believing He was good, all the time and faithful. We saw this so much these past eight months. Katy never argued with God. His way was good. She loved Him that much to trust in His good love for her. Her ability to trust also showed in the way she trusted others...

Maybe the simplest evidence of how sweet she was is that we all name her in this way, "Our Katy," because she truly gave herself to us and in some way allowed each of us to own her. Katy did not merely give time or attention or money, she gave us herself.

Now there is a question we can ask, "Why? Why did Katy do that?" And it is a question I can answer. With as little "Piety" as I can conjure I want all of us to hear this as just a simple fact. "Katy loved God." She wasn't in love with some idea of God. She didn't love God because He "worked" and made her life better. Katy did not love God because He would keep her soul from hell and Katy didn't love Jesus so she could get to heaven. She wanted to go to Heaven because she loved Jesus. And just as Jesus asked, "How can you say you love God whom you have not seen when you don't love man whom you have seen and who is created in the image of God?" We can answer our question of why Katy loved us, because she loved Jesus...

There is no doubt, that our Katy ran a good race and finished well. In our hearts, we have imagined our Lord saying to her, "Well done, good and faithful servant. You have been faithful over a little; I will set you over much. Enter into the joy of your master."

*I know I don't have a clue what it means to enter in our Savior's joy. But I want to. So our comfort is this. Our sweetest sister, daughter, friend knows the joy of her Lovely Lord. She is now forever in that joy.*

Kit's full tribute from Katy's funeral can be read on the website: *tellthemwhatyouknow.com*

When the last notes of the final song faded, the spectators moved outside where they fastened the messages they had written to Katy to helium-filled balloons and released them. They could be seen for a long time as they drifted heavenward. Meanwhile, back inside, the chairs were rearranged around tables and everyone was invited to share a meal that women in the Neighborhood community had prepared. So many remembering Katy and joining us in our sorrow.

A few days later we brought Katy back to Indianapolis and then hundreds more attended a service there. They came from Arizona, Indiana, Michigan, Ohio, Texas, North Carolina, Missouri, Maryland, New York, and I'm sure other places. Rick's cousin Frank had made the funeral arrangements for us. Our wonderful friends and family had handled everything: flowers for the casket, bulletins for the service, a catered meal for after the service. My black suit was hanging in the closet fresh from the dry cleaners. Our house had been cleaned. Our cars were gassed and washed.

The funeral in Indianapolis was held on January 10th at Tabernacle Presbyterian Church, the beautiful 84-year old gothic structure where Katy had spoken at her Thank You Dessert only a few weeks before. Visitation was held Tuesday evening and the next day for an hour before the service. Amy and Lenny met people in the parlor where the slide show was running. Patti Pate, who had often babysat for Katy and her siblings when they were little, kept the refreshment table stocked with cookies and coffee.

Colorful bouquets, sent by loved ones, decorated that room. More of them surrounded the open casket across the hall in the chapel, where

Rick and I stood greeting the hundreds of mourners who came to say goodbye to Katy. They hugged Rick and me, often in tears.

◆

A friend, Janet Starkey, described the crowd on the blog.

> *A huge line of people wound through the building and out to the parking lot, cramping inside to stay dry from the pouring rain. Thank you Jesus, for weeping at your friend, Lazarus' death and thank you that I feel you weep now. Katy, if you can hear my prayer, well done young one. I'm sure your young life reached more people than ten times your life span. You dance right now and rejoice. Thank you for being willing to be poured out for your God in your life and your death. We cling so dearly to this life we only can know, our perspectives are not eternal as yours are now. We have no answers to why you had to die so young and full of promise, and that's part of the pain that those who love you will have to walk with until they see you again.*
>
> *Oh God may the rain that drenches the ground right now like tears bring forth fruit like we have never seen before and a deep peace and comfort in all those who mourn.*

Tab's sanctuary is large, but the pews could hardly contain everyone who came for the service the next day. The tall Eternity Candle and beautiful white bouquet from Amy and Lenny flanked Katy's flower draped casket. Tab's pastor, John Bruington, officiated the service. Leah Crane's clear, beautiful notes soared. Kit repeated her touching tribute. Rich organ music accompanied the hymns we had chosen. Gilbert Orban, who had been a student in my classroom when he was only five years old, spoke. He talked about the time Katy told him she was going to be a teacher when she grew up. After the service people were invited to stay for a meal in the church dining room. Our friend Betsy Paul had arranged for a catered meal. At every place setting was a packet of

112

Forget-Me-Not flower seeds with a note.

*Katy spent her life planting seeds for the Lord all over the world. Now you can plant seeds to honor and remember Katy.*

*"For as the soil makes the sprout come up and a garden causes seeds to grow, so the sovereign LORD will make righteousness and praise spring up before all nations."*

*—Isaiah 61:11*

◆

Again, cards and pens were available for people to share special memories and stories.

*I remember her love of small children. How on any given mission trip she would have 5 kids crawling on her and I remember her beautiful smile, the Love of Christ in that smile.*

*—Kyle Ragsdale [a former youth director Katy had worked with]*

◆

*She has made us better people because she loved us.*

◆

*I will never forget the countless memories of her that give me strength now and forever. I will always miss but never forget my cousin, she who changed the world.*

*—Brian Baker*

◆

*Precious Katy—such a gentle spirit, thoughtful, quiet, but so firm in her convictions and determination to pursue God's will. It was such a blessing to watch her grow--from the days when she helped paint the "Guilford Inn" to Bible studies at our dining room table and in your home, to seeing her at Biola when she was starting to teach at-risk kids, to following her ministry in Phoenix. She was such a gift. She fought a good fight. She was faithful throughout the days God gave her. We are so thankful for her life.*

—Sue Pankratz [her mentor from high school]

◆

*We prayed every day for a miracle in the form of Katy's total recovery. Now we realize the even greater miracle that we have witnessed—Katy's life and the way that she lived it.*

◆

There were many testimonies from those who attended Katy's funeral at Tab that came days, weeks, even months after the service in the form of notes, messages on the blog, and written in sympathy cards. Katy had been gone from Indianapolis for almost nine years, except for short trips. The people there had watched her grow up, but what they knew about her as an adult came mostly from what others shared. Yet, they also spoke of the influence Katy had on their lives.

Some of these testimonies came from members of our immediate family. My sister Judy had asked for prayer for Katy in her 2005 Christmas letter. In the letter she included in their holiday greetings in December 2006, she related what had happened to Katy and the impact she had on her own life.

*…Katy touched so many people so profoundly, yet she managed to make each one of us feel like we had a special bond with her. Jesus is rejoicing in having that special bond now. She never feared death, she always knew God was with her. Easy wasn't what she expected or asked for. But she was never alone in her journey. Oh to have just a fraction of her faith… I wish I could be just a bit more like her… I'm trying.*

After attending Katy's funerals in Phoenix and Indianapolis and

114

witnessing the impact she had had on so many people, Rick's sister Jody wrote to us.

*A week ago, I could not find the right words to say, but after experiencing the love Katy showered on everyone she met, I too have been inspired. I thought I knew Katy, but I really didn't. I learned more about Katy and her beliefs in that one evening than I ever knew in the 26 years I have loved her. She was our "Reel Angel," but she is also Their Angel. Katy will live on in all of us, because she showed us the way to God.*

*I used to only glance at life and the world around me. Katy has given me insight into God's kingdom and I pray that I can be more loving and giving, like her. We have been blessed.*

◆

Letter from Tab's Clerk of Session:

*…Clearly, God called Katy for special work and she was an example to all of us in her obedience to that call. As Kit recounted Katy's journey at the service, I was overwhelmed with a feeling that we had all been in the presence of greatness…*

◆

Katy's Great Uncle and Aunt shared:

*You will forever be with us through your legacy of gentleness, serenity and compassion. You are an inspiration to all who have come in contact with you… We all should aspire "to be like Katy."… Katy, you are forever gentle on our hearts and minds.*

*Love, Great Uncle Chuck and Aunt Sue*

◆

A blog entry shows more.

*Thank you for this blog--this labor of love. I've been following it*
*since the first week, and have felt my own love for Jesus deepen as I*
*observed, from a distance, Katy's faith and trust in her Savior and*
*Lord. I was fortunate enough to be able to attend the funeral last*
*week at Tab, and left feeling sad, but in a strange way, energized...*
*challenged to be better with my family, better in my work, better in*
*relationship with the Lord, just...better.*

—Jennifer Wirt

◆

We received a condolence note from a college friend and roommate, Briahnna.

*Katy was a true friend to me. One I knew I would have for life,*
*I just thought that would be a longer time. She is one of the best*
*people I have ever known in my short life. And by best I mean*
*she was full of virtue, goodness, truth and beauty. She is one of*
*my heroes (I told her that once). Without a doubt, I am a better*
*person for having known her. She modeled Christ to me so many*
*times throughout our friendship..."*

●●●

On January 11, the morning Katy was to be buried in a family
plot in Indianapolis, we (Rick, Amy, Lenny, Heather, and I) drove
to the funeral home to say our final goodbyes in private. Agony that
had no words gripped me as I began to sense the reality of her loss.
Her shocking death had been abrupt and final. I still felt like I was
sleepwalking. We drove to the cemetery where we were joined by other
family and friends. Janet Starkey again captured the scene well as she
wrote on the blog.

*Today is Katy's Burial. The sun shines brightly today, the sky*
*is blue, not a single cloud in sight, it's nearly 60 degrees on this*

*January day. Yesterday it poured all day long, but today it's like spring, how fitting and right dear God, may it be a day of hope and joy for all who love Katy. The pain and sorrow is undeniable, but may joy be felt today, may it transcend the sorrow, Katy as you dance in God's presence today. Today may we dance with you and honor all you lived for. May that joy and dance be our battle cry to death and darkness. To Patty, Rick, Lenny, Amy, Kit, Heather, Kirsten, and all the young warriors who battled for Katy with your love, well done to you too. I know this loss you feel right now will become part of the fabric of your life. May it only be clean pain that brings redemption to you, may it drive you closer to God, not away, may it birth in you the love of God Katy has, may that be her final gift to you and yours back to her.*

The verse on the headstone that marks her gravesite reads:

> *But as for me, it is good to be near God.*
> *I have made the sovereign Lord my refuge;*
> *I will tell of all your deeds.*
> *—Psalm 73:28*

◆

I wanted the verse to reflect who Katy was. I read her writings searching for scripture that was meaningful to her. I kept finding references of her wanting her life to bring glory to God. Then I read what Luis Lemus wrote on his card at her funeral in Phoenix.

*Last time we spoke we talked about life & death. My dad died September 19, 2005. She knew I was in pain. She spoke to me and told me that God has a plan for everyone. I was so scared because I seen him die and just to feel how scary it is to die. She told me not to be afraid, that the best place to be is with God. She also said that she knew that she was very sick and that she wasn't afraid to die because she did what God ordered her to do and that is to serve*

117

*the people. I love Katy and I'm gonna miss her.*

So, Psalm 73:28 was fitting. It was a verse she recorded in her journal. It didn't focus on her life. It spoke of God's goodness and her longing to be with Him. That Spring Gilbert Orban, my former student, donated an oak tree in Katy's memory that was planted in the cemetery where she was buried. There is a plaque beneath it bearing her name and the same verse.

• • •

Yet another observance was held a few weeks later in California, at the end of January. Kristen Kinard, Katy's co-worker and friend, organized a memorial at Ocean View Elementary School where Katy had taught first grade for two years. Teachers, students, and their parents were invited to "remember and celebrate her wonderful life." Kristen shared a beautiful tribute. Part of it is included here:

> *...and then it was time. Katy's body was wearing down and never fully recovered after her second surgery. It was time for Katy to see her Father in heaven. We all wonder why things happen the way they do or why God allowed Katy to leave us, but one thing we know to be true is that we are all better people for knowing Katy Reel. She was a true example of Christ. Katy brightened a room with her smile, loved with her enormous heart and touched lives with her tender spirit.*
>
> *Her Master said to her, "Well done, my good and faithful servant. You have been faithful over a little. I will set you over much. Enter into the Joy of your Master." The Lord set Katy over much. She was a daughter, a sister, a teacher, a leader, a counselor, a confidant, and a best friend. She was Christ's hands and feet to a world in need. I believe she left a legacy of fingerprints on all of us. In Katy I spied a glimpse of Christ here on earth.*

Other Ocean View teachers, former students and their parents wrote memorial and sympathy cards.

*Thank you for touching my daughter's heart in a way she will always remember! The world is a better place because of you, Katy.*

◆

*Our love for Katy will last forever. She has touched our children and they will never forget her.*

◆

*"Your favorite student,"* signed by more than one student.

◆

*We loved having Miss Reel as a 1st grade teacher in her 1st year at Ocean View...What a blessing to every child she was.*

◆ ◆ ◆

A teacher at Ocean View recorded her condolences on the blog.

*Katy's love for others reached far beyond the love of one human being for another. Having tasted of His divine love, she poured it out freely and unashamedly on others. She lavished on each of us a love that nourished, healed, and strengthened every child and colleague that HE entrusted to her care.*

*—Ann Zwiter*

I was touched and comforted by the sympathy cards, notes and blog responses that kept coming. I knew Katy had the attributes that were written and spoken of over and over. Living in her home in Phoenix for almost a year, I had the privilege of witnessing her care for people as I watched the ones who came to sit on her front porch troubled, sometimes scared and uncertain, searching for encouragement or advice or maybe just a sympathetic ear. They came even when she was sick. They came because they trusted her and knew she would welcome them with compassion. I watched her tenderly care for the homeless she came across in her neighborhood. I watched and I learned how to look into the eyes of someone who has lost hope and see them as a child of God, worthy of my attention, not someone to be judged or dismissed as unimportant.

Then I began to think about all the unsolicited testimonies I discovered from all sorts of people about how Katy had helped and affirmed them. High school friends and teachers. College friends. Young moms, kids and staff at NM where she was working. Cousins, aunts and uncles. Staff and parents of her 1st grade students in California. Katy was quiet, even humble so she didn't bring attention to the influence her life had on people, but it was evident if you looked.

Thirteen years later, I received an essay written by a friend from Katy's time in the Neighborhood community that illustrates how difficult her death had been for some of her close friends.

*A Less Fortunate Aftermath (Thankfully, Only Temporary)*

*Her community of young adults, those who considered her more friend than "teacher," were simultaneously inspired to live in a more godly way and immobilized to move down a godly path by grief and confusion, anger and sadness.*

*For a moment, things fell apart.*

*The darkness that only profound loss can bring settled upon some of us. We were broken and we knew it, and we lived it.*

*"Katy, things were so much more… Good, when you were here. It's not fair."*

*Of course, I am not saying that Katy's death was the cause of any of this. I say it merely to show how powerful was her goodness. It touched us, moved us, protected us, seeped into us. Looking back now, 13 years later, I remember Katy with fondness, gratitude that*

120

*I experienced her goodness, awe at the power of influence that she had without ever meaning to do anything but share her love with us. So many called her an angel. I agree—she was as close to an angel as I knew and have ever imagined.*

A childhood friend's letter written five years after Katy's passing sheds more light on her impact:

*As I reflected on the person Katy became in our midst, someone who truly knows how to say yes to God, I see so many ways that her obedience and love have shaped me, healed me, taught me, encouraged me. I can't distill these things into a tidy list—I just know how good it's been for me to rub against the goodness of our God by getting to know His beautiful creation of Katy. And I know that these blessings will continue to unfold, continue to shape me for the rest of my life. Katy remains a very real model for me, and always will be..."*

—*Kirsten Guidero*

How do you survive such a loss when you are frozen and numb, praying for sadness without despair? In part by God's tender comfort through faithful friends. Meals appeared for weeks; thank you notes were written for us. Dot came over and asked, "What do you need to do right now?" and gently led me through writing checks for overdue bills. Kathy offered to help, saying she was good at organizing. We had most of Katy's things in boxes in the living room and Kathy came and labeled each one, listening as I talked. Mary took me on several trips to state parks. We talked, hiked, cried, played canasta, photographed wild flowers and ate delicious comfort food at the park's Inn. These are just a few of the many memories I have of the healing comfort of people who dared to care.

I read books on grief and God's peace that gave words to what I was feeling when I had none, until I was finally able to say, "thank you, God, for Katy." The gift was ours to borrow. I continued to seek His face and trust His love as I delved into scripture and prayed for truth. Even then, I refused to believe anything that was not true, even though it might make me feel better.

Several years later an email was forwarded to me that contained a touching piece that Pete Newlove, husband of a friend of Katy's at Biola, wrote "to document, in my own kind of way, the fact that Katy existed, and that she was a tremendous person... a gift from God, truly."

*"... Why Katy? Why anybody?" I know, I know. But seriously, Why Katy? I feel quite dumb, really, sitting here, knowing that I should try to pull together all of the best, most eloquent, superlative, and beautiful words I can think off, so that anybody who did not know her could get a glimpse, just a little feel, at least, of who Katy was. Everybody who met her walked away feeling like a better person. But no words can possibly be adequate enough.*

*There is solace in the fact that I knew her. My wife was lucky enough to meet her in college, and thus I, when we began to date. But the thing is, when I met Katy, it was like I'd known her since we were in the same kindergarten class together. She was immediately disarming, in the most sincere, humble way a person could possibly be. There was never, ever—as far as I could tell—a trace of insincerity. And even in the moments when even the strongest people in the world would succumb to a moment of weakness, and make some snarky comment about some annoyance, or lash out at somebody for something they did, Katy never made a person feel bad about him or herself. She was nothing but real. And kind. No. More than kind. She was winsome. Endearing. Perfectly good. Perfectly Katy. Ah, but even these words fall short!*

*Katy, never—not even when Death first became a reality to her physical existence—never came off as one who considered her needs to be any greater that anybody else's. She apologized when we saw her in the hospital, that April day in Phoenix. She apologized.* "Sorry I ruined the birthday party," *she said with a smile on her face that was not sad, self-pitying, or even angry, but was somehow humble and perfectly true. Seriously? I thought to myself. You just found out you have brain cancer, and you're apologizing?? But she meant it. Sincerely.*

*I lament that we could not travel to see her in her final days or even go to her funeral. More so, I lament that my kids will never know her. Yes, she was that kind of a person!*

*She died in January.*

*It was unfair.*

*But strangely, in a manner that can only be ascribed to the nature of Katy's wonderful God-given and God-taken soul, a tragedy like this only makes sense… is only fair… was only right… even if I didn't understand it… because it was Katy.*

*It was Katy. The use of the past tense still stings.*

Grief has a will of its own and pounces when you're not expecting it. When that happened I would play beautiful music, walk in the woods, call close friends to dilute my grief by sharing it, even go to a movie to distract me from my profound sadness. I don't remember being angry, only wondering why this terrible thing had happened. I understood I didn't know the big picture, the final story, but desperately hung onto God's goodness, trusting the truth of it.

Eventually, my numbness began to ease. I no longer woke up hoping for the briefest of moments that it was all a bad dream. Then questions started to float into my consciousness. "Did I do all I could have done? Was there some cure we missed?" I was with Katy as much as possible, advocating for her with all the medical personnel involved in her care.

We were all there helping, comforting, loving. I had few regrets, yet if some incident came to mind that I felt remorse for, no matter how small, I would visit Katy's gravesite and apologize over and over until my guilty feelings began to lift.

Gradually I began to wonder about Katy's quiet, tenacious faith that had driven her passionate quest to serve God. A God she knew well and loved. When did that start? What nourished it? I wondered about the effect her love had on such a divergent multitude of people and how her life was a testimony of her faith.

I remembered the journal I had found behind a bookcase in her room, then the others. Were there more? So the search began. I discovered more journals, workbooks from church, notes from friends, memos, sayings that were on the door of the bedroom she had as a child, the blog written for her, and even sometimes by her during her illness. I searched the attic for papers from school and looked for old emails I had saved. Even comments written on memoir notes at her funerals in Phoenix and Indianapolis. These have all come together throughout this book. All pieces of a wonderful puzzle: the journey of a love story between God and Katy.

# Part Two
## *Listening and Learning*
## 1987-1998

# Chapter 6
## *Hearing and Believing*

Several people asked me to share more of Katy's writings after they heard Kit quote them at her funerals. These requests came throughout the months and years after Katy was gone and spurred me to continue the search to learn how Katy became so close to God and such an influence on all kinds of people. It was agonizing at times. I would gather what I found on the dining room table and start to look at it, then realize that it was too painful and put it all away. This process went on for a long time. I would find more information, put it on the table, then be overcome with sadness and put it all away again. I needed someplace where I could lay out what I had and leave it there, coming to look at it when I could. I kept trying.

Then one day I was with a friend at the Flower and Patio Show, held annually at the fairgrounds. Kristin knew my dilemma. As we wandered through the displays, Kristin rounded the end of one aisle and exclaimed, "Here's just what you need!" There was a small, simple cabin, named a "loafing shed." Perfect. We could have it built in the woods near our house. I could put everything there and when it became too difficult, I could just leave it in place, lock the door, and walk away until I was ready to face it all again. It became my sanctuary, a place to pray, read, and write Katy's story. Bryan Paul, another friend, built a beautiful table "for Katy and you," and I was able to start working in earnest.

My search for clues to Katy's quest for God netted over 125 pieces of information, including journals she wrote in high school and college, notes, letters and cards from friends, college applications, high school essays, written testimonies for support letters, a workbook on applying your faith, and many, many others. It became a treasure hunt, and with each piece I learned a little more about how and when Katy's faith began, then grew stronger. One clue led to another. I also uncovered assorted notes and letters written by numerous people to Katy or about her. I began to notice that many of the letters and notes revealed how this light that God grew in Katy had shone on other people; it was a reflection of His love for them. A theme began to form in my mind: hearing, believing, growing, sharing. Perhaps Katy's story should be told.

I typed each discovery into my computer, then read it to Rick. He had been in Indianapolis caring for his ailing father so much of the time during Katy's illness that a lot of what I read was new information to him. I heard him say, "I didn't know that," over and over. We cried together; we laughed together. These were important moments for us that loosened the bonds of sorrow that had been threatening to pull us apart. They united us in our grief and shared history as Katy's parents.

I knew many people were eager to hear more of what Katy wrote, but I hesitated to share her journals that contained her private thoughts and prayers. Then I came across three quotes in her writings that gave me pause. First, a prayer written when she was 17.

I pray that You would use me and my life to share your wisdom and love with others around me.

128

Next, from her application to Biola University.

> As I continue to grow and understand more about the Lord's plan for my life I felt God's call to tell the world about him and it is my greatest desire to be obedient.

I found the third in a journal excerpt from the summer before she started college.

> I am still troubled by a dream I had a while ago; I was all of the sudden in the middle of a very busy place. Everyone had on white veils and headdresses. They were touching this wall that had holes in it. Then Jesus was there. He was speaking to the people; I was watching. He then pointed to me and said, "Tell them what you know."

Related to this dream, a later entry said,

> I told Avery (a college roommate) about my dream and she told me of a place in Israel, to which she has been, called the Wailing Wall where Jews go and touch and put their prayers in holes in the wall. She then showed me a post card of it and it was identical to the images I had seen in my dream.

It was such a difficult decision—should I share Katy's dreams, struggles and joys in hopes that they would inspire others, or should I guard her privacy? I continued to ponder the answer to this question even as I was recording her story. Then one morning I woke up very early, before first light, thinking about the dilemma and the answer came to me insistently: the truth of what Katy knew about God is imbedded in her own story. The details of her faith journey are hidden in her journals. The only way to share her story now was to reveal what she had written in them, even though that probably was not her intention at the time.

It felt (and still feels) like a risk daring to divulge her private thoughts and prayers, no matter how carefully I could edit them. But I realized, this was how she could continue to, "tell the world about Him."

How she fulfilled the mandate Jesus gave her when she was 18 years old, to "tell them what you know," was the theme of Katy's life. Telling her story now is a way to extend her witness.

After consulting people I respected—and much prayer—I was convicted that I would share this remarkable story of a joyful and loving life that touched so many others. My prayer is, and has always been, that the story of Katy's life would bring hope and encouragement to truth seekers.

My search continued, and I was delighted to find a testimony Katy had written for a college application that described early moments in her faith journey.

> I knew of Him; I did not know Him. This is how I would best describe my relationship with Christ the first twelve or so years of my life. I am from a Christian home and have attended the same church [Tabernacle Presbyterian Church in Indianapolis] my entire life. One week during Sunday school when I was in third grade I asked Jesus to come into my heart; I did not know Jesus, but I wanted to. In the silence of that classroom and in my sincere but childlike faith I repented of my sin and accepted Christ as my Lord and Savior. The Lord has been faithful to this promise in my life and each day I learn more about what that means.

Katy didn't tell me, or anyone as far as I know, that she asked Jesus to come into her heart that day. I was so touched when I read that had happened when she was so young. I wondered, in that moment, who that teacher was, who had presented the gospel in such a compelling way. I wanted to figure it out. Then, I found a picture of Katy at about age eight or nine with one of her Sunday School teachers; I thought maybe Carolyn Duvall was the one. Mrs. Duvall was deceased, but I shared that picture with her husband and told him my thoughts.

Even now, when I imagine Mrs. Duvall telling the gospel story to her class of third graders in such a way that it resonated in Katy's heart, I

smile. I am so grateful to her (or whoever that teacher was) and a little sad that I can't tell her how that Sunday morning sparked an enduring faith in a little girl.

Katy's story began to unfold as I sorted through all the material I had gathered, trying to put the pieces into chronological order. I remembered she had written a long thank you letter to Rick and me when she was 21. I searched among Katy's things I had saved and found it. She reminisced about her childhood in this nine page missive.

...I thank you so much for my childhood. I thank you for a brother and sister to play with and learn from.

131

Thank you for clothes to wear and a fun house to live in. Thank you for the many activities that you let me be involved in (and we know there were many). Thank you for being so supportive and taking me to practices, coming to games—and even coaching. I thank you for fun family trips and wonderful family friends.

I thank you with my whole heart for taking me to church and teaching me about loving God. Thank you for: bedtime stories, diaper changes, help with homework, rides to friend's houses, birthday parties, time with cousins, popsicles, piggy-back rides, hugs, ballet, gymnastics, soccer, softball, tennis, the clarinet, ceramics, big wheels, Christmas morning, Bolivia, Jamaica & Romania [mission trips with her Tab youth group], water balloons, the State Fair, family reunions, play group, braces, sleepovers, bike rides, the Kislings [neighbors], Christmas tree shopping, Toby [a family dog], collector dolls, kisses, the Tree Farm, wrestling matches, gingerbread houses, driver's ed, Clifty Falls [Indiana State Park], Girl Scouts, manners, the Riviera [swimming pool], frog hunts, my Bambi blanket, the newts, camping in the backyard, climbing trees, North Central [High School], math tutors, visits to Warsaw [Indiana], the mini-marathon, and Pokagon [another state park].

I am so grateful for the things you taught me in childhood that gave me such a strong foundation for the rest of life ahead of me. These are the values that continue to shape my character, and my decisions...

It was obvious that Katy enjoyed doing so many things as she was growing up. There were wonderful stories about each of these activities and events. Her childhood seemed happy, and rich with many different experiences.

But for some strange reason I wondered, "Had her childhood been happy?" A gnawing feeling in my stomach led me to search through old photo albums. What evidence would I find there? As I came across pictures of Katy as a child, I copied them and arranged them on a bulletin board in my cabin. There she was grinning at me while she blew out birthday candles, gently cuddling a tiny chick, coasting down the hill on a tricycle at nursery school, touching noses with her puppy "Happy," holding her hair down on a windy day at the zoo, sharing a drink with her cousin Holly at a Butler football game… Those heartening photos dissolved my doubts and made me smile each time I glanced up at them from my desk chair.

Katy had always loved going to church every week. When she heard the gospel repeated clearly one Sunday morning, she believed it was true and stepped out in faith. She never wavered in that decision, as far as I could tell. As she began to mature, she began to ask God to reveal Himself to her. He responded and Katy's faith grew deeper.

There were stories of Katy's childhood told by others, including what Kit shared in her memorial tribute. She highlighted the character that God was weaving into Katy even then.

*The Katy we knew and loved showed up early. She was described by her preschool teacher as "cheerful, loyal, a hard worker, persistent, a treasure. My memories of early Katy include her mothering everyone (even then) from the loft of the playhouse at nursery school."*

*When her mom was pregnant with Amy, and Katy was just 3 ½, her tired and swollen mom was resting on the couch. Katy walked by with bucket and soapy water, sponge in hand… "Preg-*

a-nant ladies should not wash floors," *she said and proceeded to scrub the bathroom floor. When Amy was just 1 ½ she had surgery on her foot, with a cast all the way to her hip. Katy carried her everywhere, even though the cast was so heavy. And when the cast came off she still carried her everywhere; Patty wondered if Amy would ever learn to walk.*

*A few years later when Katy was about 10, the neighbor across the street built a very elaborate tree house that went from one tree to another, without cutting any branches or even any twigs. Katy helped him build it, learning the tools and techniques involved. One day his son slipped through the slats on the bridge and dangled from his head. When Katy heard the calamity, she calmly took the drill, set it so it would unwind the screws, loosened the slats and got the boy out.*

*When Katy was 11, her dad included her in his morning running. He was preparing for the Mini-Marathon with 25,000 other runners. Every day Katy ran with her dad. She used the time wisely.* "Dad," *she would begin,* "the gifts you're giving Mom don't work. No more athletic equipment. What she wants for her anniversary is..." *daughterly advice for her father. Well, the event came. The plan was for her to run just the first mile. Rick was instructed to hold Katy's hand the whole time; Patty was so worried she would get lost in the huge crowd. And he did hold her hand. Katy went past the mile marker and kept on running, running the entire half marathon, 13.1 miles.*

*Boy, she was one to run a good race, wasn't she? And she ran it again the next year, but this time stopped to get something to eat midway, so their finishing time wasn't as good.*

Those were some of the stories I had told Kit for her eulogy. Putting them together in sequence, I could see the pattern God was growing in her; she was always seeking to help, wiser than her years, continually focusing on other people.

More of Katy's written testimony told how she began to know God better.

> I continued to hear about God and Jesus but I did not feel like I had changed or gained a greater understanding of who They were. However, during middle school I began asking God to reveal Himself to me and He really spoke to me and told me that the best way to get to know Him was by reading His word on a daily basis. So I began to read a portion of God's word every day and for the first time in my life God's word became alive to me and I realized that the Bible is the inspired, living word of God and a testament of His love for us. After I read more, I began to ask God to make me into the person He wanted me to be and to teach me to be more like Jesus. God began telling me that I was too concerned with worldly standards of appearance, athletic ability and popularity. It consumed me and was even more of a burden than I originally estimated. I asked, and God lifted that enormous burden from my soul and in place of my cynical attitude I found peace and joy in the Lord!

Our friend Lucia, the pastor who had worked with Tab's youth, got to know Katy when she was young. Lucia wrote about her in her online devotional.

> *I have had some great mentors in life and the way in which they live their life has served as a great example for me. Now, you would think that these are all adults who have years on me, but that has not always been the case. I probably first met Katy when*

*she was almost eleven and I am so thankful to have witnessed her*
*zeal for life and her zeal for walking in God's ways. Katy has lived*
*her life committed to Christ from the word go. She lived with the*
*same kind of dedication and goodness as the apostles and her life*
*was an example of how it can indeed be done.*

Katy's fifth grade teacher wrote a note about her to Rick and me.

*I would like to express to both of you what a wonderful job*
*you have done with Katy. She is a good citizen, tries hard, and is*
*sensitive to the needs of others. In sixteen years of teaching, I have*
*worked with many young people. Katy is without any question, at*
*the top of that list. I feel fortunate that Katy was assigned to my*
*class…*

I always feel that Rick and I have gotten a disproportionate amount
of credit for our children.

*…He who began a good work in you will carry it on to*
*completion until the day of Christ Jesus.*

*—Philippians 1:6*

Rod Smith, Tab's youth director when Katy was 14, took the youth
group to Jamaica to help in a children's home high in the mountains.
Kit discussed in her tribute how this and the other mission trips Katy
would experience in the next few years had significant impact on her.

*The mission trips Katy took with her youth group ignited her*
*passion for Kingdom living and Kingdom calling. She went to*
*Jamaica at 14 and worked in a children's home. This is where she*
*first experienced the Lord's calling—it was in Jamaica that she*
*felt He had a special path for her and that, in part, it would have*
*something to do with dispossessed children from a culture other than*
*her own. For many years after this Katy would seek the Lord for the*
*rest of God's call for her and the follow up to what this all meant.*

Katy also detailed the impact the Jamaican trip had on her in a college application.

> Another significant marker in my spiritual life was my mission trip to Jamaica. God used my time at an orphanage in the middle of this island to focus my attention from my personal growth to that of others. I was gripped by the poverty that I saw, and God began speaking to me about His heart for the poor. After my initial trip to Jamaica, I began to realize my passion for children, cultures and travel.

I took great delight in seeing Katy had lived doing what she felt called to do and loving it! It was gratifying to see my child had found her God-given passions and God-given abilities in sync. Being changed by God was a gradual process as He revealed Himself to Katy. The last paragraph in an essay Katy wrote describing her experience in Jamaica showed what she was discovering.

> ...I see five eager children racing towards me begging to be pushed on the swing. I pull myself up and before turning around I take one last glance at the rolling hills and the green grass as if they were a window into the world. I have come to realize that, even in a children's home in the heart of Jamaica, people are people. Even though people may have different appearances, customs, or culture, deep down we all have the need for food and shelter, and most of all, the need to be loved.

> *"Always give yourselves to the work of the Lord because you know that your labor in the Lord is not in vain."*

> —*Corinthians 15:5*

Lucia also has described Katy in sermons and during youth retreats, especially to challenge other youth to set out on their life mission with passion and joy. She wrote this, describing Katy during a mission trip.

*Let me introduce Katy Reel. I first knew Katy in the church youth group. Katy was always one who would step up to help. Serving others was a joy for her. Watching her in action on our mission trip was amazing. She was "at home" with each new way she could be of service. It felt like Katy had a super power to look into another person's eyes and see where she could shine the light of Jesus. She was a natural because her life was dedicated to mission. Katy had a huge heart for children. Actually, Katy had a huge heart for children of all ages. They were drawn to her like a magnet and she was fully with them and for them. Children saw Jesus in Katy. Jesus' words in Matthew 19:14, "Let the little children come to me" were in her heart and children knew it when she was around. She certainly touched my heart.*

The trajectory of those events in her young life followed the path God had paved for her. I was not surprised when, soon after that first mission trip, Katy taped this quote on her closet door.

*AGAIN JESUS SAID, "PEACE BE WITH YOU! AS THE FATHER SENT ME I AM SENDING YOU."*

*—JOHN 20:21*

With that verse, Katy declared her intention to become a missionary.

138

# Chapter 7
*Growing*

As I reread the testimonies Katy had written for her college applications, I discovered more of how God had influenced her character when she was young. I knew she didn't feel comfortable with all her peers, but I wasn't aware of the extent of her angst. In one application she wrote:

> Throughout Middle and High School, I realized that the world was empty. We all were caught in the eternal cycle of trying to fill our emptiness. I knew that drugs, sex, financial prosperity, prestige, fame, cars, big houses and anything else (people) were trying to use, would never fulfill their needs and give them peace. I cried out to God. I wanted and needed Him; I wanted Him to change me as only He could. He grabbed hold of me and I began to read the Word and understood it as I never had before. Gradually, the Lord began to change me from a very

sarcastic person who felt she had nothing to offer, to someone who is confident of her Savior's love, has a peace that surpasses all understanding, and has hope that the Lord is going to use her to further His kingdom.

Katy's activities in school and church reflected the changes she asked the Lord to make in her.

I was blessed to go to public schools for elementary and high school which has provided me with the opportunity to be a witness among my peers who don't know Christ. I am very involved with my youth group. At school I am involved in Learning Unlimited, a program in which students are given time during school on Wednesdays to do community service projects of their choosing. The three projects I chose were: helping students with special needs in a first grade classroom, tutoring ESL students from Vietnam and China, and assisting my youth director.

Reading that Katy had witnessed to her peers in high school surprised me, and I wished I had more details. I was proud of her, and I also wondered when she had gained enough courage to do that. I knew that she lived her faith, but I hadn't realized she spoke truth to unbelievers.

The Learning Unlimited curriculum required students to journal their experiences. Katy reported on her work with first graders.

I learned that I can make a difference one person at a time, that I really like working with kids and that I would probably enjoy a career in teaching. I learned that I like cutting, pasting and coloring just

142

as much as I did in first grade. I learned that I can do a lot more than I credit myself as being able to do.

Her notes from working with junior high Chinese and Vietnamese English language learners show more of what she was learning.

I really admire these kids...

♦

She just needed some encouragement.

♦

We all could learn a thing or 2 from her.

♦

I learned that individual differences are what give a person character and I must keep that in mind and try to be patient.

♦

I didn't want to waste time just wandering around aimlessly, so I went to another teacher who I know needs help.

♦

I will keep trying different activities until I find one that works well.

♦

I told him he could use Chinese words also. We both learned new vocabulary from each other.

♦

Her supervising teacher praised Katy's work with the students.

*"You are a born teacher. You obviously appreciate cultural diversity and can relate to people very different from yourself. Katy, I am being truthful when I say I can't imagine a beginning teacher doing better than you have done in creating lessons and teaching these children. I am amazed."*

This sentiment was confirmed by another friend, who wrote on a memorial card at her funeral.

*"She seeks out friends who share her values and lifestyle, but is still able to reach out to others who live differently."*

In her third semester of Learning Unlimited, Katy chose to assist Kyle Ragsdale, Tab's Youth Director, when she was a senior in high school. Later, she discussed that experience in her application for a Leadership Mentorship Scholarship at Biola University.

I believe I have had an impact on the spiritual growth of those around me because I have been able to encourage other youth, help organize activities and trips that are created to encourage spiritual growth; pray with and for other youth, and work with other youth in creating tools that encourage spiritual growth.

Kyle later said of her:

*I feel so blessed to know someone so faithful and godly. What a witness to me (and all your peers) you've been. I recognize as I'm writing, that so much of the good things we've done, you helped accomplish. I definitely am thankful for you and I'm proud of what a Christ-like example you are, even though I didn't have anything to do with it.*

I learned more about how Katy was growing closer to God from other remarks she made on that application.

> I would like people to describe me as a leader who loves the Lord and seeks His will. Also, I would like to be described as a leader who is just as willing to listen as to talk. Most of all, I would like to be described as a leader whose actions and words have the same focus: *to do justice and love mercy and to walk humbly with your God.* — Micah 6:8

When Katy was a junior in high school she said to me, "Mom, you're great, but I feel the need of another mature Christian to mentor me." We prayed together, asking God to bring Katy just the right person to mentor her. The very next day, when I was at church, Sue Pankratz came up to me and said, "Patty, God has placed Katy on my heart. Do you mind if I mentor her?" Those were Sue's exact words, fulfilling Katy's request of God. That incident was the most concrete proof of the reality of God that I had ever experienced. To this day, I carry it in my heart. I take it out to show people who are questioning, and to remind myself when my own faith needs bolstering.

Sue was the perfect person to mentor Katy. She had been a missionary in China. She and her family lived and worked with the poor in the inner-city of Indianapolis. So Katy, often with a friend, would drive to Sue's home after school for Bible study, learning more about God and how He was trustworthy. Katy sometimes would babysit for Sue's daughters. One day, Rick found a note Katy had left for him.

> Dad—I'm going to the Pankratz's to babysit. I will probably be back about 8 or 8:30. I'll call before I leave the house. If you call, the answering machine will probably answer, so don't worry. No one is going with me—everyone is busy, but don't worry, I'll be

I will admit that having Katy drive alone to the area where Sue lived made me nervous. She had a terrible sense of direction and I was afraid that she would turn the wrong way when she left Sue's and get lost in the rough, unfamiliar neighborhood. But I, too, was learning to trust God. Sue knew my concern and would stand in the street watching Katy drive away, phone in hand, and call me to report that Katy had turned the right way and would be able to find her way home. Then, when my parent's pastor and his wife were murdered two blocks from our house, I called Sue, baffled by the irony of violence in the "safe" suburbs, so far from the inner-city where she lived. Sue, who knew the Bible intimately, seemed to always find Biblical answers to life's questions. She quoted Matthew 10:29-31: "Are not two sparrows sold for a penny? Yet not one of them will fall to the ground outside your Father's care. And even the very hairs of your head are all numbered. So don't be afraid; you are worth more than many sparrows." She explained that nothing would happen to Katy without the knowledge of the Father and that God loves her even more than I do. I held that wisdom close from then on, and remembered it when times got hard.

My quest continued as I delved further into Katy's writings. One day, when I was searching through the books stacked on the floor-to-ceiling bookshelves in our living room, I unearthed a workbook of Katy's titled *Experiencing God Day-by-Day, The Devotional and Journal* by Henry Blackaby and Richard Blackaby. I vaguely remembered that Tab's youth group had worked on that study when she was in high school. The workbook had daily Bible readings followed by the authors' commentary and blank lines for the reader's responses. As I looked through the workbook, I discovered Katy's handwritten notes on many of the pages.

Clutching the workbook, I grabbed my coffee and headed out to my cabin to study it. As I thumbed through the pages, I read Katy's words with growing excitement. I couldn't believe it! Here was the clue I had been searching for that showed how Katy became such a devout Christ follower! Katy had become who she prayed she would become—God's humble follower, joyfully loving and serving others. Her prayers asked God to make her more like Him. They showed how deep her relationship with God had become by that time; she must have been a junior in high school then.

As I continued to read Katy's responses, I began to remember similar themes in the notes people had written about Katy and in the cards she had kept from friends. There were so many. At one point in time, I had begun to record those sentiments, scribbling them on post-it notes and sticking them on the wall of my cabin. The wall was covered in yellow and blue squares. I started reexamining the notes pasted there and found they echoed the very traits Katy had prayed for God to grow in her. My heart raced. Gripping her Experiencing God workbook, I stood in front of the note-speckled wall and matched her responses to those notes. Surely God had answered Katy's prayers and here was the evidence.

There were messages from high school and college friends, co-workers, students and parents at Ocean View, friends, other staff and parents from the Neighborhood community, and even from relatives. Reading those beautiful thoughts helped soften the ache in my heart. I wanted to organize them, so I took a notebook and wrote each of Katy's workbook responses on a separate page. Pealing the post-it notes off one by one, I matched them with Katy's specific prayer or statement from the book.

For example, Katy wrote the following:

> Lord I pray that I would constantly, whole heartedly seek you. Lord I pray that my seeking would be such a huge thing in my life that it would attract others and help others grow close to you themselves. I pray that I wouldn't be known as someone who seeks

happiness or praise but a humble servant who seeks to be with You and to know You.

> "The way she sought His way for her life is a model for all of us to follow."

> "Thank you for helping all of us who know you to fall more in love with Jesus."

These notes showed God's response to that prayer.

Katy repeatedly wrote about God's love and prayed to know and emanate it.

> Lord, I thank you for Your amazing love. Show me how to love through Your Holy Spirit. Help me to love those that are hardest to love. Help me to see them as You see them. Lord, show me how to express my love, that I may glorify You in all things.

> Even in times of doubt I am assured of God's love through His involvement in my life thus far. Looking back at my life I cannot deny or forget the amazing things He has done. In Jesus Christ is proof that I know that He does, always has, and always will love me.

> "You were here to bless those around you, to be a deep, true and bright example of God's love."

> "Every time you hold a little one in your arms you are an extension of Christ. Your love for Him radiates from you."

These notes were a testament to those answered prayers.

Christlike love is difficult and very painful at times. In order for Christ to love others

> "I learned how to love and show it by watching Katy's example. She could calm a playground fight with her soft words and loving hugs."

> "I am so absolutely serious when I say that your face radiates with the love of Jesus. It glows and shines. I'm sure many people have told you this very thing. It's incredible and a gift of God... your life a gift to Him."

through me I have to make myself vulnerable and forgive even when it is difficult. Christ-like love cannot look back and cannot seek revenge. Christ-like love means humbling yourself completely and letting God love through you.

My heart caught when I read two of Katy's prayers that seemed to foreshadow her struggles, but at the same time, underscored her faith. Katy was 16 years old when she wrote the words below.

Not only do I need to conform my prayer life to that of Christ, but I need to conform my will to His. He will not always spare me from suffering, but He will always love me.

> "You fought a valiant fight and you inspired everyone with your gallant demeanor and unflinching faith."

> "The way she handled herself over this last year was a real inspiration to me. May I learn to have her faith."

Help me endure hardships with patience and grace as Jesus did. Help me not to become bitter. Teach me in my trials. Lord, help me be obedient.

Ten years later, she lived these words as she battled brain cancer. I saw no bitterness, no doubt, just trust and obedience grown out of an enduring relationship with God. I was not the only one who was inspired by how Katy dealt with the gravity of her illness. Many comments from the blog, the guest book in the hospital, and get-well cards confirmed God's answer to Katy's pleas.

The results of still other prayers Katy wrote were captured in the witness of others.

"It has been sweet to watch you live. You are so real and honest. You are an expression of God's love to all of us."

"I'm amazed by you constantly—your faith, your honesty, your purity, your service to others, your heart, your sense of humor. Jesus is so evident in your life."

Dear Lord, I pray that I would find encouragement in the Word instead of in others. Help the Word to become not something that I read but something that I do and someone I am becoming.

So often we hear "God is my best friend" and "God wants to be your friend." But God is our Father, Creator, Shepherd, Savior and Lord. I need to learn to fear Him as much as I do love Him.

"Our Katy knew Jesus perhaps better than any of us."

I know that Christ brings peace that surpasses all understanding to all that cry out to Him.

"Knowing that you pray for me helps me make it through the tough times and joyful times as well. You put the concerns of others first."

"I know that the peace of Christ that passes all understanding is true for I have seen it—in, through, and around Katy Reel. While her peace, serenity were constant, her strength, courage and mission has always humbled me."

Prayer is one of the greatest gifts He has given us to help us through these times, and we pray knowing that Jesus was on earth and He knows and survived blamelessly.

I have included more of Katy's prayers, paired with comments from people who knew her well, on the website.

It is hard to adequately convey the effect this crucial discovery had on me. After all my searching, I'd found the essential key to how Katy became the humble, devout, and loving person she was: God had answered the fervent prayers she offered when she was 16 years old. I was elated to finally be able to come to this understanding. She indeed became who the Lord created her to be.

As I studied Katy's responses in *Experiencing God*, I came to three conclusions:

One, reading what Katy's friends, colleagues, students and their parents saw in her validated our (Amy, Lenny, Rick, and my) own perceptions. We weren't the only ones who knew her compassionate love.

Two, I was struck by the realization that I didn't come to her level of understanding of God's love for me until I was much older. In fact, it was decades after my 16th birthday when I experienced a sudden revelation that changed my belief in God from academic and hopeful to heartfelt and sure. I began to wonder what my life would have been like if I had known God this deeply when I was as young as Katy. Much later, after Katy passed, I could look back and see how God had prepared me to cope with her illness and death through that knowledge. I doubt I could have survived those hard days without knowing that the Lord and His heaven were real.

Finally, something stirred in me when I observed the pieces of Katy's story fall into place. I could follow the path of her relationship with God, how it had grown since she heard the Gospel as an eight-year-old. I could see how her prayers that were so mature for a teenager had come to be. Her unwavering trust in Him had been forged from her continual seeking, praying and studying His Word, and daring to live what she learned. Indeed, Katy's love for God was always real and resolute. I could only say, "Thank you, Lord. Your love molded Katy into the sweet, precious child you gifted to so many."

# Chapter 8
## *Answering God's Call*

Katy began to journal the spring semester of her senior year in high school following a suggestion she heard at Urbana, a prominent Christian student missions conference.[1] Thankfully, it became a practice she continued the rest of her life. Much of the content here is from those journals. They gave me a window into her insights and dreams; frustrations and joys. Throughout this book, I have shared what I felt would contribute to Katy's testimony—outlining her deepening faith and obedience to God, her ability to "hear" Him, her discovery of her calling, her passion to serve others. In this chapter, I've shared several of her journal entries from 1996 and 1997 that illustrate her process of discerning God's call to become a missionary.

In the summer of 1996, Dan Rexroth, Tab's youth director during most of Katy's high school years, led the teens to far off places to see what God was doing there, and how other believers worshiped Him. In June, Katy and Lenny traveled to Bolivia with a group of other young people from Tab. I was excited for them to have those experiences, but at the same time I was concerned about unknown dangers. I remember one morning in particular when I felt the need to pray for safe travel for them, so I got on my knees and prayed. When they returned, I discovered that on that day, the brakes on one of the vans malfunctioned as they were descending a narrow mountain road. Fortunately, they were able to stop after several harrowing minutes and ingeniusly repair the brakes using part of Dan's leather belt. The van arrived safely at its destination.

In Bolivia, they traveled to intriguing places like Santa Cruz, La Paz, Cochabamba, the Amazon Forest, Lake Titicaca, and the Andes Mountains. They mingled with local youth groups in fellowship and worship, and helped improve the facilities of two children's camps. I found a journal Katy wrote on the first week of that trip. Among her notes:

> ... no lanes, no stoplights and no rules about driving. If a car wants to merge onto a street it merely turns and hopes the other cars don't hit him... a little girl only about four or five covered with dirt and with an infant strapped to her back, begging for money... vendors everywhere trying to sell food and everything else you could imagine... raw meat sitting out without any kind of refrigeration... delicious ice cream!... just as earlier in the afternoon there was no water... people selling souvenirs... ducks, monkeys, dogs, cats, guinea pigs, chickens, parrots and mice for sale... park near the top of the mountain... a llama in the woods... two more... gorgeous view of Cochabamba and the other mountains... even though the songs were in Spanish and the sermon was in Spanish it was very moving... balloon volleyball... laughed a lot... climbed a hill to get to a local church... children running

around... two hour van ride to Camp Candelaria... made dinner... discovered Timmy (a mouse), Milo (bat) and caught the towel on fire...discovered that hygiene wasn't a major concern of the Bolivians... breakfast of rice and bread... chipped paint... getting the plaster and mud off the rafters required me to climb the cat walk and the brick wall of the bathroom... dish duty... kitchen duty... painted the rafters green... used gasoline to take green paint off... tree frog... prepared breakfast...cleaned the toilets... attempted to start the fire... Bolivian workers and some of the guys poured foundation... don't think I have ever seen a more blue sky... unloaded 20 2x4's and 250 bags of cement (50 #s each)... chiseling cement... popcorn and hot chocolate...evening meeting...

These trips allowed Katy the opportunity to participate in missions work as a teenager and fueled her awareness of God's love for the poor and her interest in other cultures. Kit explained how important that was to Katy in her tribute.

*She was a kind of big sister to a lot of people in the youth group. Nurture was her game and she was on it. The group took another mission trip, this time to Bolivia. One of the projects in the camp was to paint the cabin, up on the second floor. It was a rickety cabin and the ladder was even ricketier and no one wanted to get up on the homemade ladder. As they all stood stumped about what to do next, Katy climbed the ladder. She was very willing to do that. But not because she was the kind of person who did the right thing and wanted everyone to notice. She just liked doing the right thing because she CARED. She wasn't trying to care, she just cared, and it wasn't an effort with her.*

*Katy was instinctive with the Bolivian orphaned kids. They may have had diseases or were really dirty or really hungry, but Katy held them, rocked them, let them cling to her. And yet, looking back, it wasn't what she did that stands out, but the attitude she did it with, the genuineness, the loving spirit that was her.*

In July of that year, Katy flew to Romania with another group from Tab, landing at a tiny airport in Timisoara. There, near Dracula's fortress, they camped with local youth and hiked in the Carpathian Mountains. She noted in a journal:

The Romanian people were so generous and willing—they wouldn't even let us put our own tent up. We were told to bring our own food, but they fixed us some warm soup. It got very cold after the sun went down so they built a fire and insisted we take the closest seats. They started singing and people from nearby camps came over to join. Everyone asked if I was cold and when I said yes they gave me their blanket and a coat.

After camping for three days they took a train to Zimnicea, gazing out the windows at fields and fields of sunflowers along the way. In that town of about 14,000 inhabitants, they visited the church that Tab had helped build, played basketball and soccer with Romanian young people, swam in the Danube River, watched horse-drawn carts move among cars in the streets, and noticed rows of plain concrete block apartments. They again saw children begging in the street. One little child grabbed an ice cream cone that Katy's host family had just bought her. Katy didn't mind at all, but of course, they were embarrassed and quickly replaced it. They witnessed remnants of Ceausescu's reign— poverty from drained family resources and a generation of abandoned street children.

Katy revealed what those mission trips meant to her in a college application.

> Later, I was able to go on additional trips to Bolivia and Romania. Through these experiences the Lord continued to reveal His character and His love for His people, especially His children in need.

A church member encouraged Katy to attend Urbana after she heard of her desire to follow Jesus abroad. Katy traveled to the conference in December of her senior year of high school, where thousands of mission-minded young people gathered from around the globe. Her small group had mostly South Korean students who were as passionate about serving the Lord as she was. After she came home, she told me how excited she was about her small group. "At last I found people who feel like I do!" Kindred spirits. International speakers encouraged specific steps for preparing to share the Gospel. I found her Urbana commitment card. On it she pledged:

> Jesus Christ as Lord over every area of my life

She wrote these goals to help prepare to fulfill those promises.

- better steward of money and time
- less or no TV
- only Christian music
- at least 1 hour in the Word
- read through the Bible
- join a prayer group
- keep a journal

Katy took another step in preparing to become a missionary when she and I took a 15 week course in missions. I loved sharing this class with Katy. *Perspectives on the World Christian Movement* taught "how God is redeeming people from every tribe, tongue and nation and how He calls all disciples to participate with Him."[2] It was a wonderful opportunity to share this with her, especially knowing she would be going away to school in a few short months. We discussed each night's topic on the drive home, stopping for warm Krispy Kreme doughnuts fresh out of the oven. I smile when I look back and think about that time, grateful we were together. Answering the question, "How has God already led me in becoming a World Christian?" she listed her missions experiences.

A.    *Perspectives student*

B.    *Jamaica*

C.    *Romania*

D.    *Bolivia*

E.    *Urbana '97*

F.        *Missions books*

G.        *Discussions with missionaries from Tab*

As she learned more about mission work, Katy questioned the need to go to college. "I wish I could go where I am going to go and get started." She was eager to begin what she felt God was calling her to do right after high school, but I felt uncomfortable with the idea of her taking off on her own at 18, especially without connecting with a mission organization. I suggested that she would need training to do that work well. She entertained the idea of taking a gap year off from school, but changed her mind. Katy was learning the discipline of waiting for God's timing as her understanding of His plan for her was coming into better focus. So, she was obedient.

When it came time to choose a college I sought God's will, saying I would go wherever I was called. I ended up at Biola University in La Mirada, California. Deciding to go to Biola was a huge step in faith for me, as I had never even visited California and very few of my 600 classmates were even venturing out of the Midwest.

Biola was the unlikely result of the "Great Midwest Christian College Tour." Katy had said, "I'm tired of swimming upstream. I want to go to a smaller school with like-minded kids. My personal ministry goals are eventually to become involved in career missions (probably in Northern Africa) teaching English as a second language as a means of tentmaking."[3] So we toured many Christian colleges within driving distance of Indianapolis. At that time, Teaching English as a Second Language was usually offered as part of a master's level curriculum. At one college we visited, Katy was troubled by their strict regulations, including mandatory chapel worship where student attendance and behavior was recorded, a required dress code and strictly enforced dating restrictions. She wanted to be with other students whose worship was genuine, not feigned. While she researched other Christian colleges, Biola University kept coming up. Maybe God was speaking. A trip to California confirmed it, so she applied to Biola.

> I believe that Biola can assist me in my growth as a Christian by integrating the Bible and course material, so that I may be 'trained in righteousness and equipped for the work the Lord has for me.' 2 Timothy 3:17.

> I believe that Biola can challenge me to grow through in-depth study of God's word and new applications of God's word. I also believe that in requiring a minor in Bible, Biola can help me to understand the importance of God's word and the emphasis that should be placed on it. Also, I think that Biola is an environment in which I can grow through the fellowship and encouragement of other students seeking to serve the Lord. Biola can also assist my growth as a Christian by providing me with godly professors who are mature Christians and have a vested interest in teaching me and encouraging me in my walk with Christ.

> Finally, Biola can help me to grow by teaching me the skills I will need in the mission field and how to share my love for Christ with others.

Biola awarded Katy a Leadership Mentorship Scholarship, which seemed to affirm her decision. Kit's tribute explained the significance of Katy's college choice.

*Katy picked a college 2000 miles away from home. She picked*

160

*it because of this "something," this awareness that she was supposed to serve Jesus somewhere. Biola had a historical missions department; she would go there for that. Rick and Patty gave her such a freedom to follow this dream, letting their "Joy" go so far from home; this was a purposeful release to let Katy become who it was clear she was becoming.*

Katy's testimony about this time in her life shows how her trust in God was growing.

> Through the grace of God's gift of faith I have come to trust Him with the small decisions in life, which previously I was unwilling to do, so that I am now able to step out in faith and trust him with big decisions. Also, during the past two years I have grown to accept God's perfect timing and, as a result, have become very patient. I still struggle with giving God total control over certain areas of my life that I feel like I need to control.

She revealed much in this journal about the path God was leading her down.

> **April 23, 1997:** God has given me peace about going to Biola, however my heart aches knowing I will miss my family—(I won't see my sister after her first day of high school; I won't see my brother getting ready for Prom) and my friends and many others, but I believe and know that the Lord has called me to Biola and will bless my time there. Praise God that I will miss these people for four years on earth but will spend eternity with them and Him in heaven!

Oh, how those words tugged on my heart when I read them. They felt like she somehow sensed that her life was going to be cut short. But knowing she was sure that she would be reunited with the ones she loved in heaven softened the toll that premonition took on my heart.

> **April 24, 1997:** The Smiths[4] came over for dinner tonight and it was such a blessing to talk to people from Tab who have a real heart for missions. (They are leaving for Southeast Asia in June.) It was also neat to hear that God really confirmed their call through the Perspectives class.

Katy attended a Women's Retreat hosted by Tab. Afterwards, she reflected:

> **April 25-27, 1997:** Mom, Brenda Stout, Wendy and Sara Wilkerson, and I went to "A Weekend Apart" Tab's women's retreat. It was incredible! Through many different women, God encouraged and loved me so much! The speaker, Hanna Miley, was born in Germany and at seven escaped on one of the last vehicles allowed out, leaving her parents behind. She grew up in England and was a missionary with OM (Operation Mobilization) for 20+ years.[5] Mom introduced me and I got to speak with her one-on-one and she was very encouraging. Joanie Walden told me that one day she saw Lenny and I standing together and he had his arms around my shoulders and she thought, "That is how I want my kids to be when they get older." Karen Jefferies saw me walking with my Perspectives book and she asked me if I was taking the course. She then said, "I want to tell you, if you feel like God is calling you to do something, do it. If you feel like you are supposed to do it, do it. And don't let anyone stop you or tell you

you can't do something because you are young."

Hanna had us create collages from pictures in magazines and at first I thought it was weird—but I loved it. We had an opportunity to share it with our small group and I did. When I explained that I chose a child to represent myself because my peers thought of me as naïve, they both said that they felt the same way when they were young and that the childlike faith and innocence I have will be worth it and everyone else will spend time wishing they were "naïve" too. Saturday night I got the opportunity to pray with Mom and Miriam Guidero and felt so loved by God through the involvement of those two women in my life. Sunday morning we had a service and were given the opportunity to share. Mom pulled me up to the front and praised God for me and asked people to pray for me at Biola and in my calling to be a missionary. A woman I have never spoken to came up to me and said, "I cry about once a year. I never cry; but when you got up there with your mom, I cried and I hope that I can have that kind of relationship with my daughters."

**April 28, 1997:** Tonight was our final Perspectives lecture... many practical applications of a desire for missions... I sent another $24 to Compassion International.[6] I think God wants me to continue that gift, but maybe I should give to more missionaries? I am praying that God would guide me to a summer job, but so far I have received no direction. I only have 22 days of school left!... God give me patience and wisdom.

Even though Katy seemed to be eager, even excited about her calling to do missions and heading off to Biola and beyond, it was hard for her to think about leaving what she knew and loved, her friends and family. Her decisions to follow God were not made lightly, but with determination.

**April 29, 1997:** Today I went with Katie and her parents to "Champions on Ice" at Market Square Arena. I can't believe that in less than six weeks I will be sitting in the same place, graduating from high school. As I was sitting there I was trying to imagine sitting there on the floor in my cap and gown with my family in the seats. I know I'm going to cry. I had so much fun with Katie, and yet I was sad because I realize how much I'm going to miss her next year.

**May 2, 1997:** ...After that we went to the Children's Museum. It was so much fun. We rode on the carousel, walked up and down the ramps, went to the Science Works, etc. It was extremely sad. I realized that I have grown up and continue to do so—even in a few years I may not still be friends with Anne and Katie. I wasn't exactly sad, I was more reminiscent. I'm glad that in Christ I don't have to worry about the future. I was standing there looking at my friends wondering where the Lord will lead us in the next five, 10 or even 20 years!

**May 5, 1997:** Today was a challenging day. I spent four hours taking the English Literature Advanced Placement exam! After school I went to Anne's to see her grad dance dress and she helped me with Pre-Cal. I don't know what I'll do without her next year!

Katy stepped into the unknown, sure that God's plan was best and that He would always be with her. She wrote about what seemed to be a confirmation that Biola was God's choice.

**May 26, 1997:** The Lord has been so faithful and creative in bringing me to a roommate for next year. Hanna Miley, our women's retreat leader, had talked with me about missions during the retreat and told me that I reminded her of a girl named Heather that was the daughter of one of her friends. Last Thursday my mom received a letter from Hanna saying that Heather had decided to go to Biola and was looking for a roommate. What's even more amazing is that Hanna was looking for a way to contact me and tell me and the day she heard from Heather was the same day she received a letter from Mom including our address. I called Heather and her mom answered, telling me that she couldn't believe I was on the phone because they were just talking about me. I got to talk to Heather; she seemed very nice. She told me she will be working at an inner-city camp this summer for her mom's outreach! We decided to room together. Praise the Lord.

I came across a note that friends had written after Katy passed that attests to Katy's sense of confirmation from God.

*It is curious to see how God makes connections for His purpose. We knew George and Hanna Miley from our days in San Diego. Claudia invited Hanna to speak at the Tab Women's Retreat. This led to the connection with Kit and her daughter, and ultimately resulted in Katy going to Phoenix. The storyline to me is that there are no chance encounters when God's hand is in the matter, and that God will use any willing heart anywhere He chooses. Katy and her beautiful smile are forever fixed in our minds.*

—Matt, Claudia Judge

She contemplated what would be in front of her the summer after high school before leaving for Biola.

**July 4, 1997:** Today is my third day of Cornerstone Music Festival... I am loving it![6] The music is great and it has been really good to be out of my house. I feel like I am in limbo. I have brought closure to high school, but I can't really move on yet. I pray that God would use this time... I feel as if all I was holding onto was being ripped away. Maybe God is doing this to make me more dependent on Him. I almost feel numb, but I am a little sad.

**August 3, 1997:** While on the beach in Clearwater, Florida (where we—Tab's youth group—taught VBS for a week), I went for a walk by myself to talk to God. I felt distanced from him and I felt some sin was blocking our relationship. I prayed out loud that God would show me what was wrong and immediately James 3:6 popped into my head. Later in my room I looked up the reference and was I convicted! Taming of the tongue is definitely something I need to work on.

The last few weeks of the summer were filled with the typical college preparations—purchasing sheets and blankets, some new clothes (end-of-summer sales were perfect for the weather in Southern California), and other school necessities (i.e., a computer); and saying goodbye to friends and family. I was excited for Katy. I brushed aside any thoughts about how strange her absence would feel because I was so happy for

166

her to begin to prepare for her chosen life's work. All the pieces had fallen into place, seemingly orchestrated by the hand of God. How else do you explain finding a college 2000 miles from home, that you had never heard of, that equips you for exactly what you feel called to do? A place that would introduce you to your future best friend with the same heart for missions work and for the poor? It felt like she was embarking on a great adventure.

# Notes

1 Urbana Student Missions Conference is a five-day meeting of thousands of college and grad students, faculty, pastors, ministry leaders, and missions organizations from many countries, sponsored by Varsity Christian Fellowship.

2 Perspectives on the World Christian Movement is a ministry of Frontier Ventures that consists of a 15-week course designed around four "vantage points": biblical, historical, cultural, strategic.

3 "Tentmaking" is performing Christian service without pay while earning a living by other means and doing one's work responsibly as a testimony to others.

4 Name changed.

5 Operation Mobilization is a Christian missions agency.

6 Compassion International is a child sponsorship and Christian humanitarian aid organization.

7 Cornerstone Music Festival was a Christian music festival hosted by Jesus People USA that was held annually from 1984 to 2012 attracting many thousands every July.

# Chapter 9
## A New "Home"

Rick and I flew to California with Katy to help her get settled and to see where she was going to be spending the next four years. Rick's Aunt Sue and Uncle Chuck lived 35 miles from La Mirada, where Biola is located; we had items for Katy's dorm room delivered to their house. Uncle Chuck gave Katy his business card and told her he could be reached anytime she needed help. That assurance gave me great comfort. We moved her into the dorm room, toured the campus, and attended parent orientation meetings. Rick and I loved Biola! We loved the fun, encouraging atmosphere, the biblically based teaching and the interest of the faculty and staff in the lives of their students. We lingered for a while. Probably a little too long, because Katy said, "I'm ok. You can leave now." We had to tell her that we weren't worried about her, we just wanted to stay because we liked it there.

I thought I might be sad on the plane ride home, but I wasn't. My friends kept asking if I was unhappy that my daughter was going to school so far away, but I was not. I felt like God had led her there; it was an important part of His plan for her. The next day I was reading a newspaper article about how upset President Clinton was that his daughter was going to college in California. For some reason that article triggered something in my heart, and I sobbed and sobbed. I thought, "Who can understand how it feels to have their child leave home and go so far away?" It soon came to me that God would understand. Jesus left His Father's side to come to earth. So, I prayed, telling God how much Katy's leaving hurt, and I "heard" in my heart, "Let not your heart be troubled." Comfort from the Lord. Two hours later Katy phoned me, "I just want you to know that you are the best mother anyone could have, and I love you." My anxiety melted with God-given peace.

Katy journaled about how she felt at Biola. It was the right choice for her.

The Lord was extremely faithful and met me at Biola with many blessings including fellowship with amazing peers, biblically based courses, encouraging professors, great times of worship and much more. However, one of the greatest of my blessings was having Heather Danley as a roommate. Once I got to know Heather and her family, I began to hear about Phoenix and Neighborhood Ministries. The more I heard about what God was doing [there] the more it began to strike a chord with my own heart and what God had been teaching me.

Communication was a strength of Katy's. She stayed in touch with family and friends back home via email and phone calls. We knew what was happening on the surface, but what she wrote in her journals revealed more. In her emails, she told us about the activities and new friends that kept her busy along with carrying a full load of courses. She mentioned raising funds for her dorm by being part of the audience for a tv show, retreats for the Leadership Mentorship Program, GYRADs (Get Your Roommate A Date), watching soccer and flag football games, worship services, computer difficulties, having many overnight guests, shopping at thrift stores, sharing textbooks to save money, day trips to Catalina Island and the beach, interesting chapel speakers and museum visits. Occasionally, she mentioned some incident of dorm drama but didn't dwell on it. She always asked for news from home and wanted to hear about family and friends because "it is important that I know so I can pray for them."

Her journal entries showed another aspect of her life there--her yearning for God.

> **Sept. 3, 1997:** *The Lord is a stronghold for the oppressed, a stronghold in times of trouble. And those who know your name put their trust in you for you, O Lord, have not forsaken those who seek you.*

> **Sept. 7, 1997:** I just got off the phone with my family. Lenny called me! I was so happy. I also talked to Mom and Amy. I pray that God will lead me to a church and to someone who could give me a ride.

Her emails were usually brief, but they gave me a glimpse of her life at Biola, for which I was grateful. I missed her terribly and reading her emails helped ease the pain of separation. I printed out each of them and bound them together in a binder. Now they serve as precious reminders of her. I have included below the ones that outline some of her feelings and experiences in a college so far from home and family.

> **September 17, 1997:** To answer your question, I am doing great. I just have a lot of work and a lot of reading that I am having trouble keeping up with. I

still love it here and I can't wait until Amy visits.

**September 23, 1997:** Hello! Amy it is totally fine for you to wear my clothes, that is why I left them there.

**September 30, 1997:** Helloooo?!!! What is this about my baby sister driving? I go away to college and look what happens. Parents lose all sense of rational thought and the next thing you know children are driving. We are going out tonight for a late dinner to some restaurant because it is my friend Julie's birthday tomorrow. We are wearing our pajamas.

**Oct. 6, 1997:** I am sorry I haven't written in so long. My computer has been busy with essays and assignments of many people at all hours of the day.

**Oct. 15, 1997:** My exams were alright and I am very glad they are over. I have such cool friends here. You wouldn't believe how many of them were praying for me and I didn't even ask or know they were. I was walking into one of my exams and passed my friends Julie and Karen and they asked how I was and I told them that I was about to take an exam and they and a guy I don't even know prayed for me while I was taking my test. Also it is rad because here your teachers pray for the class because they want you to do well.

Amy, I can't believe that you are coming next week! We are going to have so much fun!

**Oct. 25, 1997:** The Torrey Bible Conference was awesome.[1] I learned so much. One of the main speakers was Keith Johnson of the Biblical Foundation Academy International.[2]

**Nov. 3, 1997:** Amy, thank you so much for coming to visit me. I had a great time and it was wonderful to see you.

**November 12, 1997:** 26? It is 60 here today and these ridiculous people are running around with layers of clothes, hats and jackets. I just laugh at them. I actually am looking forward to the cold. I am taking only GE classes next semester so that I can get them out of the way. I am taking water aerobics, Intro to Psychology, Christian Thought 1, Nature of Mathematics (help me Rhonda), Art Appreciation (for three hours on Tuesday nights. AHHHH!) But I have friends in there to keep my company. That is 16 units. Does that sound good to you?

**November 13, 1997:** I am sorry I missed your orchestra concert Amy. I can't wait to see you... two more weeks.

Her journals, on the other hand, illustrated how her experiences were fostering her growth and deepening her determination. One entry showed concerns she had about how living in such a close-knit group of people was affecting her. She seemed to always be aware of what God was doing around her; she caught herself when she was distracted and losing her focus. She wanted to serve God above everything else.

**November 14, 1997:** I get to go home in less than two weeks; I am so excited. God has been doing some amazing things lately from arranging another ride for my field trip so that I wouldn't have to miss classes, to leading me to a local church (and a ride) with emphasis on missions, to finding me a possible ministry with children. I have been feeling really claustrophobic lately. I am afraid of the "group mentality" I have developed, and I yearn for time that I can be alone just to think and be an individual again. I love my friends here, but I feel I am compromising so much without realizing it.

She wrote about some of the exciting and hectic moments of life at Biola.

**November 17, 1997:** I just had an awesome weekend. I went to a missions conference at what I hope is my new church. It was awesome. One of the seminars that I went to was taught by Meg Crossman, the editor of our Perspectives text.

**December 4, 1997:** All of my classes are coming to an end; I have one more paper (that I am going to write this afternoon), a quiz, two more tests and then four finals. Other than that I am done.

The plan was for Katy to stay in California until her Christmas break, but as Thanksgiving approached, no one (including Katy) thought that was a good idea. It was just too long for all of us to be apart, so we changed the plan and bought her a ticket home. We (Amy, Lenny, Rick, a few cousins in town for the holiday and I) eagerly drove to the airport to greet her. As she was flying to Indianapolis, her former youth group was gathering to welcome her home. Everyone wore a funny hat. Someone made a "WELCOME HOME KATY" sign. As we all waited at her gate, other passengers started questioning, "Who's Katy?" Wow, was she surprised when she saw everyone there for her!

Saying goodbye when she returned to Biola wasn't hard, knowing she would be back in a couple of weeks.

Katy continued to journal when she came home for Christmas vacation. As I read what she wrote years later, I could see her struggles to reconcile where she fit, where was home. It was ironic: I had always encouraged my children to follow wherever God led them, but I assumed they would always be eager to return to the place where they grew up; their first "home." She grappled with this over the next few years, finishing at Biola, teaching first grade in California for two years, and then moving to Phoenix to work in urban missions.

**December 19, 1997:** Well, I'm home! It doesn't really feel like home... well it feels like home but it doesn't feel the same... it almost feels like I don't have a place here anymore... I don't feel like I fit. Amy and Lenny have both grown up so much... I miss everyone from school so much... I feel like I identify with them so much. I am really looking forward to church and seeing everyone. I pray that I would grow much during this time and that this time would not be wasted. I don't know how I am suppose to act... I have never been the kid coming home from college for Christmas break before.

**December 29, 1997:** Enough! It is time to get serious and get focused. It is time for me to get serious about my Bible reading, verse memorizing, healthy eating, exercising, reading, and letter writing. It is time for me to stop watching TV, sleeping in late, staying up late, day dreaming, and eating bad food. Somehow, somewhere I lost my focus and I need to get it back before I fall apart.

*To live is Christ and to die is gain.*

*—Philippians 1:21*

**January 18, 1998:** Wow! I can't believe it is already '98! This year has flown by so fast! I can't believe that I'm getting ready to start my second semester of college. I have really enjoyed this six-week break at home. It has been fun to be at home without school work. And it has been great to see the family and friends. Unfortunately they are all back to school and work schedules and routines and I still have a week left at home. I am excited though, because I am babysitting for Zach and Jordan Fisher all week and I get to oversee their homeschooling.

A few things I learned from first semester and need to work on for this semester and a few other things to remember: daily devotions should not be the elective daily activity; I am not a very good judge of character and shouldn't be judging anyone anyway; with a little extra effort I should be able to get much better grades; remember the Urbana commitment card; look for God and expect to find Him in everyday things; no work gets done in the lobby; and God has sent me to Biola thus far and has provided financially so I don't even have to have a job.

I kind of feel like I live in two different worlds and when I am in one, the other almost seems like a dream. With the first few days of my visits home comes the feeling that I am a schizophrenic or that I have multiple-personality disorder. My own bed feels unfamiliar and it took me until now to finally sleep well and through a whole night without waking up.

All I know is that God is so faithful, good and patient. Who would have thought that I would be going to college thousands of miles away where I know no one in a state that I have never been to? God has been so faithful in providing the finances, giving the 'rents and I peace, providing friends and so many other things. I think God is asking me to go to Phoenix for the summer... it will be a big sacrifice for me to give up summer at home, Cornerstone, and seeing friends and family, but somehow I am not concerned with all of that and I am just excited about the possibilities in Phoenix. Even my grandmother thinks I should go. We will see. He is the master planner and is waiting for the perfect time to show me what move to make.

**January 20, 1998:** today was my first day with Zach and Jordan. They are such neat kids and I, myself learned a lot today. Their mom told me that homeschooling is easy and if missionaries knew how easy it is they wouldn't send their kids away to boarding school. She said I might keep it in mind as an option for my kids—interesting thought. I got a letter from my roommate, Heather. Praise the Lord that He is receiving priority in her life as she is seeking His will constantly. ...I am so thankful for the friends the Lord has provided at Biola.

I went to dinner with Dad tonight. I had a really good time and we got to talk a lot. Also I helped (actually he supervised me) Lenny put photos up on his wall. So many memories... I can't believe he is a junior and much taller than I... I have been so blessed with such a wonderful childhood... I have gotten to go so many places and do so many things... always with 100% support from my family.

Katy was beginning to experience the costliness of discipleship. Following where Jesus led was not always easy.

I go to Biola a week from today. In some ways I am ready but in others I am not. At least I know I will be having visitors: Liz and Heidi, Katie (for a whole week) and probably Lenny. It is hard to leave not knowing when I will return.

Katy returned for her second semester and continued to keep us abreast of her daily life via emails. She kept busy with new ministry opportunities, church, exercise with "practically the whole end of the floor and several guys on open house nights. (There will be no freshman fifteen for me.)" and visits from friends.

**January 28, 1998:** It is really weird to be back here but good to see everybody.

**January 29, 1998:** I had psychology this morning and it is such an awesome class. The prof is great and I know tons of fun people in the class. It is so wonderful to have great friends here. Have a great weekend.

One of the highlights was Lenny's visit in the Spring. She wrote:

**March 2, 1998:** Ah ha! Just as I suspected... everything was going great with Lenny's visit and all, he was meeting people and going places... until tonight... just like I predicted, he bonded a little too well with the Stewart boys and they all ganged up against me. They joined forces and Lenny was the ring leader. He told them exactly what to do to irritate me. Everybody knows him; if he stays here much longer he is going to have more friends than I do.

Staying in touch with us continued to be a priority for Katy.

**March 14, 1998:** Hello it was great to talk to ALL of you today! I hope you have a great weekend and stay warm... spring is coming... death to El Niño... I love you guys!

Katy's journal entry at the end of her freshman year shows her thoughts and feelings about the changes that happened in her life during that year, the challenges she was facing and her plans for the summer. She continued to deliberate over what "home" was and what it meant for her.

**May 24, 1998:** well, here I sit, my first year of college completed. I cannot believe it; I didn't realize how fast life is until I graduated from high school. This year was my fastest yet, but what a blessed year it was; full of new friends, experiences, adventures, mistakes, ideas, and most of all a new home. Home. That word has a whole new connotative meaning for me. Home used to be my house with Mom, Dad, Amy and Lenny. It used to mean familiarity, comfort, safety, memories, support, and consistency. I knew what to expect and I trusted it for 18 years. This year I went on to a new home with a new "family" and each time that I returned to my Indianapolis home, it became less and less like a homecoming and more and more like a vacation or a short visit to a place and time and a person that I once was. It feels familiar and comfortable but I feel less and less like I belong, and yet California doesn't feel completely like home as Indy used to. I feel somewhat like a vagabond, really belonging nowhere. It is a strange feeling and yet something in me tells me that this is what life is. This has all made me realize that I must find my "home" in the Lord for He never changes and to Him I will always belong.

The Lord has blessed me so much in this past year. I have some incredible new friends who have encouraged so much growth in me; I have had wonderful Christ centered learning and I have had many life-changing experiences. There were some really hard times I'll admit, but the Lord was so faithful and my family was so supportive that I can do nothing but run to obey the next direction the Lord gives me.

Through all of this though, the one thing that I continue to struggle with the most is the feeling that I have abandoned the brother and sister that I left behind. It breaks my heart that I can't see them every day and be there to protect and encourage them when things go wrong. It hurts me so much that I didn't get to see my sister's graduation from 8th grade, my brother's Junior Spec performance. I didn't get to help Lenny go tux shopping for the prom or Amy for graduation, that I don't get to go to Lenny's soccer games or Amy's viola recitals, that I don't get to ride with Lenny to school in the mornings or come home late to find him waiting up for me, that I don't get to be there for Amy when she gets frustrated with her homework (or Mom) or when she has a bad day at school. I feel like I am missing them grow up and missing out on one of the most important times of their lives. I know that I have to be away and I know that they understand that but that doesn't stop the aching I feel in my heart.

There are so many things that I wish I knew about my future... I wish my future was now. I fear that each day I sit at Biola is a day I should be already gone... I know that the Lord is not ready for me to go yet and I appreciate the time that I have at Biola.

I got to see both Anna and Frenchy and Grandma and Dad Dad [her grandparents] today. I am truly blessed to have the privilege of knowing all four of these people. They represent over 100 years of marriage. Amazing. Mom and Dad are such a blessing as well. When I think of how much and how unconditionally they love me and then I think about how much more God loves me, I am overwhelmed.

This summer I think that God is calling me to spend a lot of time alone with Him, reading the Word and reading encouraging books. I am going to try not to spend so much time and money on insignificant (eternally speaking) things such as movies. Hopefully I will know what my major is supposed to be by the end of the summer. I don't know what it is supposed to be; all I know is that I love the Lord, I love kids, and I want to take care of them and I am willing to travel. A friend told me of a guy at Biola who wants to take a group of people as soon as we graduate and go to India and start an orphanage. I said, "Sign me up."

I miss my friends. I miss being around people.

At the end of her freshman year of college, Katy packed up her dorm room in LA, put most of it in storage and, along with Heather, moved to Phoenix, Arizona, for a summer internship with Neighborhood Ministries.

1 Torrey Memorial Bible Conference is a three day symposium at Biola named after Biola's first dean, Reuben Archer Torrey, a well-known evangelist. Sessions have been taught by faculty and others, such as Josh McDowell, Jill Briscoe, and Elizabeth Elliot.

2 Biblical Foundation Academy International was started by Keith Johnson. They create material for those seeking a biblical foundation for their faith through tv, radio, books, internet, DVD, and live presentations.

186

# Part Three
*Serving in Love*

# Chapter 10
## A Summer of Urban Missions: 1998

### Part I: Profound Insights

I was happy for Katy when she told me that she had an internship with Neighborhood Ministries. It seemed like a good opportunity for her, but I was a little sad I wouldn't see her until August. If I had known how the experience of her time there would impact her life I would have been thrilled. But I missed her and had looked forward to being with her. She would spend most of that summer in Phoenix. When I discovered her journal entries from that time, I was struck by Katy's exquisite awareness of God. This chapter is largely comprised of her words directly. Katy summarized that summer and the impact it had on her in a letter she wrote to Tab's Mission Committee five years later, as she prepared to become a two-year intern with Neighborhood Ministries.

I became an intern for Neighborhood Ministries the summer after my first year at Biola. That summer I experienced God like never before. In letting Him love his little children through me, I was able to see His children as he does. I felt their brokenness and His brokenness for them. In seeing their vulnerability and weakness, but strength in the Lord, I realized my own need for the Lord and how much I rely on Him. Within a short time of being in Phoenix I began to feel an overwhelming sense that, somehow, I belonged there. When I left after the summer I knew I would return and I prayed that God would call me soon.

**Katy journaled every day at the start of the summer internship.**

**June 1, 1998:** Today was my first official day as an intern. There is so much going on; in a lot of ways it feels like starting college did: a new home, a very small room with a roommate, many new people, a new church and I don't have the slightest clue how "things" work. I feel a little overwhelmed now but I know if I just hang in there I will eventually get the hang of things. I am very excited about this summer; I think the Lord is going to teach me a lot. I am also really looking forward to working with the other interns: Heather, Amber, Kenny and Seth.

**In a note Katy wrote on June 2, 1998, she talked about the interns.**

Dear Family,

I am really enjoying working with the other interns; there are five of us including Heather and I. One just graduated from Wheaton, another from Arizona State and the third is starting ASU in the fall. It is neat to be part of a team of interns my age. It makes me wonder how much Kyle[1] would benefit from having a team of college (or younger) age students as interns during the summer or even during the year.

Looking back years later, Kit described the interns who served that summer.

> ...*highly capable young people who had the capacity to carry a very heavy load as a team. Before Kids Club started, they did all the program planning, did the structural set up, trained the work crew, oriented the teachers, reviewed the curriculum, and registered hundreds of kids, among other tasks. Then when it started, they did whatever job each were assigned. Kids Club today has the same components as it did then, maybe with more kids, but now there are many more interns to handle all the work.*

> *Amber was kind of the team leader; she was older and had been a summer intern for several years, since she was in high school, so she had experience running the program. Seth, like Amber, had been an intern with Neighborhood before that summer. Kenny, also a volunteer at Neighborhood for years in various capacities, was a Kids Club veteran. Heather too had been involved at NM in a myriad of roles before that summer. Those four interns brought invaluable experience to Kids Club and the other summer programs that year.*

Katy was among like-minded people. She continued in her journal...

We spent the day driving around signing the kids up for Kids Club. It was really good for me to see these kids' homes and meet their families. It is funny how each time I think I am the most culturally

191

sensitive and unbiased person, God shows me an attitude or thought in my heart that needs to be changed. I think that while I have compassion for the poor, there are a lot of attitudes of my heart that need to be worked on.

I am excited because all of us (the interns) are going to do devotions and work out at the "Y" for an hour each day as a group. All of us are so different and are in different places and come from different places, but even just after a day I can see different gifts represented and being used for the benefit and balance of the group.

I want to be a godly woman. Sometimes I have been distracted from this, but this summer I really want to stay focused on Christ and becoming the woman He wants me to be. I want to spend more time reading and studying rather than watching TV or "bungling" around wasting time. I think that God keeps "encouraging" me to come out of my comfort zone and I keep forcing myself out so that I can't become too comfortable with my surroundings or too comfortable with myself. I am thankful but that is exactly how I feel—uncomfortable.

**June 2, 1998:** "Today was a good day!" I began to feel more a part of the team of interns today. I had some paper work to do first thing in the morning. I feel like I am beginning to understand that part of things more. We got to work out at the "Y" today for a while and it was a really nice transition between the paper work and going out on the road doing registrations. I went out with Kenny at about seven and tried to do registrations. We prayed in the van before we left; then it started to get dark. We were having trouble trying to find places and what is worse, it was too dark to read the house numbers. One house that we spent a long time trying to find, 1018, we eventually gave up on. As Kenny got out of the van to check one last number, he dropped Kit's cell phone. We thought it was fine, but we worried for a minute. It wasn't the right address so we gave up and headed for home. But God didn't want us to give up that easily. As we continued driving we noticed that a piece of the phone was missing, so we needed to turn around and find it. Very "purposefully" the driveway we chose to turn around in was 1018. We had been on the wrong street the whole time. We first went to get the piece of the phone (which, by the way, clicked right back into place) and then we went back to 1018 and got three forms from some very excited kids. The Lord had used the phone to lead us right to the kids. The Lord is so good and has such a sense of humor!

Phoenix has such a nightlife. There are so many people out, even little kids, but they were fearful of the van when we drove slowly trying to find the addresses and with good reason. Maybe the Lord is giving me a heart for urban missions. I know I want to work with kids and Kit still has her family, house and job and is in constant contact with kids. So who knows? There are more ways to be a "missionary" than I could have ever imagined. I am feeling much better about this summer; yesterday

I felt so overwhelmed and out of place but I feel so much better after just one more day. I am a little sad that I am not going to be home this summer, but I realize the longer I am away from home the harder it is to be at home. When I am there I feel like I don't fit in and I am more of a guest... it feels more like a vacation than like I am coming home from vacation. I can't sleep at home and I have dreams with a lot of people that I know in them and they leave me feeling emotionally drained... I am sleeping better at the Danley's but I am still having these dreams that I remember leave me feeling not very rested. I think God is using my feelings of detachment to make me totally dependent on Him and to get my attention.

**June 3, 1998:** We had teacher training led by Kit. She truly has the spiritual gift of teaching. I didn't realize what a huge responsibility I have. Seth and I are teaching a fifth grade class. This is something that I know I definitely cannot do--it is going to have to be entirely the Lord. I am in no way gifted or prepared for this, but the Lord wants me to do it— again He is pushing me out of my comfort zone. I am continuing to have troublesome, bizarre dreams.

Lenny got his wisdom teeth out today.

**June 4, 1998:** What an amazing Savior! He truly doesn't wish that even one lamb is lost. These kids move so much, but the Lord keeps leading us to them. Every time we are ready to give up on finding one of them He says, "Wait, don't give up on them, I haven't." Today we met two really great fathers in a row that is more than I have seen the whole rest of the time doing registrations. I think that the Lord is teaching me to praise Him in all things, just for who He is and then for what He has done. I pray that the Lord would help me to see these kids as He does.

Soon Katy, the other interns, and a few high school students were sent on a short missions trip to Mexico to help build much needed housing, partnering with a ministry called Amor.[2] She wrote of God's direction for her life.

**June 12, 1998:** Mexico was yet another adventure with the God of Comfort who keeps putting me in uncomfortable situations to shake me from my hold on the comforts of the world. He keeps calling me to new experiences in new places with new people. I am beginning to see my life as a collage of colorful experiences and lessons that are all connected and very significant. The Lord leads me from one to the next, without dwelling in one for too long or looking back. There are times I just want to give up and go home to a place I know so well and people who I know and who know me, and then I am reminded that while home is familiar it doesn't really feel like home; it too is changing. The people that I know are changing too and I am not the person they know. The Lord is the same yesterday, today and forever. My heart feels homeless because I don't really know where I belong. I know I belong to the Lord and that is all that I know.

I wonder why God chose me. I wonder why God made me a white, American, Midwestern female in the 1990's. Why this specific time? Why this specific place? Why this specific body and specific weaknesses and abilities?

Being in Mexico just confirmed my desire to work with kids and just love them. I may not speak their language or be able to fix their past, or build them a house, but I can let Christ love them through me and transform their lives for eternity.

*"You then, my son, be strong in the grace that is in Jesus Christ. And in the things you have heard me say in the presence of many witnesses entrust to reliable men who will also be qualified to teach others. Endure hardship with us as a good soldier of Christ Jesus. No one serving as a soldier gets involved in civilian affairs—he wants to please his commanding officer."*

*—2 Tim. 2:1-4*

Next, they went to California with the junior high kids for a Young Life camp and a trip to Six Flags.[3] California brought another layer of depth to Katy's experience of God and his children.

**June 14-18, 1998:** My love of challenges was definitely tested this week from many different angles. At times I really felt out of my realm of gifting and I was amazed by Amber's obvious gifting and ability in many different areas in relation to working with this specific group of kids. As I watched them interact in total disrespect for one another and total disregard for each other's feelings and started to think critical thoughts, I was reminded of my own uncertainties and fears at that age.

Amber did everything; I feel bad that I didn't help her more. I wanted to, but there really wasn't room for that especially since I really didn't know the kids well or what was going on.

Amber and I had "cabin time" with our seven girls after each presentation of the Gospel and it really amazed me how little the girls knew about the basics. The whole experience left me wondering, "Why me Lord? Why did you choose me? Why do I understand?" It makes me incredibly thankful, but it also makes me feel like He really wants to use me for something great, but I am humbled because at this point right now I am feeling a little useless, but I know that He can use me and I just pray that He will...

The fam is in Sanibel this week; I am kind of sad

that I am not with them; it would have been really fun, but, oh well...

It was really bizarre. The strangest feeling came over me when we were in California—I felt like I was at home--almost as much as I do when I am back in Indiana. I didn't expect to feel that way; it really surprised me.

I am so confused about so many things right now—like where home is (I feel rather displaced), what I am in Phoenix for, what I am majoring in, etc...

**June 20, 1998:**

*Lord, I pray you would give me the Spirit of wisdom and revelation, so that I may know you better.*

*Also I pray that the eyes of my heart be enlightened that I may know the hope to which you have called me, the riches of your glorious inheritance in the Saints and your incomparable great power for us who believe.*

*—Ephesians 1:17*

Then began the preparation for Kids Club, an intense two-week day-camp for hundreds of children, kindergarten through 6th grade, full of field trips, singing and skits, crafts, learning about God, and special events like Lake Day and Carnival Day. Each child was placed in a group of kids near his/her own age with the same leaders for the entire two weeks. Katy helped teach one of those groups and was also responsible for part of the Work Crew, a team of high school kids that help run Kids Club.

**June 28, 1998:** Here it is, the night before Kids Club starts and even as I sit here it is hard for me to imagine what is going to be taking place here in these next two weeks; I feel so much anticipation for all the amazing things God has for this week and knowing all of the amazing things He has already done in preparation. God has been a part of and provided every detail from our car situation to Work Crew to helping us find missing kids. It has been just amazing to see God's hand in every detail of this work. I am compelled by *Ephesians 4:2-6:*

*Be completely humble and gentle; be patient, bearing with one another in Love, make every effort to keep the unity of the Spirit through the bond of peace.*

*There is one body and one Spirit—just as you were called to one hope when you were called— one Lord, one faith, one baptism, one God and Father of all, who is over all and through all and in all.*

My Work Crew is great. I can already see how uniquely gifted they are. It will be neat to see them grow.

Most of the time I make myself so busy that I don't really realize what is going on inside of me or outside of me and how that's affecting my heart. It is the times when I stop and think that I really experience God and His work in my life. I am in Phoenix. I am a sophomore in college. I am teaching a fifth grade VBS (Vacation Bible School) class. I feel like my life is going so fast that I don't realize where I have been until I am somewhere else. There is a line from a song that I think describes my life perfectly: "Every new beginning is another new beginning's end."

**June 29, 1998:** The first day of Kids Club. Completed. Today was an amazing day, more than I could have imagined. It was a day full of excited and overwhelmed kids, government lunches, junior leaders, Work Crew, roller skating, swimming and more swimming, name tags, candy, heat, buses, new friends, running in circles, walking in lines, chasing kids, classrooms and questions. I came in expecting to be a teacher and a guide to the Work Crew, but I was totally blown away. The Work Crew is amazing. Sincerely, they are probably the best group of high school students I have ever worked with. They are such a blessing and really minister to me. It is also so encouraging to see how much they love and care for one another. They are coming from all over to minister to inner city children and they act as if they have been lifelong friends.

I am a little nervous about teaching...

I am pretty exhausted because for some reason I couldn't get to sleep. I laid there for three or four hours, so frustrated.

I also got to talk to one of the Work Crew today and he told me that he didn't have a Bible. I felt immediate shame because I have so many and I don't read any of them as much as I should and don't appreciate them. I got to give him a New Testament.

**July 1, 1998:** Today in class Seth taught about the parable of the Lost Sheep. I am continually amazed at how God is so whole heartedly and persistently seeking after these kids. I am truly amazed at how He has brought each one here. God has had us chasing them around when they move or stop coming or change families. He truly does wish that not one would be lost. I am also noticing God's hand in the diversity of our class. We have Bosnians, Hispanic kids (from all over—some first generation), African Americans, and a few white kids. I am finding myself very frustrated that I don't feel like I am getting to build any sort of semi-deep relationships with the kids in my class. I feel like I have too big a role as a disciplinarian and organizer. It is the relational part that is important to me and that I yearn for, but maybe God has a different role for me in these two weeks. Besides, I am getting to build relationships with the Work Crew.

Today we took the kids to the water park. It was an indoor wave pool. It was there that I felt the least connected to the kids. Most of the time they do not listen to me.

The weird thing about these first three days is that I am finding myself desiring to be with the junior leaders more than any of the other kids. At first I thought it was just because of familiarity or maybe because I had forgotten how difficult that week in California was, but I think I am falling for those kids.

I know how stubborn and determined and needy that each one of them is, but for some strange reason I am regretting that I can't stay in Phoenix and work with them.

I am getting frustrated with myself because I don't feel like I am good at this whole teaching thing. I think it would be easier for me to accept, if it weren't for the fact that it is supposed to be my major and if I don't major in something to do with teaching then I am really lost.

God told me something last night when I was praying—**I will find the feeling of home and total comfort in Jesus**—and that is kind of what heaven is all about—it is a place where we fit; it gives us a perfect sense of belonging and comfort.

My prayer for myself (and all the teachers) is *that whenever I open my mouth, words may be given me so that I will fearlessly make known the mystery of the Gospel.*

*—Ephesians 6:19*

Katy walked in the footsteps that God set before her, and He confirmed her path in many ways.

**July 2, 1998:** The Lord is so amazing! I can think of only one or two times, no actually I have never felt God's presence like I did today. Yesterday I prayed Ephesians 6:19 and that is exactly what happened. Today when I was teaching, the kids' eyes were glued to me and they were so engaged in what I was saying I almost stopped talking because I was so excited to look out and see all of them looking back at me. Also today we reviewed all three stories and even Adolfo knew all of the answers.

Today during class Mateo asked me a question about psychics on TV and I told him to sit with me at lunch so that we could talk about it and so I could explain thoroughly. (This was my chance to get more on the relational side like I wanted.) We ended up sitting with Araceli and the two of them asked me questions for about 45 minutes. I prayed that God would give me the words and wisdom to tell the Truth and I could feel the Holy Spirit pouring answers out of my mouth faster than I could think. My lips were moving so fast; I was never hesitant and I could feel God using me. We talked about how Jesus was not a created being but part of the Trinity, how God has always been and always will be, superstition and the reality of Satan, why bad things happen, sin and free will, death, God's purposes for everything, God's love, heaven and hell, Christ's second coming, idolatry, ghosts and spirits and lots of other things. The whole time you could see their hearts joyful as they heard the truth. Everything I said—they understood.

**July 3, 1998:** Today was Lake Day at Canyon Lake. The bus ride was about three hours. When we got there, there were boat rides, swimming, feeding ducks and lots of other things. I really enjoyed getting to spend some time with the kids in smaller groups outside of the classroom, especially Adolfo. He really is a good kid and has a lot of potential, but he just needs a little help. I am so thankful that I have been able to continue that relationship and see it grow; it makes me sad that I won't be here after July.

I can't believe the first week of Kids Club is already over and it is July already. I get to go home soon; school starts again soon.

Everyone keeps asking me if I am going to do Kids Club next year—I would love to but I just feel like there are so many other ministries out there that I should be a part of too.

**July 4, 1998:** Today was kind of a strange day. We got to sleep in until 11:30. In the afternoon we went out to the Capitol to watch the fireworks. Kids Club sits the same place every year so our kids know where to find us. One of our kids came running up because she had just watched her aunt stab her mother in her own house. I felt like the wind had been knocked out of me. I am filled with an overwhelming desire to save, rescue and shelter these precious ones. I know that God does everything for a reason and He is able to use everything for His purposes but I am still overwhelmed with the pain that these young ones endure. I felt like I was in a movie where I was frozen and everyone around me was moving. Don't these people understand that while they are having fun there are children suffering, oppressed, alone and hopeless?

*I keep asking myself why I have had such an easy*

*life and had everything that I wanted.* I have been so loved, encouraged and protected, while so many others are fatherless and out in the cold. I feel the only way I can live with the contrast is to offer my life back to Christ and serve Him through loving His children, constantly pouring myself out and eliminating my own ambition. I have been so selfish with my life and with my love.

It was an "aha" moment for me when I read those words. I think that paragraph encapsulates what motivated Katy to serve God.

**July 7, 1998:** Today was an amazing day! Four kids in my class accepted Christ. After we had our lesson, the parables of the Hidden Treasure and the Pearl of Great Price, we broke up into small groups and discussed various things we have been talking about. I picked the toughest boys to be in my group—Pedro, Carlos, Adolfo and Miguel. As we were talking about things Pedro seemed to really understand and really believe God's truth that he had been hearing. I talked with him for a while and then I asked Seth to join us. Pedro prayed and said that he had forgiven his dad for leaving him. As he tried not to cry, he and Seth prayed and asked God to forgive him and help him live his life. God is already at work in his life; he shared that he had recently decided to stop hanging out with gang members because he felt that God wanted him to.

Today was also hard because I had to watch some of the Junior Leaders go through some painful things. I want so much for them to know God and how much He loves them.

The more I think about it the more I hate that I have to build relationships with these kids and not get to be with them throughout the year, or probably ever again.

**July 9, 1998:** Without air conditioning, our class soon turned to chaos. The auditorium was so hot and muggy, I felt like I was in the jungle. When it came time for me to teach I felt like no one was listening; one of my Work Crew ran off to the freezer to cool himself off. I couldn't blame him though, I just wanted to lie down and take a nap myself. Even in these conditions and our tiredness the Lord was at work. During our small group time I talked to Pedro, Juan Carlos, Sofia, Leonardo, Dylan and Matthew. I was excited to hear Leonardo share that he had already accepted Christ years ago. Pedro has such an awesome understanding of the Gospel and it is evident that the word has really taken root in him. Ian took Adolfo out to the playground and just loved him, and told him that he wasn't bad and not to let people discourage him. As he heard these words of encouragement he accepted Christ.

**July 10, 1998:** I can't believe it is over. As I sit here I can't believe I have been here for only two weeks. It feels like I know these people too well to have only known them for two weeks but this week especially has gone by so fast.

Today was a great day! The morning started off by Lucia (one of the junior leaders who I went to California with) saying she had a song for me and she sang a song about how she was going to miss me and how I had been like a mother to her. Then I saw Mateo coming in the door and he gave me a Barbie doll that his mom had sewn clothes for. When I went into the auditorium Camila, my little pre-K friend that I met at the lake said, "I was looking for you," and jumped in my lap.

In class everyone wanted me to sign their shirts and Adolfo poured water all over me. The Work Crew gave testimonies. Mateo also gave all of the leaders a cross that he had sewn.

I was so happy because when we went into the auditorium all of my kids wanted to sit by me. When Kit asked for volunteers to say their verse Rosa Mari went up there and said hers perfectly. Juan kept showing me his loose tooth and played with my camera. Araceli gave me her picture. When we went swimming, Camila grabbed me and told me that she was looking for me all day and then she gave me a big hug and in her best English said, "I'm gonna miss you." I was so worried that I wouldn't get to say goodbye to Sofia but then I found her and later Rosa gave me a bracelet. Manuel and Victor smiled at me all day and kept hugging me; in fact, Manuel grabbed me real tight and gave me a hug and kiss on the cheek.

Debriefing took a long time but it was awesome to hear how God had worked in everyone all week.

**July 11, 1998:** The enemy is very upset at all the

victory this week. We experienced broken vehicles and air conditioning throughout the two weeks, but the worst destruction was today. Someone smashed the windows in two of the buses that were parked at the old building. After we had spent all day cleaning we took one last glance at the locker rooms to make sure they were clean and noticed that a huge mirror that had been hanging in the weight room had come off the wall and shattered all over the floor. The timing made us think—there had been several guys sleeping under it both weeks but it happened to fall just as we were finished cleaning when no one was in the room.

**July 13, 1998:** I had to speak in church yesterday morning—my worst fear. I was so nervous but God continued to be faithful and gave me the words.

It is so weird—to be here I mean. I feel like I am in between again. Home is in sight, I am starting to think about school again and I still have lots to do here. I need to focus on here but it is hard. I kind of don't want to go back to school. It is not just the work I don't want to deal with but I think it is also that I know things are going to be similar, but not exactly the way they were but people will treat them as if they were. For some reason I can deal with things that stay the same and things that change but things that get treated as if they haven't changed when they really have irritate and disturb me. I don't know why.

A few final thoughts about Kids Club: Kids Club is one of those things you just really have to do to experience so it is hard for me to express exactly what went on these two weeks but a few words come to mind: excited and overwhelmed kids, government lunches, junior leaders, swimming, roller skating, parables, "the green bus", candy, work crew, lost sheep, new friends, a welcoming Father, running in circles, walking in lines, prayer, cooking, laughter, water park, decisions for Christ, worship, crafts, team, patience, chasing kids, questions, memory verses, open hearts, mopping, mopping and more mopping, snacks, family, provision, joy, skits, Lake Day, tears, air conditioning, carnival, frustration, boats, hope, protection, debriefing, exhaustion, break throughs, water fights, forgiveness, smiles, confession, basketball, the wave pool, *truth spoken and lives changed.*

## Part II: *More Revelations, More Questions*

After Kids Club, Katy spent a week in Kids Camp, a mountain camp for fifth to seventh graders near Payson, Arizona. Katy helped register campers, plan cabin assignments, supervise work days in preparation for camp and serve as a counselor to a cabin of junior high girls. Katy's journal on her time preparing for and being at Kids Camp expands on her life-changing experiences there. This was a time when Katy dealt with a lot of difficult questions and emotions. The beginning of the journal she wrote about Kids Camp stated:

This work is in no way complete; it is merely a glimpse into amazing memories, unrevised dreams, unpolished responses, and amateur thoughts....

**July 14, 1998:** We had a camp meeting today. As of now I have a cabin of 5th and 6th grade girls, including some from my class at Kids Club. I am thankful to continue those relationships.

I have learned a lot from Wayne and Kit about how ministry centered families work.

Dad sent me his first place medal and a t-shirt from Cornerstone. I miss him so much.

I am starting to get anxious about school again. I am so confused. I don't really have a specific reason I need to be at Biola anymore and I can't justify the expense. I could just as easily go to IUPUI [Indiana University-Purdue University Indianapolis] and work while living at home and save my parents about 80 or 90 thousand dollars. If I can't find a reason to stay soon I really might consider a transfer. I never thought I would say that but...

I don't feel like I know anything. I am just going to have to totally trust God, but I am scared.

I still feel like God gave me this summer to think, read, learn, and observe, but the more I do, the more options I realize there are and the more confused I get. I am thankful because I have learned a lot this summer and I have processed a lot that I never took the time to before. In some ways I wish I could just be a house mom in Indianapolis and have a nice house and a nice husband and go to Tab and live near my family... but... I know I would never be satisfied with that and neither would God. I just need to remember that the easy thing is not the best thing. I also just wish I could go to where I am going to go and get started, but again I know that wouldn't be best and I need to wait for God's timing. I am beginning to hate getting attached to people and places and then having to leave them behind. They and I know how temporal our relationship is and its depth reflects that.

I feel confused and frustrated but I am trying to keep my guard up for fear the evil one will try to attack during this vulnerable time in my life.

**July 15, 1998:** Today was a busy work day at the office, but it was still good. We had to start getting all 60 kids signed up for camp and scheduled for workdays. I remembered when we were registering kids for Kids Club and there were so many names and addresses and I just felt so overwhelmed. Today I realized how many of the kids I know or what's more—know me. Addresses and families are familiar. It was such a great feeling. Also when we were at lunch I realized how close I have grown to all of the interns.

I am afraid that in my eagerness to go home I might mentally and emotionally check out before this camp happens and that really isn't fair to the kids.

More and more I am realizing that I like nice things and nice houses and I don't feel like I should. I feel like I am doing something wrong or liking something that I will never have, so I should get over it now and avoid later disappointment. I can't sleep. I continue to have terrible dreams and wake up all through the night.

**July 16, 1998:** The whole bus incident happened again last night—they got the rest of the windows. There is nowhere to put the buses and local churches aren't helping; however, it did appear on the 10 o'clock news, so we'll see what happens. Again, I slept horribly last night and had terrible dreams.

**July 17, 1998:** We didn't do much work today, although because it was hot the little we did do seemed like a lot. We only stayed at the office for a couple of hours and then brought the rest of our work home. Heather called the rest of the kids that we hadn't been able to get a hold of and she got almost all of them. Mateo can't go to camp but wanted to help us out at the work day anyway. We got to go visit Sofia to see if she wanted to go to camp and she gets to go! I am so excited!

Amy called during dinner and I got to talk to her for awhile. She's so excited about her New Mexico trip.

I tried sleeping on the floor last night—it didn't help. Heather thinks I'm stressed.

**July 18, 1998:** Two weeks from today I will be at

home. I feel a bit like I just morph to one place, wherever is next on my agenda and the last place where I was disappears like Brigadoon.[4]

I went house shopping with the Ryans. I think it is a good experience for me to see them as they try to re-acclimate themselves in the US in case I ever have to do the same.[5]

Amy and Lenny are getting ready for New Mexico.[6]

I just finished reading *The Screwtape Letters* by C.S. Lewis. This part feels especially applicable to my life right now: "The human lives in time and experiences reality successively. To experience much of it therefore, they must experience many different things. In other words they must experience change." I think that is so true. I think God is nudging me to so much change in my life right now because He has so much to teach me and I have so much to learn.

A few thoughts on life and my future: What's the plan? I feel scared to dream. I don't know what God has for me so I can't allow myself to start picturing myself doing certain things or being in certain places. I just want to do God's will. I know I want to have an open house. I want it to be safe and welcoming. I want it to be filled with people, especially children, who want love and freedom. I want myself to be more concerned with taking care of others rather than myself. I want to be overseas, but yet now I can also see myself in an American urban setting. I want to be challenged. I want to be deeply involved in the lives of at risk children and teens. I want to allow God to love them through me. I want to know what the next stop for me looks like. I don't want to go back to Biola and back to being the same person that I was. I am scared to go back and start regressing, start gossiping, and lose perspective. When I am at Biola I feel like my world shrinks. I am really having trouble justifying why I am there. Why was I there? I know I love it and I love the people, but... I am getting very eager for life to start. I know I need to go to college for the experience and I do learn a lot, but I really am starting to feel anxious about going back. I don't have the same peace about going, maybe it is just that I have been away from home for so long. Home. There is that word again. I'm still really struggling with that. I am so confused about the present regarding that word; the future is even foggier and almost feels lonely.

I need to give all of the before-mentioned to God. I think my anxiety is causing my sleeplessness. I think that I haven't truly let myself dream for so long that I have unconsciously blocked myself from doing it. Frightening.

When did I let the uncertainty of my future go from being exciting and hopeful to being frightening and anxiety-causing?

**July 19, 1998:** (Sleep last night was the same—I didn't.) Today was my last Sunday at Open Door.[7] The pastor spoke about James and the tongue. It was rather convicting. After that I called mom and got to talk to her and Amy for a while. She is so excited about her New Mexico trip. Then Kit and I worked on the camp list some more and realized that we have exactly the right amount of kids.

**July 20, 1998:** (Last night I didn't sleep either and I had a nightmare. In it I was running with someone else; we were trying to hide and help other people hide because after we signed a kid up someone would come and blow up their house.)

Seth and I did paper work at the Danley's until a woman called saying that her husband was in the hospital and she and her 3 young children had no food, so Seth and I took her to the Food Bank and gave her what we could find.

Everyone keeps asking me if I like someone here, why I don't have any romantic interests in Phoenix. I am so glad that I didn't think about that at all this summer and I could stay focused on the reason God had me here—for the kids and to learn. Another reason I'm scared to go back to Biola: when I am doing ministry I am so focused on others that I don't have time to think about myself, but at Biola all I am encouraged to do is think about myself and that is what I put most of my energy into.

**July 21, 1998:** No sleep again. I got up at about seven and we had to rethink the work day. We ended up with only three kids instead of nine. We came back here and I did laundry and wrote thank you's for Kids Club. I told Kit about my dream where we were running and trying to hide the kids. She said that it was a stress dream and that I was aware of the war going on and I feel like we were losing. I guess I am under a lot more stress that I realize. I am getting excited for camp, but I am even more excited about going home. I don't think I have ever been this excited or ready to go home.

**July 22, 1998:** I didn't sleep at all, maybe an hour. I set my alarm so I could get up and call Amy before she left for New Mexico but I missed her by half an hour. I was so upset. I already feel so incredibly terrible for leaving her and being gone for her birthday. This is just another event in a long string of not being there for her. In the middle of the night last night, in my weakness and frustration, I had one brief moment of wondering if it was worth coming here, "Lord, look what I had to give up to come here." I immediately stopped. What I had to give up was nothing compared to what He had to give up—everything. I recommitted to go wherever He wanted.

Today Seth and Amber let Heather and me sleep in until 9 when they dropped off 10 kids. So we had a work day with them at Nueva Esperanza.[8] It could have been so hot while we were pulling weeds but we were blessed with rain instead. I love rain so much; it made the work so much better.

I talked to Mom on the phone. She said that Amy told her, "Finally," as she was getting on the plane for her first mission trip. I am so excited for her. I am so glad that she and Lenny will have that time together. I will never forget having Lenny with me on my Jamaica and Bolivia trips. After being so airsick flying to Bolivia I was so scared that I would be sick the whole way home. I will never forget him reaching across the aisle and holding my hand during takeoff. I didn't even tell him I was scared, he just knew and he knew what to do. I envy so much the time that they will have together these two weeks. I also really envy the time they will have together this year—Lenny's senior year and the college selection and Amy starting high school and driving. I wish I could be part of that, but my time is through there.

Reading how deeply she missed Amy and Lenny broke my heart. Katy intentionally made a difficult choice, sacrificing her own comfort and happiness to follow God's lead.

I told Mom that I want to have a big talk with her and Dad about my future major, etc. when I get home.

I really think that I am starting to become exhausted physically, mentally, and spiritually because I can't sleep and that adds to my stress.

I am really excited about camp, not just for myself but for the kids. They are looking forward to this so much. I am excited about the opportunities to get to talk to some of the kids more seriously and in depth. However I feel bad that I have to go and continue to build relationships that will end August 1st. I feel guilty. It is not fair to the kids.

I think I am feeling pre-separation anxiety or something. I hate getting attached or involved in a child's life and then be just another person to leave. I did it in Jamaica, Ridge Center, Kids Club, my own family.[9] I hate it. It makes me feel like I have abandoned them.

**July 23, 1998:** I didn't sleep well last night either. Today was a huge workday; we had over 20 kids scheduled to work. I took 11 to pull weeds, pick up trash and cut down trees. The kids worked so hard. Vincente, who we hadn't been able to get a hold of to come to camp randomly showed up at our door.

**July 24, 1998:** The Lord provided for the broken bus windows—a glass company is going to replace the windows for free. I slept better last night but I still had bizarre dreams. Today we are having a half day of prayer. We had one at the beginning of the summer and so much has happened since then. I can't believe I only have nine days left. I have learned and grown so much this summer; I have met and gotten to know some incredible people here that I am sorry I have to leave. Heather and I will have to take a road trip out here sometime during the year so I can come back and visit.

Things I've Learned:

• Being still is often much more pro-active than moving.

• God doesn't wish that even one small child will perish—He has a rescue planned that is incredible and in perfect timing.

• Fatherless children, destruction, grief, violence,

poverty, despair, child abuse, abandonment, drugs, gangs, addictions, anger and hate are all symptoms or side effects of the spiritual war that is going on in this world.

- God is a father to the fatherless; He brings hope, joy, peace; He brings new creation, a fresh start.

- He has not forgotten the lost.

- Forgiveness is a wonderful gift and it is one that if we give it we will be set free and healed.

- I love kids!! I want to be part of God's plan to rescue and bring hope to lost children... somewhere.

- I wouldn't mind so much living in the US and doing urban ministry.

- If my purpose of being created and being here on earth is to praise and bring glory to God, why didn't I take more time out of my busy schedule to have quiet time at Biola?

- I love my family so much and I am so encouraged to see God at work in amazing ways in each of their lives. It is out of my love for them also that I am able to go places and serve the Lord because I go on their behalf—they are (in addition to God) part of me. I represent their encouragement and love for the past 19 years, their sacrifice and hurt and all the things that go along with truly loving a person.

- Apart from God I can do nothing but Christ can do all things through me.

- I was saved by grace. It is no less of a miracle that I was saved than anyone else whom I deem impossible.

- Satan's work is destructive but God is in the reconstruction business.

- Do not be discouraged by what seems to be huge losses because God has the ultimate victory and He uses all things.

- Sin is not a private, personal, quiet thing; it is all-encompassing, paralyzing, destructive, wounding power.

- I am getting impatient for my "real life" to start, but I think God wants me to be still and abide in Him.

- God is my comfort. He loves the poor and the weak and the defenseless and He wants them at His wedding feast.

- God is My Provider—every good and perfect gift.

- God can even work through me—in my exhaustion, fear, impatience, pain, and in my weakness.

- There is power in the cross and in the Truth.

- Hope is a rare and incredible thing in the life of a child who has never had any; it is everything. It changes lives.

Katy's "Things I've Learned" read to me like a list of godly precepts. Her eyes were opened to those truths through the experiences she had as an intern that summer.

Again, it is hard for me to believe how fast these two months has gone. A week from now I will be packing for home! We had a time of debriefing today with all of the interns; it felt weird. I remember sitting with those same people two months earlier feeling awkward and overwhelmed, wondering if I would ever fit in with those same people that I now consider friends.

This afternoon I found out the father of the Smiths[10] threw away all of their clothes and everything else they owned. I got to go to the food bank and help them get clothes. The younger ones were fine, but Zoe was so embarrassed and ashamed. The reality of their lives hit me hard.

Fears:

I am so scared of going back to Biola and falling into old, bad habits and loosing new good behaviors; I'm scared of going back to being the person I was or of letting that place or the people get to me. I'm scared that I will fall (or slide, rather) back into self-focus. I'm scared I'll begin to think life at college is normal. I'm scared that I won't work up to my potential merely out of boredom or burnout. I'm scared that I will begin to believe that each social problem at school is a crisis or of great magnitude. I'm scared that I will take it for granted again. I'm scared that I waste money when there are kids without food.

What Neighborhood Ministries is doing right:

·Follow-up  ·Monday Nights  ·Team of Interns

·Day of Prayer  ·Multi-ethnic sensitivity and
staff  ·Transportation  ·Sharing the Gospel with
full assurance  ·Passion and Purity  ·Food Bank
·Clothing Bank  ·Work Days  ·Spanish option
·Registrations  ·Availability  ·Tutoring  ·Sports
·Shoes  ·Bibles  ·Leaders

•••

*My God is so big, so strong and so mighty.*
*There's nothing my God cannot do.*
*The oceans are his;*
*The mountains are his;*
*The stars are his handiwork too.*
*My God is so big, so strong and so mighty.*
*There's nothing my God cannot do.*

•••

**July 25, 1998:** Today started before nine when
Ricardo pounded on our door insisting that Kit told
us to make him pancakes, so I got up and made
him and Patricia breakfast. I started packing all of
my stuff for camp, home, and Biola. The worlds of
my life are about to shift once again. Amber and I
called all of the kids and made sure they had rides
for the morning. I realized today that I have lice—
beyond a shadow of a doubt. As I sat on the front
porch with Heather studying my scalp I just had to
laugh. I should say that after realizing Heather was
infected too—we share everything—even head lice.
We washed each other's hair and I just laughed.

Now that I think about it—I feel really unprepared
for this camp. I want my kids to have a great time.

Again, as I start to connect with these kids I hate that I have to leave. They all keep asking if I am doing Kids Club or Monday nights and when I tell them, "No" they say, "Why" and tell me I should stay. "I would love to," I tell them. It's too bad I'm back to Biola.

**July 26-31, 1998:** Neighborhood Ministries' Kids Camp memories and a few thoughts.

I was out the door at 7:45 as kids were starting to walk down the street to our house. The parking lot was pure chaos and I had to try to check everyone in. Believe it or not, we managed to leave for camp with all but one of the kids we were expecting. The two hour bus ride turned out to be a 5 ½ hour bus ride with a trail of cars behind us. At times I think we were only going about 15 mph, and at one point we actually had to get all of the kids off of the bus and have them stand on the side of the road. But all things considered, the kids were good and there were relatively few complaints or fights.

Our cabin is across the creek and there are nine of us: myself and Paula[11] my co-counselor, Ashley, Matias, Sofia, Rosa, Alicia, Ana Maria and Patricia. On the bus they made up this huge soap opera, saying that Romero and I were married—little did I know that it would last all week and that eventually they would say they were our kids and start calling me mommy. This week is even more intense than Kids Club—you are with them "24/7" so you see them in all their glory—good and bad and my own strengths and weaknesses surface as well. Because I

223

am writing about this week as one collective group of experiences, in no particular order I will mention and try to capture significant moments and memories of this week... finding a sad Diego and playing ping pong with him, seeing my girls sing at the top of their lungs during barn time, having Alicia paint my nails, hugs from Jose, taking my girls for showers, to the nurse, to the water fountain, being the last ones to everything because "you don't need hair spray, you need a salon", listening to Juan tell me that he "sucks at everything" and he "wants to die", thunderstorms, hearing Matias say "aspiration" instead of "ass", crossing the creek with Sofia on my shoulders, having her sneak into my bunk when she thinks no one is looking, wearing sombreros to breakfast in our pajamas, "My God is so big, so strong and so mighty there's nothing my God cannot do", having my girls wake me up in the morning, capture the flag in the meadow, archery, BB guns, carrying Araceli to the nurse, smiles from Enrique, sitting on a sleeping bag under thousands of stars and speaking the truth to seven very scared girls, having Juan hanging around and tell me that he doesn't suck at everything and that he knows Jesus and I care about him.

**July 30, 1998:** God continues to amaze me. I realize how little I dare to hope and dream for these kids. Tonight I saw the most incredible movement of the Holy Spirit that I have ever witnessed. We had had an especially difficult day. We all went to the barn and while we were singing "It's Amazing

How You Love Me" the Holy Spirit swept the whole room. Everyone began to cry. Matias and Ashley said that they couldn't stand it and asked me to take them outside. They began to sob and as the Holy Spirit was convicting them they apologized for being so hard on me and disobeying and all of their own volition went up to each person, especially counselors that they had wronged and apologized to them. In the meantime everyone was pouring out of the barn and the Holy Spirit was moving, convicting, reconciling and healing. After my girls confessed they began to deal with the hidden pain in their hearts. All I could do was hold them while they grieved and told them of God's promise to never leave them. What else do you tell a child when they are hard and defiant all week and then you suddenly find them in your arms broken and grieving, telling you that they want their daddy who promised never to leave them and then committed suicide a year later? What do you tell her when she says she just wants to die so she can see her daddy? I watched the Holy Spirit expose pain in children's lives so they could deal with it and name it for the first time. Ana Maria also sobbed because her father is still alive but chooses not to be a part of her life. Then Francisca, who had been making a joke out of her dad's drunken behavior and having to leave him and hold him back from hitting her mom broke down and was overcome by her grief. I watched her say that she just wanted to die and kill herself because it hurt too much. I saw little Adolfo protect those who were crying from a few boys who were mocking them. I saw Rosa grieve the death of her cousins in a drive-by. I watched God reconcile girls that had been viscously battling all week. I watched Manuel cry like a baby. I saw counselors ministering to kids and to each other. I watched Juan whose suffering has been so long and suppressed walk around moaning and weeping. I watched kids pray for each other. I saw children giving and asking forgiveness from enemies. I saw some of the hardest hearts soften and open. It was one of the most incredible experiences of my life.

The presence of God was thick as we all stood outside the barn. The sight of the body in motion was beautiful. Just when someone felt that they couldn't stand the pain another second, someone would come alongside of them and hold them and pray for them. There was deep healing. The ladies in the kitchen came like angels out of the darkness and helped Francisca and others giving them courage and hope.

On the way to our cabin Francisca still didn't have the strength to stand and I watched Jose minister to her and tell of his own father who God changed after 20 years of prayer. Back at the cabin I watched the girls who usually pick on each other united in grief and in prayer. I watched Josefina come to Francisca, who moments earlier hadn't been able to walk either, climb into bed with her and pray for her. The Holy Spirit did such amazing work in so many lives. Amber told me that Manuel said that he had been waiting a long time to cry.

**July 31, 1998:** Our bus ride home took from 2-8. The bus broke down 3 or 4 times. The kids were so hot and tired—I lost all will to keep order. Once we got to the church we had 60 kids to find luggage and parents or rides for.

It is so weird for me to imagine that I will be with my family in less than 24 hours. I am feeling right now that as soon as I get off the plane I am going to want to treat my lice and then not have to talk to anyone until I have some rest and time to process all of this summer. I started on laundry and packing. I am sad—I have made some great friends here and I have seen God work in some amazing ways in kids' lives and I want to stay to see what happens next.

Francisca came home to discover that her mom went back to her dad and he beat her up really badly. Time to put on the armor on her heart again. It is hard to watch God expose a soft heart and walk in it and then the kids have to harden their hearts again to survive in their world.

Heather and I spent our final evening together treating our lice again.

**August 1, 1998:** I can't believe this summer is over. Amber and Heather drove me to the airport and waited with me. It was fun to go over some of the summer's highlights and lowlights. It is going to take me a while to process all that happened this summer. *One thing I know for sure is that I experienced God and His power this summer and I will never be the same.*

I don't know what my future holds but I do know that I saw God work in the lives of broken and wounded children. I saw Him give hope and change hearts. I saw God search out the lost and forgotten and take them to a place of hope, safety, love and comfort. I saw God work in my own weakness and in all of my humanness and selfishness. He brought divine love, patience, and healing. I think that part of my hesitation in leaving comes from the fear that I am leaving God behind and that I won't experience Him in such a significant and similar way anywhere else—especially not the familiar places I am going to, like home and Biola. All this thinking is ridiculous because it is not the place or the people but the Savior, and He can and will work in familiar places too. I think I am more eager to go home than I have ever been before.

This appears at the end of the Aug 1st entry, exactly as written.

...having Francisca tell me that when I come to visit I can stay at her house, watching the cousins play on the wagon, Freddy telling me to go to Juan because he was crying, watching Juana catch fish, painting nails instead of going to kickball, having Mateo, Rosa, Gabriela, Cesar, Mario hang out with me on the nature hike when my girls refused to come any farther, having Ashley and Patricia come to me and tell me that they prayed for the other girls when they were lost and then teaching them that it is hard to do the right thing because people often laugh at you and don't appreciate you, watching Diego worship in a mighty way, sundaes for being the winning team, counselor hunts, having Rosa stand up for me when the girls were talking back, watching Rosa and Sofia become good friends and then wrestle and giggle together, watching my girls all sit and play together and stick up for one another on the bus, the girls sneaking out the back door, calling Rosa out of the darkness by the bus, toilet paper football, hearing screams at the mere mention of spiders, singing "Lean on Me", Guadalupe standing strong when kids teased her about being from "Boston", having Adolfo tell me that he has no more clean clothes, having someone ask what time it is and Sophia grab my hand just when I was almost asleep and saying, "Here, let's look at Katy's watching", having Sophia take me out back to tell me that my camera was dropped because she thought I would be furious, saying goodbye to Kit and having her say, "It feels like we should all just be going back to the house," Dave saying, "You will be missed", seeing Paula and Guadalupe read the Bible together, watching Ashley read the Bible of her own volition, Ashley sharing with me about her sister running away and being abused by her boyfriend, seeing Patricia finally find her place and voice in the group, being the pregnant woman in the doctor's office skit, counselor meetings, Juan's buying salmon eggs at the gas station, Maria saying, "I've known you since California. I was cold and you took me to the restroom and gave me clothes." Miguel sharing first that God had given him patience and helped him not to fight, snack bar time, seeing Kit hold

Veronica, hugs from Veronica, thunderstorms, seeing Ricardo wear the same sweatshirt for days and refuse to take a shower, seeing the disappointment on the kids' faces when I told them I couldn't do Monday Nights and then having them insist that I go to college in Phoenix, seeing my sweatshirt on a different kid every time I was at a group event, treasure hunts, holding onto hula hoops, horn-toed frogs, "Jilly bean", water fights, "cattle roundup" and "jail break", the girls confessing sins, flashlights after lights out, moose and gel on the front porch to trap the boys, Sofia climbing on the rafters, Francisca looking out for everybody, tucking them in and waking them up.

In 2008, Rick, Amy and I ventured to Mountain Meadows Camp to teach crafts in the open-air ramada. Lenny had been helping at Kids Camp for the previous three years as a counselor and part of the program staff. I had been searching for a way to be part of what God was doing at Neighborhood Ministries, and Kids Camp seemed like a good way to help. Part of my wanting to go was a desire to be where Katy had so profoundly experienced God, a sort of pilgrimage. Little did I know that I was going to witness so much of Him in the lives of those children.

Passing the church bus belching black smoke as it chugged up the mountains I didn't know existed in Arizona, I wondered what was in store for us. Such a beautiful setting: pine and oak trees shading red-tinted soil, a Carolina-blue sky, rosy sunsets disappearing behind the mountain ridge, night skies packed with bright stars. It was so different from the familiar brown dust of center-city Phoenix. Here the kids ran and laughed in the meadow, hunted frogs, splashed in the creek, stared at the giant moth on the cabin wall, and screamed at the occasional mouse that found its way into their cabin. Kids being kids—hiking, exploring, sometimes ignoring or teasing their leaders, singing joyfully at barn time, and always being friendly.

The NM staff did such a great job of providing a safe framework for fun. The theme for that week was, "Telling Your Story." As the days went by, the campers became more confident in their groups when they were encouraged to share their stories. I saw them begin to trust the pain of their lives to others. I saw so many signs of comfort: counselors holding broken kids and kids with their arms around each other sharing God's love, assuring each other that they weren't alone and that they could trust God with their hurts. After all, they had just learned that "God is Big" at Kids Club.

Billy Thrall, NM's pastor, heard that I wanted to see the cabin that Katy and her group of kids had stayed in. Although that part of the camp had been sold and was off limits, Billy led Rick and me across the creek to her cabin. We didn't go inside, but sat on rustic benches left from camp and allowed our imaginations to take us back in time. It's hard to describe what I felt as I sat there, where Katy had been. I know that I was on the brink of tears, and an ache caught in my chest. It was terribly important to me to be there. I dared to let my mind connect fully with memories. Billy gently reflected on his impressions of Katy and caringly counseled us about the nature of grief.

Later that day, Kit asked me to share my story with the campers. My stomach churned at the thought; talking to anyone about Katy's passing still made me tremble, much less a barn full of young teenagers I barely knew. But as I considered what I would possibly share with these kids whose lives were so different from mine, I concluded that Katy's enduring faith in the midst of her illness could encourage these young teenagers who faced such hardship. That evening, I stood in front of ninety junior-high kids and counselors and surveyed their faces as they stared expectantly at me. Katy had only been gone 2 ½ years; most of them had known her or at least had heard of her. I started to tell my story. My voice shook as I skimmed through my pre-Katy life, but as I told instances of Katy's confident trust in God through her entire illness my voice became steadier. No one made a sound; there weren't many dry eyes as I disclosed how deeply she loved God, her family, friends, and the Neighborhood community and how that love and trust carried her through such difficult times. After I had told my story, kids began to take me into their confidence. One young man reached for my arm as we slid down the hill through the rain-soaked earth to our cabins. He shared that his girlfriend was a friend of Katy's and really missed her. Others revealed some of the hard realities of their lives: one young man approached me to say he had witnessed a fatal drive-by; another wanted to tell me about seeing his cousin die. They knew I could relate to their stories because they had listened to mine. Others shared happy stories about Katy. A counselor said that she never met Katy but felt like she knew her because so many kids at Neighborhood were named after her. After that evening I was always greeted by name and a smile. God did use my words.

My experiences that week were similar to Katy's. I was grateful to have had the opportunity to taste her life there and picture her laughing among her campers, and telling them truth under the stars.

## Part III: *A Difficult Re-entry*

When Katy came home at the end of her internship with NM it was obvious that she was distressed. Re-entry from such intense experiences was hard. She was restless and unsettled. Trying to reconcile the children's lives of poverty, neglect and abuse she had witnessed with the ease of her life was challenging. She had changed and was unsure how to conserve her new God-awareness in such familiar settings. We took long drives and had intense discussions. She attempted to explain her frustrations with trying to live her new reality in her old world. Katy's "End of Summer" journal shows her concerns.

**August 4, 1998:** Well, coming "home" again is proving very difficult. I am still trying to process my whole summer experience, but I came home to find that my sister is taking driver's ed, my brother is a senior and my two best friends are moving closer than ever towards marriage. I am really feeling all of my worlds colliding and reality seems relative.

We picked Amy and Lenny up at the airport as they were returning from New Mexico. They are so mature and independent.

I feel so much like I am floating. I have been on so many trips and such but I have never had this much trouble with re-entry. I learned so much and I feel like I changed so much through experiencing God to an extent that I never had before. I am having trouble reconciling the grief that I saw and experienced.

I am so scared of leaving that place behind because I know that is where I experienced God in an amazing way... I know that God is not connected physically (or limited to) a specific place but it is hard for me to feel peace about returning to somewhere (Biola) that doesn't nurture the character strengths I gained this summer or where I became a person that I don't like. I loved Biola and I learned a lot there but I easily bought into the Biola view of the world that is very small. I lost passion for everything and became completely compliant and submissive. It took me a long time to shake those things, too.

I am finding it hard to justify spending $20,000 a year on a place where I don't feel certain important things are nurtured in me. I just want to be in God's will. I don't want to just assume that I will be at Biola for four years. I don't have the same peace about going there as I did (and last year I had every reason to be anxious).

I have changed and I am scared of regressing into the person I once was. I feel like I could live at home or even have my own apartment, go to IUPUI; that only costs $1500 and be involved in a lot of ministry.

I love challenges. When I am challenged I know that I grow. At Biola I am way too comfortable. I don't feel like I am challenged, so I don't feel like I am growing. Few things about it are hard; having

things be so comfortable and easy seems almost unnatural.

I just want to make 100% sure that I am supposed to stay at Biola before I spend $20,000 when I know kids who need food and clothes. I was telling Mom about how disoriented my sense of the word "home" is now. I was telling her that I don't feel really connected to anyone. I feel like I am floating.

So much has happened since that conversation that it has faded from my memory, but I shuddered when I read those words in her journal. To hear your daughter say she can't relate to "home" was upsetting, but I understood that she was finding her own way in the world. I found myself empathizing with her pain.

I am doing collages to help me sort out some of my feelings (and I get to use my creative energies.) I have been so hyper and restless, I can't sit down and I think it is because I am used to constant motion and purpose and activity. I just feel like a vagabond.

One of the collages Katy made pictures a young woman driving a light blue Beetle convertible, top down, along a country road. She wrote phrases in the sky that I speculate show her priorities.

working with kids ◆ family ◆ keeping in touch with friends ◆ being obedient ◆ building community ◆ growth ◆ being a part of what God is doing ◆ hope ◆ taking risks ◆ reading ◆ being connected ◆ working with the poor ◆ being out of comfort zone ◆ balance ◆ faith ◆ health, fitness ◆ financial responsibility ◆ relationship with God ◆

235

**August 6, 1998:** I am compelled by the words Paul wrote in prison to the Ephesians:

*Pray also for me, that whenever I open my mouth, words may be given me so that I will fearlessly make known the mystery of the gospel for which I am an ambassador in chains. Pray that I may declare it fearlessly, as I should.*

*—Ephesians 6:19-20*

That is my prayer as I share about this summer and as I return to Biola. As I fight this spiritual battle that is my life, I recognize one of my greatest enemies: apathy and a loss of passion.

For the first time really all summer I thought about Biola and people from Biola. It was weird. It is going to be both good and strange to be back there.

**August 9, 1998:** I am scheduled to speak at the Missions Committee meeting on Wednesday for 10 minutes. There is so much I want to share that I can't fit it all into this short amount of time.

Maybe I could just move to Phoenix, get a job, go to school and work for Neighborhood Ministries. Even though that is my gut feeling right now, I know that I shouldn't and I can't because that would be quitting or taking the easy way and I am not capable of either. I shouldn't.

I am still thinking about next summer; I really want to go to Africa (I have for as long as I can remember) but I also want to do urban ministry in the US. Who knows, maybe God has an entirely different plan. Perhaps He will reveal to me why He still has me at Biola.

I am keeping terrible hours—I can't sleep until late at night and I feel like I sleep all day. Oh well, there will be none of that at Biola.

Reading this journal of Katy's was exhausting, exhilarating, disturbing, and eye-opening. It showed me that Katy was consumed with working with the Neighborhood children, becoming aware of the perilous lives they led, learning to love them, witnessing God work in remarkable ways, and yearning to become part of the "rescue operation". It also showed me the difficulty in her awakening. I knew the facts, but experiencing them through the thoughts she penned enhanced what I knew.

**August 10, 1998:** Today I slept in until 11. I hate sleeping in because I feel like it is a waste of time and I hate wasting time. *I figure my time here on earth is short.* I should be awake for it.

Once again I am so quick to forget about God's provision. He reminded me today that I need to look to Him for everything. It has already started. I am so comfortable that I am not seeking God and looking to Him for all of my needs. I have a problem with that; as soon as all of my basic material "needs" are being met, I forget that I need God and that I have a heavenly Father who loves me and wants to meet my every need. I was trying to figure out who I should get to pick me up from LAX [Los Angeles airport] and I didn't know who I should call and have kind of been worrying about it. I put a call in to a friend, but she wasn't home. In the meantime another friend called and told me how she loves to be the one picking me up at the airport and before I knew it I was giving her my flight information. The Lord is so amazing; He even provides when I forget to ask Him.

I can't believe I go back to Biola in exactly two weeks. I can't believe that I am a sophomore in college. It is such a nice feeling to be going to a place that I already know and to a routine I know and most of all—people I know and love; it is more like going home...

It is hard to believe that it was just a year ago that Mom and Dad were getting ready to take me to Biola. I just wonder where all of my stuff is and how I am going to get it back to my room. There I go again forgetting that the Lord will provide—I feel like Israel—I am so quick to forget.

On this last page, I look back on the most amazing summer so far. I will remember it as one of the times when I was met by an amazing God who changed me so I will never be the same, see the same, think the same, love the same, hear the same or live the same. He interrupted my life, my plans, my dreams, and my expectations—for that I am truly thankful. I commit my life to loving Him and being obedient to Him.

*For we are God's workmanship, created in Jesus Christ to do good works, which God prepared in advance for us to do.*

*—Ephesians 2:10*

**August 11, 1998:** Today I went to lunch with Mary Beth (a missionary friend). It was really fun to recount my summer and have her be so enthusiastic about it. I told her about being unsure of a major and she seemed to think that TESOL was the way to go.[12] She said maybe even some urban studies type thing might work. I told her that all I know is that I love kids and want to work with kids of any age from pre-K to high school, and am really into the long term, relational part of kid and youth ministry. It was really nice to talk to her because she is so encouraging, supportive and wise.

**August 15, 1998:** Well, the inevitable happened... Katie and Ian got engaged last night. As the maid of honor my most important duty is to pray for the bride and groom. It truly is an honor, but also a great responsibility. I want to (and am supposed to be) Katie's big support... I am feeling more and more like I need to be around next summer.

Today Katie and I went dress shopping. It is kind of strange when I think about it—one year prom dress shopping, the next grad dress shopping and now wedding dress shopping. Weird. I really am sad that I am going to be so far away and unable to help her in planning everything else.

I just finished the book *Redeeming Love* by Francine Rivers. I got so involved that I basically stopped life and read it in 2½ days. It really helped me to see into the heart of not just one prostitute but into the heart of used and oppressed people in general. It is so hard for someone to accept and understand if they have never experienced love in the first place—or the only thing they have experienced in the name of love has been painful or dominating. After reading this book the "tough act" that many of the kids put on this summer makes a lot more sense to me.

I got an email from Heather—she is so wonderful. I feel like I have taken her for granted. I can't wait to see her at Biola and catch up. Again her heart and mine seem to be the same (in some ways anyway). She wants this year to be a lot different from last and she has the same anxieties about this year that I do.

Oh the randomness. Jose called tonight using his Pepsi taste test calling card.

I didn't sleep well last night at all; I had the strangest dreams.

I am really excited about going back to Biola but I am feeling really anxious too and I am not exactly sure why. I think my biggest concern about going back is going back as a changed person and having to fight falling back into old, bad habits again. Maybe Heather and I can make a contract and she can help keep me accountable. I need to work on not gossiping, time management, not losing perspective, being more consistent with quiet time, not being so concerned with other people and their problems that I lose who I am, finding a ministry that really has eternal value and uses my gifts, and lots of other things. I want to listen more and talk less, walk more and eat less, watch less TV and read more, give more and spend less, pray more and complain less, encourage more and criticize less, serve more and consume less, trust more and spend less, sleep more and visit less... I have so many hopes and dreams, anxieties, and fears for this year. Last year I felt so much peace—this year chaos and turmoil. I am so torn. I am really enjoying being at home, but I know once I get back to Biola I will love it and want to be there.

The following is from Mother Teresa's *Meditations from a Simple Path*. I think it touches on a lot that I am feeling right now as I look toward another year at Biola:

*Deliver me, O Jesus...*
*From the desire of being loved,*
*From the desire of being extolled,*
*From the desire of being honored,*
*From the desire of being praised,*
*From the desire of being preferred,*
*From the desire of being consulted,*
*From the desire of being approved,*
*From the desire of being popular,*
*From the fear of being humiliated,*
*From the fear of being despised,*
*From the fear of suffering rebukes,*
*From the fear of being calumniated,*
*From the fear of being forgotten,*
*From the fear of being wronged,*
*From the fear of being ridiculed,*
*From the fear of being suspected.*

**August 22, 1998:** I am feeling really anxious about going back to Biola. I don't know why, though. I haven't been sleeping, but what else is new? I think much of my anxiety comes from my deep yearning to serve Christ and be used and I know (last year at least) at Biola I don't feel I do either.

*"I want to know Christ and the power of His resurrection and the fellowship of sharing in His sufferings, becoming like Him in His death and so somehow to attain to the resurrection of the dead."*

*—Philippians 3:10-11.*

Kit concluded in her tribute the effect Katy's summer had on her plans for her future.

*Before school started, she went to Tab to report about her summer in Phoenix, her work with the children, how she was getting a greater glimpse of the passion residing in her. The guest preacher that day overheard her report. He was an urban missionary from New York. As he spoke that morning, God gave him a word for Katy. He told her she was being called to urban work in the US. Until then Katy thought she was heading overseas. But that word, combined with her summer, changed her course and became the next piece to the puzzle.*

# Notes

All the children's names in this chapter have been changed to protect their privacy.

Bold text has been added for emphasis.

1 Tab's Youth Director during that time.

2 AMOR works with local pastors and mission teams to provide adequate housing in Mexico, South Africa and other locations to keep families together.

3 Young Life is an international Christian organization whose mission is to introduce adolescents to Jesus Christ and help them grow in their faith.

4 Brigadoon is a delightful reference to a mystic village in the movie of the same name that miraculously rises out of the mists every hundred years for a day, then disappears.

5 The Ryans were long time friends of the Danleys who had just returned from ten years of service in Bahrain. Katy had gone with the Danleys to greet them at the airport earlier that week.

6 Tab Church youth group mission trip..

7 Open Door Fellowship is a nondenominational Christian Church in Phoenix that was connected to Neighborhood Ministries in the early days of their organization.

8 Neighborhood Ministries church for Spanish speakers in 1998.

9 The Ridge Center was an after school Christian center for children in an underserved community near Clearwater, Florida, where Tab's youth group helped with VBS (Vacation Bible School.)

10 Name changed.

11 Name changed.

12 Teaching English to Speakers of Other Languages. Katy had considered this profession as a means of supporting herself so she could share the gospel in countries that were not open to Christian missionaries.

# Chapter 11
## Turmoil, Mercy and Clarity

Returning to Biola proved to be very challenging for Katy. She had difficulty reconciling her summer of missions work with what she had experienced in college. She had built relationships with children in poverty living lives of near desperation. She had seen such need and wanted to help. College life with its dorm drama seemed frivolous in comparison. I remember having similar feelings after a summer job during college working in a mental hospital as a student music therapist. The incongruity of the lives of the patients I worked with who had nothing, not even their sanity, was such a stark contrast to my college and home life. During that experience, I too was confused and had doubts. Still, it was hard reading in Katy's journal how she struggled to reconcile the discrepancies she saw first-hand.

## Sophomore Year

**August 25, 1998:** Well, here I go again. Back at Biola. I have never felt so much like bailing in my whole life. I keep reminding myself that I "love challenges" and I "hate quitting", but I have never felt so much like packing and going home (again, where that is—I don't know). It has always been my policy to be content wherever I am no matter what the conditions. I always finish everything I start, fulfill every commitment that I make. I feel so overwhelmed. What is going on? I haven't slept well and have had terrible and bizarre dreams ever since second semester of last year. My soul is not at peace. I am trying to get control of my thoughts, but really I just need to have faith that God will be faithful and get me through this and in fact this is all for some purpose.

We got a plant and named it Avery. The Danleys got me a fish so Heather and I both have one. Avery still comes often to visit and just sit in our room. It is good to be back here and see everybody but somehow I feel like it is just adding to my anxiety. I can't do this... I want to leave. I can't spend a whole semester feeling like this, let alone another day. Somehow I feel that another year of Biola is a huge step back for me.

**August 26, 1998:** We went to Huntington Beach with a few Hell boys [lower level of Hart Hall] and some Stews [Stewart Hall]. We went to Chuckie Cheese for a birthday...we ate and played games. Some of us went to Common Grounds. Despite being surrounded by friends, being at my favorite place—the beach and having a beautiful new room, I can't feel happy. I still feel like there is a storm inside me and it is starting to rage. I can't handle this. I don't want to be here but I do. I feel I am being totally self-centered. No one needs me. I am a 19 year old who has gotten everything I have ever wanted, who still doesn't have a job, wastes $20,000+ a year on college and who still needs spending money. I don't want to be here but I don't know where I want to be. I feel selfish feeling this way. I love my friends here, but when I'm here I can't help but think of myself and that gets me nowhere.

It was painful to read Katy relate how hard it was to return to Biola after her summer internship at Neighborhood Ministries. I had known her plight, but reading her description of those dark days gripped me. It was difficult to envision her as unhappy, but in the back of my mind, I knew she had to reconcile those conflicts herself.

**August 27, 1998:** It has been great rooming with Heather again so far. We are getting along better than ever; we have long talks every night before we go to bed and last night we decorated the room together.

**August 28, 1998:** I felt even better today. I had one class and was done by 9:20, so I had the rest of the day to play. I bungled around and took a nap. Three of us got dressed up and took lots of pictures then headed out to Santa Monica/3rd Street. We had a blast: shopping, drinking coffee and people watching. It was so much fun.

It is good to be back here again with my friends...

**August 30, 1998:** I went to the Harvest Crusade with friends.[1] It was so hot, but it was great and thousands came forward to accept Christ. The music was great too.

I am surprised, but I am actually glad to be back at Biola. I feel myself slipping into selfish mode again— save me, Lord, from myself.

The difficult reentry process continued, but as the semester developed its own rhythm, Katy began to come to terms with her life back in school. She saw God work in the midst of this struggle.

**August 31, 1998:** The Lord truly does answer every prayer in His own timing. I saw prayers prayed today and some prayed a year ago answered today. I was feeling really frustrated about my classes this semester, primarily my American Culture and Values class. I just wasn't feeling good about taking it, and the time is getting closer to when I have to commit. I prayed a lot about it today and (on the advice of Heather) decided to attempt to see my advisor. She has strange office hours and is always busy, but when I went to her office today she was there and had time to see me. She knew exactly who I was because she had talked to Kit at a conference last weekend. She suggested a class she teaches that fits perfectly into my schedule: Intercultural Communications. Also, she told me about a new major possibility—Liberal Studies with an emphasis in ICS [Intercultural Studies], so I am really excited to see what that is all about. God answered that prayer immediately.

Indeed, Katy did change her major and included a minor in teaching at the elementary school level.

Today I noticed a change in the character of many of my sisters on the floor and I have also seen difficult relationships turn into friendships. The Lord is such an awesome provider. It is exciting to see Him working in the lives of the people all around me.

**September 6, 1998:** This was a really strange week... it seemed to drag on. I got to talk to friends from home. Also my mom called me every day this week, many emails and letters as well. I think she can sense the unrest in my soul and is worried about me and feels totally powerless so far away.

Heather is in Phoenix this weekend. It has been kind of nice to have the room to myself but I realize how much I value her and her friendship. She knows me better than a lot of people and certainly better that anyone else at Biola. There is something just so comforting to being around someone that knows you so well.

I am feeling better every day about being here. I hope it is sincere and not just my survival "suck it up" instinct.

I want to get involved with a church and ministry through that but transportation is a huge problem. Also the job situation...

September 10, 1998: Lenny called me yesterday and told me he is interested in a school in Alaska. How cool would it be for Lenny to go to school in Alaska? I just pray that the Lord would give him a vision and give him the boldness to do it.

I am really enjoying my classes (especially personal defense, as Heather and I get to "attack" each other in our karate uniforms), but I am really having a hard time staying awake and my short-term memory is seriously failing.

**September 11, 1998:** Today we had our GYRAD. My date was Diesel, whom I didn't meet or even see until tonight. We went thrift story shopping and picked out outfits for each other and then we went bowling.

Briahnna [friend who lived across the hall] and I talked about how much we want this year to be different... we want to be different. We want to know God and be godly women. We want to make a contract with each other and God. I think God has really brought the two of us together this year to sharpen one another. What a blessing.

**September 19, 1998:** Today was the first Saturday of intramural football and I watched three different games. It was so fun.

I want to get involved... I want a serious ministry... I don't know what or how.

**September 27, 1998:**
*When my heart was grieved*
*And my spirit embittered,*
*I was senseless and ignorant;*
*I was a brute beast before you.*
*Yet I am always with you;*
*You hold me by my right hand.*
*You guide me with your counsel.*

*And afterward you will take me into glory*
*Whom have I in heaven but you?*
*And earth has nothing I desire besides you.*
*My flesh and my heart may fail,*
*But God is the strength of my heart*
*And my portion forever.*
*Those who are far from you will perish;*
*You destroy all who are unfaithful to you,*
*But as for me, it is good to be near God.*
*I have made the sovereign Lord my refuge.*
*I will tell of all Your deeds.*
*—Psalm 73:21-28*

By the beginning of October, it seemed Katy had resolved the conflict between what she had experienced in the summer and life at Biola. She focused on preparing for her future, still wondering about the unknown, but trusting God.

**October 6, 1998:** I had so much work last week. I am so thankful that the Lord has been so faithful to help me stay awake and get all of my work done—which is truly a miracle.

Some days I feel like everyone here is trying to hook up. I just want to finish school and be out and go wherever. I don't want to be concerned about or focused on the petty things and yet—I am.

The Lord is teaching me so much in my classes and giving me such better knowledge of the Bible. What an awesome thing that I can be here.

**November 20, 1998:** Wow! Life is so fast! Here I sit three weeks away from completing my third semester of college. I have a new major and absolutely no idea what the rest of my life looks like... but really, who has time for all that.

It is kind of ironic because I always assumed that my life would become clearer with time, but in reality it has become much more complicated and confusing. The world is so full of possibilities. I have never been so eager to go home. I think I am homesick. Once again I am preparing for my two worlds to collide. In bracing for the impact I find it hard to be connected to either world. So many thoughts and feelings fill my heart and throat and yet I push them down so I can move forward towards home... towards interterm.

Four semesters until I graduate, four till I am old, responsible and an adult, four semesters too few.

The Lord continues to be faithful in the lives of those at Biola and at home... it seems as though some are wandering and others are finally settling down.

Oh, there are so many things I wish I knew... so many things I wish I was... if only I could be... without distractions.

**December 18, 1998:** As I reflect on the completion of my third semester of college one thought prevails—God's faithfulness. God has been so faithful in so many ways: in keeping me healthy, allowing me to survive academically, bringing new people into my life, leading through a change of major that was virtually hassle-free—but that is not all—I can't ignore all the really hard and painful things that He was so faithful to see me and everyone else through as well. This semester was a semester of self-examination. I am exhausted in every way. God took care of me and gave me exactly what I needed.

Katy continued to journal through her winter break in Indianapolis, her first "home."

**January 11, 1999:** Life continues to amaze, confuse and surprise me. I had Kirsten, Alice and Heidi over; I haven't seen them for months and yet our relationship always seems to pick right back up where it left off. It did my heart so much good just to get to see them and laugh with them! Then today at church I got to see more people that I love and miss; people that I have so much history with. Just being around them brings me much comfort.

I don't know what I am supposed to do this summer. There is Lenny's graduation, Katie's wedding and I need to take some classes, so it looks like I will be staying around here for a while.

**January 25, 1999:** Ok, so another semester finished and I am going back for more. WOW! This sure is going at light speed.

I just got my grades today... almost a 3.5; I am very excited and I give the glory to God because it was such a difficult semester for many reasons and I had some difficult classes.

Once again there are so many things that I want this semester to be. I want to be more consistent with devotions, exercise and healthy eating. I also will be taking 18 units (God willing) so I need to keep my studies up. I also want to find a church and get more involved with some sort of children's ministry. Several of us need to finally start our accountability group that we always talk about.

I am still praying about Spring Break... I don't know what I am supposed to do.

I was thinking the other day about something that someone has said to me (and my family) on occasion, "I think you are perfect... don't tell me anything to make me think otherwise." That is like someone telling you, "I don't really want to know you, I just want to know the part of you that I am going to like." One thing that I have learned is that to truly love somebody as Christ loves us and intends us to love others we have to know the whole person: the good, the bad, and the ugly. That is what makes a person who they are; that is what makes them human. I don't know, just a random philosophical thought...

Her ability to see through someone's shallowness (no matter who they were) and then reframe it in Christ's perspective impressed me. I have prayed that my children would not be drawn to worldly things no matter how attractive. And here it was in Katy's own words—confirmation that God answered that prayer.

She also recorded her thoughts on the flight back to LA.

Saturday I went with Mary Beth to pick up Dr. Michael Johnson, a missionary surgeon from Kenya. It was very fascinating to hear his thoughts on the current state of affairs in Kenya and the US. His advice to me was that I get the most education I can now. He said that I am not going to want to be in school any more than I do right now, so it would be better to just get it all over with. He also said that if we spend our energy caring for the elderly, feeding the poor and visiting the prisons people would come to Christ and lives would be changed. We need to be spending our energies wisely.

This flight is 4 ½ hours because of a 115 mph headwind. I am rested; in a short time that word will be just a memory. I am glad I am going back early so that I can get settled in and play a bit before classes start.

As she settled into the new semester, her writings show how acutely aware she was of God's persistent role in her life. Katy started recording her prayers in her journal. They are heartfelt and thankful and illustrate ways to share one's deepest thoughts with the Father.

**March 3, 1999:** I stand in awe of your faithfulness Lord. Forgive me for my own persistent unfaithfulness. Forgive me for relying on myself, and then crying out for your help after I have given it a try on my own. Thank you for being patient with me when I fail to ask for help and give you all of the glory.

I thank you for your faithfulness this week getting me through all of my tests. I thank you for placing me in the perfect classroom at Scott Ave. Thank you for your faithfulness to my family. Thank you for your amazing work in the lives of my friends. I thank you that you know me and love me anyway.

I thank you for the rain.

Katy still used email to stay in touch on occasion.

**March 18, 1999:** Hello! How are you today? The missionary staying in my room is very nice and I got a chance to talk to her some tonight so that was good.

That guy that I went to Les Mis with left roses in my room today (by climbing in the second story window)... he said they were to replace the one he gave me that had wilted... why me? No worries... I will get Heather on the case... she is very protective of me and will break it down for him as soon as she comes back.

The conference is going really well and the speaker tonight was excellent. It was nice to hear a woman speak. She is only the third female speaker we have had... I am tired of hearing middle-aged Caucasian men.

Have a great day

Love
Katy

However, she wrote her inmost thoughts in her journal.

**March 22, 1999:** These days when I day dream, I think of home, my family, friends and driving on familiar streets. I don't know what this means... I don't know whether it is a "the grass is greener" thing and I would rather be where my homework and stress aren't or I am actually homesick.

This week was Missions Conference and we had a missionary with WEC stay in our room.[2] It was great to talk to her about missions and refreshing to be around someone that is not in college.

It has been on my heart for some time now, that I would disciple a younger girl and Lord willing I will have that chance with a girl in Watts through World Impact.[3]

I feel myself being sucked into the desire to be an elementary teacher in the US, have a house, get married and have kids. That has never been for me and the Missions Conference was good to get me refocused.

I am trying to figure out the summer with classes, work, the wedding and maybe Romania. It just doesn't seem to be coming together.

Sometimes those thoughts seemed to be random, as if she would suddenly miss one of us and stop what she was doing to write them down.

## *My Brother*

*1.* Drying my hair for my high school graduation open house.

*2.* Holding my hand on the plane in Bolivia when I was sick.

*3.* Buying gloves for me in Copacabana.

*4.* Using a cold hair dryer to cool off my sunburn in Jamaica.

Katy kept us close as she shared her West Coast life through those emails. She reported on the possibility of student teaching in New Guinea, a dream about visiting Rick's old rugby friends, the beautiful California weather, Rick's race results, how long until school is out for the summer, the Biola baseball team, and other matters. As I revisited her emails, I loved coming across lines that showed her sense of humor.

"I would love to help out on race morning. Can I wear my pajamas?"

"Betas are always such pillars of society. Too bad I was born with double X chromosomes."

Her journal writing revealed more about how she was processing life. And she expressed her more personal emotions there.

**April 14, 1999:** Thou my best thought, by day or by night. Waking or sleeping. Thy presence my light.

Mom and Dad came for Spring Break/my birthday. How weird to be "grown up" and with my parents on vacation. They got to see my room and meet some of my friends, so that was great. They had a surprise beach party planned, but then it rained, so we went to Friday's and shopping. We also went to San Diego and stayed in La Jolla. We went to the zoo and aquarium. Then we went to visit Aunt Sue and Uncle Chuck in Pacific Palisades. With them we went to Third Street and Universal Studios. We got to hear lots of wild family stories.

I am really excited about this summer and seeing everyone. A thought: what about doing/leading a college Bible study this summer...?

**April 24, 1999:** The Lord has been so faithful this

week (and this semester.) I have been able to get all of my work completed—and on time at that. And through it all I have been able to have joy. I am getting more and more excited about going home every day. Romania isn't going to work out, but summer school has been narrowed down to two classes. I have a job babysitting in the works.

I went to the beach last Sunday with a guy. He took me to Laguna Beach to see the tide pools. It was so fun... we hiked around and saw starfish, crab, and lots of other sea creatures. We were talking and I asked him what he wanted to do with his life and what his passion was. Word for word he said the exact opposite of how I answered: he said that his passion is marriage; he doesn't like kids, but he thinks maybe he could learn to like his own; he wants to live in California in a quaint town and he would maybe consider living outside of the US but definitely not in a third world country and the only place he would really live is France; he doesn't need a big house... just a really nice car. He wants to work for a big corporation and his whole life and happiness is built around his future wife. He said nothing of wanting to do something great for God... it was all about his fulfillment of the American Dream. Ha Ha! I had to laugh... God does have such a good sense of humor. We hardly talked on the ride home... we both knew what had happened, but neither one of us was going to bring it up.

**May 16, 1999:** I don't exactly know how to articulate this, but I will try my best. For weeks now I have been having nightmares. The one thing they have in common is that they all have children in them. I don't remember all of them, but I do know that when I wake up I feel very disturbed and tense, often crying. I remember one in particular—I was at a concentration camp and I was in charge of taking care of the children. They kept asking for more food, but I could give them none. In another dream I was in charge of a bunch of kids. We were in a different country. It was very hostile. The children wanted to get out of this house that we were hiding in, but it was too dangerous. I had to keep them inside all day and make them lie down perfectly still and be silent. I began to cry out to God and we were spared. I don't understand the meaning or the purpose of these dreams.

At Singspiration tonight I was singing and all of the sudden this overwhelming sense of sadness came over me and I couldn't control my tears—I could barely breathe and as I was praying to God about how I could possibly love Him as I should, these words I heard almost audibly, "Love my children."[4]

I really began to cry and I felt overwhelmed, like the wind had gotten knocked out of me. I said, "Me Lord? How can I possibly do that?" He replied "In my strength." I still felt overwhelmed with a deep sadness. I realized that I was feeling my heart breaking for these children.

I stumbled over to the prayer chapel and continued to sob. I read Matthew 18 where Jesus says that He doesn't wish that even one of the little ones should perish. I said that I would do all that I could, even give my life to obey this.

Being home for the summer was a nice break from her studies, but it turned out to be another radical change from her college life. She discovered that things at home didn't stay stagnant.

**May 30, 1999:** well, I find myself home again— but not without first having the totally exhausting experience of packing, finals, storage, leaving and flying. It feels good to be home and even better to know that I get to stay in one place for a bit. Everyone around here is getting so tall, not to mention so old.

I am really looking forward to this summer. It is so hard to believe that it was just about a week ago, when I felt like school and the work would never end.

**June 17, 1999:** Being at home for the summer is proving to be quite an adjustment. I feel like I am in a time warp and have in fact been gone for 10 years instead of two. I feel like I have missed a step.

## Junior Year

During her junior year many of the things Katy had been praying for happened, but she still wondered about her future. In spite of her uncertainty, she continued to trust in God's faithfulness.

**September 6, 1999:** This Sunday I went to a new church, Calvary Chapel Saving Grace. It was awesome and I was really challenged. I am beginning to realize that since I have been at Biola I haven't lost my vision or my focus, but that I have lost much of my enthusiasm. It feels so distant... so impossible. All of my focus has had to be on studying and my equipping; I haven't stopped to see that this chapter of my life is drawing to a close and a new chapter will soon begin.

A man spoke at church about his ministry in war-torn Sudan and I was reminded of what I want my life to be about and what I want my life to look like.

I need to begin serious thought and prayer about what will happen in two years. I don't even know what state I will be living in or anything. I have nowhere to picture myself... I have to trust God and His timing. It is so exciting and yet frightening all at the same time. I can't wait to get to a place where I know I might be for at least a little while. Having one home would be nice.

I wonder what my life is going to be like. I realize now that I have not allowed myself to dream... for fear that I might want something that is out of God's will... as a result I feel somewhat lost.

Both Amy and Lenny called me tonight... It did my heart so much good to hear their voices.

Dear Lord, I just thank you for your comfort. I thank you that no matter where I am, I am always in your care and protection. I thank you for this weekend and the time of relaxation and encouragement. I pray that you would be glorified in all of my words and actions. I give this semester to you. I pray that

I would be a good steward of the time, gifts, and opportunities I have been given. I pray that you would help me to be diligent in my studies and help me to have a good attitude. I pray that you would soften my heart and open my eyes and ears to what you would have me learn this semester both in and out of the classroom. I pray that you would use me as you see fit in the lives of those around me. Please make me sensitive to the needs of others. Please show me what ministry you would have me involved in. I give this semester to you. Change me Lord, make me into the woman you would have me be. Amen.

As I read another of Katy's prayers, I was encouraged that the storms she felt the year before had dissipated. She still wondered what God had in store for her future, but she seemed more curious than anxious. As she found peace, my uneasiness from her distress lessened. She had clearly been confident in God's faithfulness.

This entry shows more of Katy's thoughts as her first semester of Junior Year flew by.

**October 14, 1999:** What a wild and eventful semester it has been already. So many things have happened, but the one thing that has been constant, and has been an overtone for this whole semester (and whole college experience) is God's faithfulness. He has been so faithful to provide for me to return here each semester. He has given me the strength and desire to be diligent in my studies. He has been faithful in providing friends and nurturing those friendships especially in the hard times. Those are just a few... there are so many others.

I had three cumulative midterms this week. I didn't think this week would end well but God was faithful in giving me the strength—despite my lack of sleep. I was just looking at the list of things I was really praying about at the beginning of this semester, and God has answered many of them already. First of all, I have found a church that I really like and have been able to attend quite regularly. It is called Calvary Chapel saving Grace, in Yorba Linda. The services are two to 2 ½ hours long, but the teaching is awesome.

Secondly, I joined the Big Brother/Big Sister program, and I have a "little sister" named Alexandra, and I go every Monday afternoon and spend time in her kindergarten class.

A third and most significant answer to prayer was redeemed friendship between people in my dorm. Praise God. These friendships mean so much and are much needed too. God has used all this to make me realize that we are all growing up here together; He is molding all of us and we are sharpening one another. He has us here for a purpose, and we all serve different purposes in each other's lives.

We have Torrey next week and then Amy is coming to visit. I am so excited!

I am feeling much confusion in my life right now (what else is new). I am really eager to get done with school and get on with things. However, I am trying to treasure the time I have left here because I know I am still here for a purpose, and also this is a very unique time in my life that will never be again and I will probably be wishing I were back here once the real work begins.

I keep praying for direction in my life, but have no idea what is in store for me yet. God willing, I will graduate and be fully credentialed in the spring of 2001. That is coming so soon and I still don't have an inkling of what I will do after that.

I am more and more attracted to the idea of teaching in the US at a public school for a while. I don't know if that is because that is what I think would be comfortable now (that idea scares me) or if it is Satan trying to distract me or if that is God's will working in my heart. Who knows?

I am scared of choosing for comfort's sake... I never want to do that. I want to obey and I want to be stretched.

Katy was spending Winter Term at Biola when tragedy struck. Her friend Julie, who lived down the hall, was killed when her car slid on a patch of ice. Julie was spending that January at home in Washington when the accident happened.

Several of Julie's friends, including Katy, took a train to attend her funeral. The Biola community surrounded them with sympathy and more: other students helped them pack, drove them to the train station and provided food for the trip; professors excused them from classes and postponed tests. Everyone gathered to pray. Katy and the other friends were devastated; that group of young women were so very close. I made an effort to console Katy through phone calls, notes and emails, but it was difficult trying to help her from so far away. She grieved. They all grieved. Julie's mother and I have talked from time to time. We try to encourage each other, especially on difficult "anniversary" days.

Her journals go on to express her desire to be faithful to God above all else.

> **March 5, 2000:** Forgive me, Lord Jesus, for how quickly I forget your faithfulness and resort to my own resources. How quickly I forget your many mercies and mighty acts. This continues to be the most painful season of my life and yet it is the time that I have been the most blessed and felt your nearness. There are so many changes going on and so many decisions to be made.
>
> Forgive me, Lord, for worrying about them and for not having the faith to turn them over to you. In my weakness Lord, may be your strength. In my brokenness, your opportunity to work, in my confusion, your chance to bring clarity, in my pain, your way to heal. Lord I just give this semester to you. May you be glorified in all that I say and do. May your work be done in your strength through this vessel.
>
> I pray that you will use my brokenness to mold me into a more godly woman—and the person you desire me to be. I pray that my own notions of reality would not hinder your work and your will in my life. I pray that I realize that all I need is you—you are my hiding place and your name is a mighty tower that I can run to. I pray that I would know you as I never have before. Please give me wisdom in my decision-making, in my day-to-day life and in my relationships. Amen

*Sacrificed*

*Loved*

*Protected*

*Hugged*

*Taught*

*Given*

*Understood*

*Hoped*

*Endured*

*Shown*

*Prayed*

*Comforted*

We visited Katy during that spring break. It was so good to see her friends, be immersed in her community, see Southern California, and spend time in person with her, especially since she'd lost her dear friend Julie just a few months earlier. After we got home she sent us an email.

**April 10, 2000:** It never ceases to amaze me how you can still be such a part of my life even when I am so far away. Thank you for that. I am so glad that so many of my friends from here have gotten to meet you; that is so important to me. If I can't have all the people I love in the same place, at least I have the privilege of having the people that I love know each other. That is a blessing. See you soon!

Love, Katy.

Her statement foreshadowed her future. She often said she wanted all the people she loved in the same place—that happened after she became ill.

In her tribute at Katy's funerals, Kit commented on Katy's journal writing.

*Katy understood deep kingdom values at such a young age. She valued the things that Jesus places as most important. And so, her only fear was that she might veer from those, that the comforts, the predictable and easy things would rob her of and keep her from remaining inside the costliness of following Jesus.*

The costliness of her obedience to God's leading can be seen in this poem I found among Katy's things. Her joyful spirit concealed how much she yearned for home and family even while she determinedly took the next step in the path He was revealing to her. Reading this was so difficult for me. I struggled to cope with the thought of her grief over missing her family. I never knew how hard it was for her; she had covered it well. At the same time, I marveled at her resolve to pursue God's plan in spite of her heartache.

Reading this poem renewed my grief as I realized I "grieve over the small things as much as the big ones... Over Friday night pizza as much as the biggest holiday meal." Nothing is the same as it was. But one thing she worried about, "Being the one who is always gone and everyone is used to it," never happened (and never will). But at first I worried it would. The hole of her absence is always there, deep down, as I struggle to balance 'doing life' and the pain of the empty space where she belongs.

The evidence of the worth of her California years, the time away from home, was apparent in the many notes and letters we received from her peers and colleagues from there at her funerals and afterward. One that stood out was sent to Lenny, two years after Katy passed.

*You don't know me, but I knew of you. Katy spoke of you often. I was friends with Katy back in college and I want you to know that she was perhaps one of the greatest individuals that I met during my time there. It was a sad day to learn that she had gone to be with her Savior—whom she has such a love for. But my memories of her are true and fond and she was a person who loved God,*

270

## And to Those I see over Turkey and Stuffing

Know that I love you.
Know that I miss you.
Know that I grieve over the small things
    as much as the big ones.
Over the rides to school as much as
        your first day of college.
Over the average Tuesday as much as
        your 21st Birthday.
Over Friday night pizza as much as
        the biggest holiday meal.
I miss a lot of things.
I missed out on a lot of things.
It makes sense though, most of the time.
It feels worth it though, most of the time.
        Until you are the one who is always gone—
            and everyone is used to it.
    Until you go from being the oldest
        granddaughter to being unrecognizable.
    Until you realize your brother could
        marry someone you have never met.
    Until you realize you missed out on
        your sister's entire adolescence.
    Until your realize the family you neglect
        the most is your own.
    Until you realize that while you are busy
        living your important life, those that
        you love are growing older and
        experiencing life—and doing it
                without you.
    It makes sense. It feels worth it.
        Most of the time.

*loved others and from the day I first met her, her passion was for the unfortunate and the lost. She knew where she was going at the old age of 19. Again, though you don't know me, please know that your sister was a special person and that she touched my life in a very special way. God bless. —Jeffery Hachquet*

Determined not to waste money Katy took extra classes many semesters and graduated in 3 ½ years. After student teaching, she described herself on an application for a teaching position in a nearby school district. She was ready to take the next steps down the path God had laid for her.

A well-trained, enthusiastic and diligent teacher who is interested in speaking hope, confidence and academic excellence into the lives of children. Children are precious and I have been privileged to fill a great deal of my life with activities that have allowed me to encourage, teach, love, learn about and learn from them. I am thrilled to begin teaching because it is a perfect blend of my two loves: children and teaching.

1 Harvest Crusade is an evangelical festival that is held at Anaheim, California to bring Christianity to young people. Over 272,000 people attended that year.

2 WEC International is an interdenominational missions agency of evangelical tradition which focuses on evangelism, discipleship and church planting.

3 World Impact is a Christian Missions Organization committed to facilitating church-planting movements by evangelizing, equipping and empowering America's unchurched urban poor.

4 Singspiration is a weekly evening event at Biola that consists of "conversing with God through an extended time of worship singing hymns and spiritual songs."

# Chapter 12
*Ocean View: 2001*

Katy finished college and took a job teaching in Biola's backyard in Whittier, California at Ocean View Elementary School. Her first class of first-graders was particularly demanding, but Katy persevered and learned a lot about teaching challenging students. She called me a couple of times when she was frustrated about reaching especially difficult students, but she never gave up on them. She regrouped and tried other ways to reach them. She wrote about her time there.

I was given a great opportunity to work at a school in one of the districts where I student taught. I took the position hoping to gain teaching experience and finish my Clear Credential (required by California within five years of teaching.) My first year was very challenging as I had a class with diverse and severe needs. I learned much from these experiences and developed great relationships with my students.

Kit told more in her tribute.

*What did she love about Ocean View? Everything, the kids, her co-workers, the kids' parents. Bloom where you're planted. That was Katy. And yet there was something missing about continuing to live in California and teach there. The pieces were still forming, the next chapter not written.*

Other teachers at Ocean View noticed Katy's efforts in her classroom and the difference it was making in her students' lives. One of those teachers made an acute observation.

*Everyone who knew the makeup of your class and saw you in action with them were impressed by your skills, attitude, and love for them. Those that knew you well know where that strength came from. It came from your love and devotion to the Lord and wanting to serve Him and allow Him to work through you. You are such a light and joy to work with.*

Kristen, the teacher who became a close friend, shared details about Katy in her first-grade classroom that tell more about Katy than her teaching techniques.

*One of my fondest memories of Katy was when the orange cards would come back from her students that first week of school. She would study them as if they were windows into her students' lives. You see, Katy knew every detail about her students. She knew their parents' employment, phone numbers of all immediate family members including babysitters and family friends, day care schedules, names and ages of siblings, academic strengths and weaknesses, t-ball schedules and dance performances. Katy knew it all!*

*For fun I would quiz her and try to stump her with questions like, "What was so and so's mother's maiden name?" or, "What does so and so like on his cereal?" But somehow Katy always knew the answer. It was then that I realized that Katy's love for her students went far beyond the classroom.*

*Katy was notorious for charts and graphs which she would tape to the student's desk to reinforce desired behaviors. What worked for one student didn't necessarily work for the other. It was like she was a detective looking for clues to solve and curb behavior. Katy continued to smile and continued to love.*

*One day it seemed that the many failed charts and behaviors had discouraged Katy. She was overwhelmed by the many needs in her classroom. I entered the room and saw her at her desk in silence. I knew exactly what kind of day she had had. I grabbed her hand and we went around to each and every desk and prayed for that student by name. You see, Katy knew that God had placed her at Ocean View for a reason. It would be by the Lord's strength that she would be able to make it through. I remember that day so vividly like it was yesterday. Katy was a person who thrived in difficult situations. She was never angry or willing to give up. Katy only got stronger in the midst of adversity.*

I learned more about Katy's years at Ocean View when I read what the people whose lives she touched wrote on the blog during her illness. Parents of her former students reached out to her.

*We felt very honored to have our son in your class at Ocean View Elementary because it was very easy for us to see that you have a special gift for working with children. You always made the parents feel so comfortable and you cared about our concerns for our children. A group of parents from our son's 1st grade class were able to form special friendships and still remain friends today and we always credit this to you. May God bless you and may you have a complete and speedy recovery.*

*Love, Christine, Robert, Tristan and Vincent Navarro*

◆

*Dear Miss Reel, Our love and prayers go out to you. I just want you to know that Marcus says you were the best teacher ever. He thinks about you all the time. We still have your picture of you in the fairy costume up on our desk. Erin says she loved helping you during school. I think that was why she decided to become a teacher. They are both doing great and they wish for you to get better.*

*All our love, Rachael, Erin and Marcus*

◆

*Dear Reels—Katy was my daughter's first-grade teacher. She is now in fourth grade and still talks about Miss Reel and what a wonderful teacher she was. I had the honor of meeting Katy a few years ago during parent teacher conferences and school events and I could tell she had a special gift.*

Some of her former Ocean View students wrote to Katy on her blog. They seemed to remember how much she cared for them, how much she was interested in what they did in and out of the classroom.

Hi Miss Reel, remember me? I was in your first grade class at Ocean View and my Grandma and Pops taught art. I am sorry you are sick and I hope you get better soon. I still have my dog Spike and I am going to a new school for fourth grade.

My new teacher is really nice just like you. But you are the prettiest and the nicest.

I miss you.

Bye for now. Love, Courtney

◆

I was in your first grade class two years ago and we're all thinking about you at Ocean View. We are all praying that you get well soon. We miss you very much and thanks for being such a great teacher to all of us. We love you!

Love, Justin

◆

Dear Miss Reel, I miss you very much. We pray for you every night before we go to bed. My report card was excellent. You would be very proud of me. I still remember when you came to my birthday party. You are a very special teacher.

◆

Dear Miss Reel, Hi! We hope you feel better soon. We will pray for you every night and ask God to keep all His angels with you so they can take care of you. We will keep you close to our hearts. Thank you for coming to my baseball games and being the greatest teacher. We love and miss you.

Love, Ezra and Kaetlyn and family

◆

The blog entries from other Ocean View teachers gave me an insight into what Katy's peers saw in her.

*You have had and will continue to have a positive influence on all the people that you meet. We were fortunate to have you as a teacher at Ocean View.*

*Jennie Mischenko*

♦

*…you had and still have a special gift in dealing with children, as well as adults. Working with you was truly a heavenly blessing which I will always cherish. I always will remember, as you will always remember, your first class.*

♦

*You were always so generous to me. You helped me set up the sight word vocabulary program on my computer and you gave me the rocker with the broken slats… You gave me support when I needed it; you listened to me and always made me laugh. I appreciate all that you have done for me, what a blessing you have been to me! … working with you was such an incredible and awesome experience. I'm positive that all whom you have touched at some point in their lives feel the same way. Your sweet and caring spirit has been surely missed around here. You were and still are a one of a kind, one in a million… a once in a lifetime kind of friend that only few in this world are lucky enough to have found.*

*Your friend always, Pano*

♦

*All of us at Ocean View are so lucky to not only call you our co-worker, but our friend. You lit up each morning with that bright smile of yours and even though that first grade class of yours was a challenge you always kept on smiling. Thank you for your daily inspiration that today (and every day) is a great day.*

I knew that even though Katy was invested in her Ocean View students, she felt a longing to return to the children and families she had come to care for so deeply in Phoenix. She felt God's call to go back there, but obediently waited for His timing, as usual, willing to be taught. She wrote these words in her journal.

> I prayed that I would be in Phoenix for my second year of teaching, but it was not God's timing. I returned to Ocean View for my second year. I now realize that the Lord still had much for me to learn from this school and my students. With a new group of students I have learned many things, and have been able to work on different skills than I was able to last year.

Her friend Kristen shared her perspective.

> *The first year came and went. Katy knew that Ocean View would not be her final destination. We would have late night chats about her passion for children that were less fortunate. She was grateful for the lessons learned in Ocean View, however she felt this was the stepping-stone for the next chapter in her life. God had prepared her for something more. In Katy, I spied wisdom beyond her years.*

After her second year of teaching at Ocean View she moved to Phoenix to join Neighborhood Ministries. As Kit explained:

> *And then the time was right. We needed Katy here, and her experience as a public school teacher was the perfect match for the launching of our Head Start class. We asked her if she would become a two-year intern and be our NM staff for this classroom. We now know that God's preparations in Katy's life were for this.*

Katy weighed her options and sought the Lord's lead. As she pondered, she recorded her thoughts in a journal.

> I was walking at the Rose Bowl the morning of the day I was to talk to Neighborhood Ministries. As I walked I prayed that God would make His will clear to me. I already knew that God wanted me in Phoenix, but there was still a small part of me that wanted to hold onto control of my life. That was the same part of me that knew how much change was going to come with deciding to move. God spoke to my heart and I realized that I must seem so foolish to pray for God to answer while at the same time want to decide for myself. So at that point I let go and I prayed saying that I would go wherever He called me. I made my decision later that day.

> As I prayed I felt that the Lord was saying that now is the time. It is time for me to step out in faith and move to Phoenix. I am thrilled. I feel that the Lord has been equipping me for this through the various trips I have been on, my time at Biola and my teaching experiences.

The decision was made and Katy expectantly followed God's lead once again.

> **April 22, 2003:** It has been about two weeks since I made a commitment to Neighborhood Ministries and I feel such a peace about it. Every time I am in Phoenix I feel a longing to stay. Ever since my first summer there I have felt God saying, "This is your future." I just have been unsure of the timing.

> My greatest fear in life is that I would get too

comfortable with my life to do what God really has as His "best" for me. At this time in my life I feel myself at a crossroads. I have two choices: I can either continue with the life I have and all that implies (acquisition of bigger and better belongings, job security, safe, developed relationships, familiar people, places, and experiences) or I could step out in faith and do what I have always felt God calling me to do.

I have noticed that my biggest challenge in decision-making has not been choosing between good and bad, but in choosing between the easy, comfortable way, and the more difficult, stretching way. I forced myself to imagine being 70 years old looking back on my life. I realized that if I continued to work at Ocean View, got my Master's degree, bought a house etc. I could be proud of my life, but I also realized that I would miss out on what God really had planned for me.

I like my organized world, my independence, my well-developed friendships. I like that I am responsible in the eyes of the world. But at the same time those things are not me. I want to grow. I want to be stretched. I want to be used. I want to be a part of what God is doing. As much as the change scares me, I can take confidence in the fact that God has always been faithful and has provided above and beyond what I have needed.

I feel like this is God's will and God's timing.

Looking at Katy's decision to move to Phoenix confirmed in my mind how brave and determined she was to obediently wait for the opportunity to follow the desire God had planted in her. She was so patient to wait for the right time.

# Chapter 13
## *"...trust, love and obey...": 2003-05*

I found a chart Katy made in one of her journals when she must have been contemplating the move to Neighborhood Ministries. It confirmed that NM honored the values that Katy deemed important.

### October 24, 2003:

| California | Arizona |
|---|---|
| easy | chaotic |
| calculated | peaceful |
| comfortable | simplified |
| self-serving | focused |
| well-maintained | other-focused |
| predictable | unpredictable |
| focused | messy |
| practical | unplanned |
| conventional wisdom | crisis |
| responsible | faith |

| | |
|---|---|
| *matured* | *comfort* |
| *wise* | *exciting* |
| *well-refined* | *supportive* |
| *pride* | *home* |
| *logical* | *me* |

Katy wrote to friends and family letting them know of her move to Phoenix, asking for their prayers and support.

Dear Friends,

As I move toward an exciting new phase in my life, I see many of the seeds that God has planted over a lifetime come to fruition. At long last, this is the year for me to move to Phoenix and begin the next exciting new phase of the life God has for me.

I have committed to a two-year internship with Neighborhood Ministries, which is set to begin in August. My primary responsibility is brand new to the ministry. Recently, the city of Phoenix let NM know of their desire to locate a federally funded Head Start program on the campus of the Neighborhood Center. The Board of Neighborhood Ministries felt very strongly that a faith-based component be added so these precious small children would hear the love of God. An additional hour and a half was added to the Head Start 6-hour day, and has been named the "wrap around piece". Amazingly, despite the prohibitions placed on faith-based programs, the city agreed to this partnership. Many have taken notice of this new working relationship, including the President's Faith-Based Initiative leaders who want badly to find a way for the faith-based community to embrace Head Start. Neighborhood Ministries has asked me to help design the faith-based curriculum that will be the wrap around piece for these four- and five-year-olds.

I am thrilled to be a part of what God is doing in central Phoenix. I know that this next chapter of my life is going to be very challenging, but I can't wait to see what God has in store. I am humbled and overwhelmed by this enormous responsibility. I know God has faithfully prepared me for this exciting new adventure.

The Head Start class at Neighborhood Ministries had launched in May of that year with Ericka Boltz as the main teacher, supported by aides and volunteers. The plan was for a 9-5, year-round program with only two weeks off in the summer for Kids Club. Katy arrived in August to find a weary staff who described themselves as "looking like deer in the headlights." They had been through several aides. The roof leaked, so there was a large trash can in the block area to catch the water when it rained. They were spending hours on the bus in the morning and afternoon picking up the kids and taking them back home, sometimes even driving it. Katy's comment was, "Oh this isn't going to work." So, she put the wrap-around curriculum development on hold and pitched in, joining Ericka and the others in the classroom full time. Kit described more about Katy's early days at Neighborhood Ministries.

*Of course, you know that Katy took on more than teaching in the Head Start classroom. She immediately moved into the neighborhood, and stepped into Mom's Place and co-led that. Relationships, Katy's strength, grew all around her. She was in homes every day. She gently woke up moms and got the kids*

*to school. She sat for hours every day in the Head Start van,*
*managing the new days of living with our families. She helped*
*create order in the classroom and helped create hope in hundreds*
*of lives. Katy was thriving. It was like she had found it, the exact*
*place and time she was created for.*

A long-time volunteer with the young children shared her observations of Katy when she joined Ericka in the classroom.

*Working with Katy, I have seen a remarkable love produced by*
*the Maker of Love. Katy didn't just "have" faith, or "get" faith,*
*she LIVED faith! From the moment I met her, I realized she was*
*the gift we needed for the kids—and the moms—(actually the*
*families) of all involved in the Head Start program. We literally*
*muddled through those first few months… but Katy's love poured*
*out through her endless willingness to love the families who*
*didn't even know they were being loved. She and Ericka endured*
*terribly long hours at school only to have to write reports, clean*
*the classroom, rearrange the classroom for weekends, knock on*
*doors to awaken children, make endless phone calls to arrange for*
*transportation needs of the children, etc. This list is minimal. They*
*did so much more and really NEVER complained. They have both*
*been examples of living the call of Christ on their lives. Katy didn't*
*just work her 9-5, Monday through Friday job, she continued after*
*hours and all weekend, depending on the needs.*

Katy delighted in all of her responsibilities at the Neighborhood Center, including helping with the young mothers in Mom's Place. As Kit explains,

*Katy became the most loved friend for the moms in Mom's Place.*
*The girls all related to her. We laughed at them always wondering*
*why she didn't have children yet. She would tell them they all had*
*enough for her to love! Katy became a friend, a sister, and even*

*though she was young, a mother to these moms. Her devotion and selfless caring for their needs has imprinted their lives and they are all stronger in faith and character for knowing Katy.*

Katy loved to tell her supporters about her Phoenix experiences and thank them for their part in making it all possible. In January of that year, she wrote to them to communicate her experiences at Neighborhood Ministries.

Dear Friends and Family,

Happy 2004! I cannot believe how quickly my time in Phoenix is going. It seems like just yesterday that I was unpacking my U-Haul wondering what this new life would hold. As I sit here five months later I am amazed at the way God has answered so many prayers.

After a short stay in a family's guest house, I found a house three blocks from the Neighborhood Center and close to many of our families. I live with two roommates, who also attend the Neighborhood Church and are involved with the ministry.

I jump-started my work here by going to a three-day Head Start conference the day after I arrived and I have been working full time ever since. Thanks to your generosity and prayers I was able to raise all of my support by September!

I was hired to coordinate the "wrap around piece," as well as do some casework. We quickly learned that the needs of our kids were so great that we needed as many hands as possible in the classroom. As a result, I am now a full-time teacher in the classroom, working alongside the teacher and assistant provided by Head Start, Ericka and Silvia. Ericka is a long time NM volunteer who has experience in many areas of our ministry and is incredibly dedicated to our kids and families. Silvia is new to us as of November and loves and prays for our kids daily.

We have 16 precious three-, four-, and five-year-olds who represent 13 families, including a set of twins, an aunt and niece, and many, many cousins. There are various significant factors that complicate the lives of our children. Since the school year began we have had over 20 moves and the most cases of lice of any Head Start around, according to our caseworker. With the exception of three children, our kids come from homes where they live with at least one, if not two other families, often in a small apartment. Many of our children were exposed to drugs and/or alcohol before they were born and several of our parents still struggle with addiction. Also, seven of our kids failed the Head Start developmental screening and 12 failed the behavioral/emotional screening. Finally, many of them are considered either below or above weight for their age as a result of poor nutrition.

While all of this sounds very discouraging, we have much to rejoice about. These 16 beautiful children receive two healthy meals and a snack each day during which they sit at one long table passing food to one another and have sweet little conversations. During the day these energetic preschoolers sing, draw, run, climb, listen, share, paint, count, set the table, dress up, play house, ride bikes, wonder, slide, throw balls, build, read, explore, hunt for bugs, clean up, laugh, take naps, solve puzzles, use scissors, imagine, dance and go home exhausted. Also, our parents are establishing good school routines with their kids that will benefit them throughout their time in school.

Five of our moms are involved with Mom's Place, our mentoring program for moms that includes weekly Bible studies, monthly family activities, parenting help and much more. We are also blessed to have several dedicated volunteers that come from a partnering church to play with and nurture our kids. Finally, this partnership has the attention of the President's Faith-based Initiative Committee, who fully supports us and is coming to visit our classroom in February.

I am thrilled to be a part of what God is doing and I am incredibly thankful for your support. May God bless you in this New Year!

Please pray for:

*A CDL bus driver who will be dependable, love our kids, and whose schedule would allow us to start the "wrap around piece"

*The safety and health of all of our children, families, and teachers

*Wisdom in navigating our partnership with the city while staying faithful to our calling (especially

preparing for our federal review at the end of the month)

—Katy

Selina Alonzo was a case worker with Neighborhood Ministries when Katy started teaching there. She shared her observations at a fundraiser several years later that describe Katy in the classroom in detail. Selina has become a special friend who I cherish like one of our family.

*Katy in the classroom was Kingdom work and the Gospel lived out. In the beginning I remember questioning with her whether public education would satisfy our ministry call, but while she taught those little children in California, her stories solidified for me that teaching, even in a public school, was really ministry.*

*Katy, as the preschool classroom teacher intrinsically lived the mission of the Neighborhood Center, and I am not afraid to say that she, in her natural self and daily life, also exemplified this mission. In order for a preschool model to fit the mission of Neighborhood Ministries, it would take someone very special.[1] Katy and Ericka were exactly that.*

*A normal day of preschool for Katy and Ericka was quite different than the average city preschool. Katy's days began the evening before when she was making phone calls and house visits, reminding moms that their preschooler needed to get to bed so they would be awake when she came to pick them up in the morning.*

*Then, it would continue early in the morning as she drove to her student's home and lovingly and gently woke up those same moms, that she had just reminded hours before the exact time she would be there—that still weren't ready.*

*In the very beginning, she would get kids dressed if they needed to be dressed and feed them if they needed to be fed.*

*Katy, compassionate Katy, displayed this kind of love before her official school day even began.*

*She knew that her work was communicating the importance of school—and she hoped that if she continued to teach this way, that the parents and children would grow to love preschool so much that they would begin to gain the responsibilities that were once foreign to them.*

*It worked.*

*This way of teaching and learning is not new. Don't we love because Christ loved us first? Don't we know how to live because Jesus demonstrated His life first to us in His word?*

*Innately, as a teacher who followed the Greatest Teacher, Katy knew what to do with this new endeavor of preschool at the Neighborhood Center, so Katy demonstrated her love first, so that others could learn and follow.*

*When children refused to learn because they didn't know how— they were loved into learning.*

*When kids fought and hurt each other, they were corrected in love and shown forgiveness. When children spoke harshly and crudely to their classmates and teachers, they were spoken back to so lovingly that after a while, they had so much experience with love that it became natural for them to give it back.*

*This was Katy's classroom. This was the only way that Katy knew how to do it, and it remains the way Lenny does it, and is the only way Neighborhood Ministries will ever do it.*

*We know now, because of Katy's hard work and wisdom, how to truly teach preschool children. The preschool at the Neighborhood*

Center has continued to thrive because it still carries within its walls the essence of Katy.

Her love, her compassion, and her desire to see the lives of children changed have never left that place.

It will never leave because it is impossible, it was too big and has impacted too many of us. It will never leave because the essence of Katy in the preschool classroom is the demonstration of the way God loves all of us.

The government's response to the need for early childhood education programs for low-income families is called Head Start. With all government programs there are many restrictions and rules. The success that Katy and Ericka shared in the Neighborhood preschool classroom was not because of government

*rules but because of Kingdom values. This sometimes became problematic because the only way we could afford a preschool at the Neighborhood Center was to be in city partnership with Head Start. Her preschool data was undeniable. Katy's classroom was among the best in our city. She acquired notice from city officials who were previously unsupportive of programs that appeared unorthodox, but God always wins.*

Eight months after starting at Neighborhood, Katy wrote in her journal.

**April 2, 2004:** Lord, I cannot even believe how much has happened in my life since one year ago. Last year at this time I was living by myself in Monrovia, teaching at Ocean View, taking grad classes at Biola, preparing for my move and the onslaught of weddings. I was struggling to make sense of so many events in my life. As I sit here at the Abbey in Sonoita, AZ, it is hard to articulate the flood of blessings and answers to questions that I have received. I learned so much about myself and my relationship with You. I was afraid that I would stop hearing (or more so) listening to Your voice in my life. It confirmed in me Your faithfulness to my process and the work of the Holy Spirit in my life. Even though my job/internship is extremely difficult and at times feels bizarre to the rest of the world, I love it. I am so blessed by doing what I do, I can't believe that You allow me to be involved with this work.

At 18, I never could have imagined where I would be at 25, or where I would have already been and what I would learn. It has been an incredible journey so far. I cannot imagine the next 25 years.

Shortly after Easter that year I was able to go to Phoenix to visit Katy and see where she lived and worked. I stayed with her and her roommates, Dianne and Jana, never imagining that I would move there a year later when Katy became ill. Visiting the Head Start classroom was a highlight of my trip. I fell in love with those precious little ones, who were learning how to "use walking feet" and to "use gentle hands," discovering how to do school for the first time. I was so impressed with how seamlessly Ericka and Katy worked together to help the children. They were loving, gentle, creative, and energetic as they managed sixteen three-, four- and five-year-olds in two adjoining classrooms, on the playground, down the walk outside to the restrooms, to the room where they ate lunch and over the fence as they bolted. What fun those children had! It was obvious that Katy and Ericka were both gifted in teaching these challenging children. When I picture that classroom, lovingly orchestrated by those two passionate and enthusiastic young teachers so in sync as they served and cared for the lively little ones, I think of "Camelot."

That spring, Katy reported about her work in a letter to the people who supported her and, again, asked for their prayers for her new, fragile community.

Dear Friends and Family,

Easter greetings from Phoenix! I pray that this letter finds you and your family in great health and joy in the knowledge of God's love for you. Here in Phoenix we have already had several days above 90 degrees, and I am becoming suspicious that spring is taking a leave of absence this year. It is hard to believe that the school year is beginning to wind down and the whole ministry is gearing up to transition into all of our big summer programs.

Last weekend we had our third annual Mom's Place retreat in Scottsdale, Arizona. There were 17 moms and 29 of their children in attendance! It was a sweet time of fellowship, teaching, worship, prayer, and play. What an incredible blessing for these moms to hear about God's love and experience it firsthand through the women of Scottsdale Bible Church, who helped organize, fund and run the retreat. Please pray for these moms as they face the daily challenge (as we all do) of following Christ's will in their lives instead of relying on their old ways of doing things. Also, praise God for one of our moms who accepted Christ on Wednesday after our Bible study. She has a very dangerous lifestyle, but wants to trust God to change her. Please pray that she would have the strength and faith to trust God to make the changes she needs in her life.

Ten of our Head Start kids will be completing preschool in June and moving on to kindergarten in the fall! While it is exciting to think of all that they have learned this year and all the progress they have made, we still have some lingering concerns. We are finding that although Head Start is geared toward families in poverty and desires to give families a variety of resources, our kids' and families' needs are off the charts in every category. Our Head Start supervisor recently told us that she has "seen classrooms with one or two kids like ours, but never a classroom full."

In an effort to help others understand our kids, the

best way we have found to describe our classroom is to liken it to an emotional ER.

Descriptors of the Children:

*Abandoned
*Angry
*Exploited
*Nameless
*Hopeless
*Violated
*Abused
*Depressed
*Unstable
*Confused
*Emotionally desperate
*Malnourished
*Wounded
*Under-stimulated
*Language deficient
*Violent
*Transient
*Exposed to evil
*Outcast
*Socially warped
*Health concerns
*Inadequate hygiene
*Drug and alcohol exposed
*Generationally fatherless
*Have teen mothers
*Lacking prenatal care

Pray for wisdom as we desire to love and nurture

our kids through deep pain and an environment of chaos. Also, please pray that others would begin to understand the lives and hearts of our kids and would be committed to their holistic growth instead of just concerned with their (academic) performance.

We are having a series of meetings with the Neighborhood Ministries Education Director and the city of Phoenix Head Start Director to plan and organize how we can restructure our program more effectively for next year (and what is left of this year). Please pray that the Lord would direct our decisions and that our hearts would be softened to hear what He has for the future.

Thank you again for your faithful support and prayer. As Ericka says, "What an awesome thing that we get to provide them a childhood." It is an incredible privilege to be living out my faith here in Phoenix, and it would not be possible without your support. May God bless you for your faithfulness!

Love,

Katy

<u>Additional prayer requests:</u>

*Parents struggling with alcohol and drug addictions (including a pregnant mother)

*A therapeutic kindergarten for a child who at the age of four has lost both father and step-father to violence

*Jobs for our moms that are struggling to support

their families without a high school diploma

*Pray for wisdom to know when to be gracious and patient with the city and to know when we need to speak the truth in boldness on behalf of our kids

The challenges of the early years of the Head Start program at Neighborhood Ministries are evident in an interview where Katy was asked to recount a highlight of their classroom. Ericka wasn't able to be there, so Katy also shared what she thought Ericka would consider a highlight.

Thank you for your support!

Katy Reel
Neighborhood Ministries

My name is Katy Reel and I am a two-year intern. I started last year in August. I spend 47 weeks out of the year at the Head Start classroom that we have. There are so many highlights, the small moments during the day are what I treasure, but the biggest highlight, I think, has been seeing how our partnership with the city has grown. At the beginning we were very nervous about having a Neighborhood program that had to meet federal standards, Board of Health standards and things like Fire Marshall Standards and being closely watched. It really has been incredible to see how God has worked through so many different relationships. In the beginning, it was difficult to work with the city because they didn't necessarily trust us and we didn't know if we could trust them, but over this past year we've really built strong relationships, especially with Ericka's boss. In the beginning, she was skeptical of us and thought we did things very backward and didn't understand why we were knocking on doors, helping kids get dressed, waking moms up; she thought that was ridiculous. But by the middle of the year, she noticed we had the best attendance record out of everyone and we were able to hold on to all the kids we started with (that's rare for Head Start) and that we had a waiting list for next year. In the beginning, she didn't understand our families necessarily, but she listened as we described our families and their situations and she's really become an advocate for us. Any time anyone criticizes us or doesn't understand why we do things the way we do, she'll start in with the things we've told her about our families. It's been incredible to see how God's worked through that and through other people we work with like our case worker.

Our case worker has my cell number and she'll call me on the weekends with, "I have this idea for this family" and, "I want to help with this." That's just been incredible because it seemed so daunting in the beginning. It's been really great to see how that relationship has grown and how there's a mutual respect there now.

Ericka was unable to be here, so I'm going to speak on her behalf. Ericka is our Head Start teacher. She is a city employee. Many of you know her. She's involved practically everywhere and she kind of grew up here. I think Ericka's highlight of the year would be stories of individual kids, knowing where they came from last year. We've had some (kids) for two years now. Some are continuing with us. Seeing their growth. We just finished scoring their developmental tests. Several kids started in the concern area. There are three areas: concern, right on track, and strengths. Several of our kids who started in the lowest of the concern area now have strengths and everywhere else are performing on a normal level.  It's so exciting to see.

I think she would also want to express to you that it's been great to see the growth in families and the relationships we've built there. We have some parents of kindergartners who don't want to volunteer in their kid's new class [but] who want to come back here and volunteer because they loved it so much.

She would want you to know how incredible it's been to work with each individual family and to see growth as a whole family unit. As I said, we used to knock on doors and help kids get dressed, especially on Mondays, but we don't do that anymore. Now we have parents calling us, dropping off their kids, volunteering in the classroom, going on field trips and reading to kids in the classroom.

It's great to look across the classroom and see kids playing appropriately for their age; it's nice to hear kids calling each other "stupid face" instead of the things they called each other last year that you can't believe kids call each other. It's been an incredible journey and it's neat to continue with some of the same families and see the growth in the family.

Such amazing growth, such amazing change. Kit shared a memory about Katy and one of her students at a fundraiser.

*Let me tell you a love story, one about Katy and a little guy named Jose[2]. We have known Jose's mom since she was a little girl. She grew up in our programs. A month before Jose was born, his biological father was murdered. Jose's mom struggled for years afterwards; when she birthed a second son, that father was also tragically murdered a month before his birth. As I'm sure you can imagine, this traumatized household suffered, mom went back to using drugs and little Jose was a handful. He came into our preschool, messy. He struggled on every level and in the classroom his behavior was unmanageable. Katy took him on. He was hers. His life would be rescued. He would be loved unconditionally. Lots of things in the classroom helped Jose but what undergirded it all was Katy's love for him. I am telling you this story, because Jose is still in our church programs and he is doing great. I had the privilege of baptizing him this summer. His testimony was genuine and powerful; his love for Jesus and his church family tangible. I looked up to heaven and said to Katy, "Girl, you did a great job with him!"*

Katy loved the Neighborhood children. I found this list among Katy's things. Ericka confirmed that Katy was the author.

If you get teams going and time it just right, you can make it so that one teacher spends virtually the entire day in the bathroom.

Most accessories meant to keep kids in only slow teachers down when they get out.

Bites from missing teeth still hurt.

A trip to the bathroom has infinite possibilities for entertainment.

When you are three there is strength in numbers, especially when you strategically run in separate directions.

There are countless places to hide in a 15-passenger van.

Without experience, nap time quickly becomes padded pandemonium.

Silence is a very concerning sound.

It doesn't take Houdini to break out of a car seat, just an opportune moment.

A three-foot-tall child can easily make it over a fence if there is at least one cousin to help.

Almost everything tastes better dunked in milk.

During this period, Katy's journal entries became infrequent, probably due to a lack of time and energy after long days working with Head Start and Mom's Place. The following entry is from November of 2004. It shows her heart better than almost anything else I have found in her writings.

When I look back on my life I want to be able to say that I lived it fully not being inhibited by fears, insecurities, or apathy. I want to have learned to fully trust, love and obey. To have learned to rely on a strength that is not my own, and trust a direction that I have not contrived. I want my life to have meant something. As I grow older it is my desire that my life become more simple, more honest, and less my own. I want to be able to say that I made hard choices, took the great risk, and chose the extraordinary over the comfortable. I want to have lived a life of passion—I hope I am still called a spit fire even when I am 80 and should be "slowing down" as culture suggests. I hope I am always going to and living in scary places and being in community with people who know no other way

305

to be than be themselves. I want to live a life of no regrets. I hope that I am more true to myself and given passion with each passing day.

A few months later, Rick and I were in Scottsdale attending a work-related convention. When it was over, we moved into the San Carlos hotel in downtown Phoenix to visit Katy for a few days. Then, we flew home. Little did we know that everything was about to fall apart until the night Kit called with the terrible news...

1 Mission Statement of Neighborhood Ministries: To be the presence of Jesus Christ, sharing His life-transforming hope, love, and power among distressed families of urban Phoenix to ignite their passion for God and His Kingdom.

2 Name changed.

# Part Four

*Home: Glimpses of Heaven*

Since Katy has passed, people have shared stories of encounters with her. Whenever anyone told me one, I asked for a written version in their own words to keep the details as accurate as possible; I believe that these people shared what they actually experienced, and I am convinced that what they "saw" was real. They were assurances from God that Katy was with Him rejoicing, healed and whole. I have included some of these unsolicited stories here. They gave me comfort and hope in very difficult times. Certain elements in them brought specific scriptures to my mind, so I added those verses following the texts.

*Sunday, January 15, 2006*

*Dear Patty and Rick,*

*I have delayed writing this note to you because I didn't know whether I should do it or not. Some would say that it is very inappropriate for such a time as this, but I can't get it out of my mind that it is something I would like to share with you.*

*When I got the call about Katy, I was really down cast, felt almost betrayed—why were our prayers not answered? This was my frame of mind and spirit for quite a while. Then suddenly I heard an inaudible voice say, "Why are you complaining!" (That's the word He used, nothing at all sympathetic. It was almost like a reprimand.) "I did heal her!" Then I saw, as up in heaven, a lithe, slender, graceful figure all in white, dancing around jubilantly, arms outstretched upward, like someone who had just been let out of a cage. I never met Katy, I don't know what she looks like, but I knew that's who it was.*

*Why her release was on the other side instead of here on earth I don't know, but it immediately occurred to me that in terms of eternity, our time on earth is really very short and sometimes there is a hiatus in our relationships when we each go our separate ways for a while only to be reunited forever later. This does not obliterate the fact that the person is sorely missed every day they are away, of course.*

*Jesus was anointed not only to preach the Gospel to the poor, but to heal the broken hearted and my prayer now is that He will be with you every step of the way and heal the sense of separation and void in your family as only He can do, and use this difficult experience to enrich your life, in some way which no other experience could duplicate, knowing that you will all be together again in His good time.*

*May He wrap you in a cocoon of His Love until it melts away every obstacle that lies between you and Him, so that one day you will have a real understanding of why things happen the way they do.*

*With all love, in His name,*

*Betty Brock*

I want to share a little bit about Betty here. She was a devout woman in her mid-eighties who spent a lot of time in prayer and Bible study. She was confident in the reality and mercy of God, a quiet soul, not given to saying, "God told me this or that." God's message through Betty that He did heal Katy resounds in my heart to this day. No more suffering, no more frustration from trying to work with a diminished body, only joy in her release and in being united with the Father she had loved all her life.

*After this I looked and there before me was a great multitude that no one could count, from every nation, tribe, people and language, standing before the throne and in front of the Lamb.* **They were wearing white robes** *and were holding palm branches in their hands.*

—*Revelation 7:9*

**There will be no more death or mourning or crying or pain,** *for the old order of things has passed away.*

—*Revelation 21:4*

◆◆◆

*Maundy Thursday 4/5/07*

*Dear Rick and Patty,*

*I've been meaning to write you this letter for a while now and today seems a fitting day to do so. Commemorating the servant love of Jesus is very bound up for me in commemorating the servant heart Katy always kept and the never-ending flow of love she poured out on others.*

*I spoke with Patty back in August about an experience I had while praying after Katy's death, and she asked for a written version. This is what I give you now.*

*It was January 25th 2006, almost two weeks after Katy had been buried. After I got home from work, I went off to a Prayer and Worship Service at church. I had been busy the past few weeks asking God what on earth He was doing, why He was allowing such a tragedy, and how we were supposed to see Him when so many hopes had been left unanswered. I was also deeply desiring some reassurance about where Katy is now, and how she had been taken care of during those last few days when she couldn't see or hear anyone around her. I sat in a chair, sort of mulling these questions over in my mind in prayer, simply telling the LORD that this all hurt so much for all of us. I wasn't asking for a picture to come in response to my questions, but that is what happened.*

*I saw Katy walking on a path. It was pitch black all around her, and the road was really just a narrow dirt and rock causeway. It was smooth and level, but very narrow. It crossed a deep chasm and had no guards or rails on the sides—it was like an isthmus connecting two bodies of land, but instead of water on the sides, there was a deep empty space. Everything was dark. The only way I knew that the path existed at all and that Katy was on it was because she was not alone. She was walking with Jesus right beside her. There was only room for the two of them on the path. He was robed in white and was holding a lantern up in between them so she could see where to step. I couldn't see His face, and she couldn't either, because His arm holding the lantern was up between them. She was focusing on the path in front of her, walking with determination and purpose, no pausing or hesitation. Her hair was long, back in a ponytail, and she was wearing a black tank top and khaki pants.*

*She was talking back and forth with Jesus and it was clear to me that they were very close companions. He was asking her about her life in a way that made it clear that He knew all the details and*

*deeply understood her perspective. She said, "Uh-huh. Exactly,"*
*in that Katy way she always had, and then they laughed about*
*whatever it was.*

*I knew in that moment that she was safer than safe, that she was*
*going home to a place she already knew because of whose she was,*
*because of who she was with, and that she would be filled with joy*
*when she got there.*

*Over the past 15 months, what has been the most difficult for me*
*to grapple with besides the loss of continuing to know Katy present*
*and here with us has been the sense that God did not answer our*
*prayers. But what has been made clear to me through this picture*
*and through the memory of other specific guidings during prayers*
*just before Katy died is that God really was moving in Katy's life*
*and in all of us throughout her entire sickness. At no time has Katy*
*(or any one of us) been outside of His love and His plans to protect*
*and save. That is His gift.*

*And as Kit said, the very magnitude of our loss shows us just*
*how richly we were blessed to know Katy, and that also is truly a*
*gift of the LORD.*

*May the hope of the Resurrection be known to you this weekend*
*in a new and special way.*

*Love, Kirsten.*

Kirsten Guidero, who wrote this letter, has been a friend of our
family for a long time. She was one of the members of the Tab youth
group who was especially close to Katy.

*Do not let your hearts be troubled. Trust in God, trust also*
*in me. In my Father's house are many rooms; if it were not so,*
*I would have told you. I am going there to prepare a place for*
*you. And if I go and prepare a place for you, **I will come back***

**and take you to be with me that you also may be where I am.**

—John 14:1-4

♦♦♦

Hi. My mom called last night to ask if I would write down what I saw in my own words—and I would love to. I haven't really shared this with anyone until the other day with my mom. As I was telling it, I realized that it should be told because it was something very special.

Just to clarify, what I saw wasn't a true vision, but it was beyond my own imagination. I believe it was God giving me peace and understanding in an "image" form.

It was the night of January 1st around 9 or 10 p.m. and I was praying before I went to sleep. I was praying for healing and just felt in my "gut" that the answer was no. That, of course, was not the answer I wanted. I didn't want to think that God would say no to Katy's healing. So I continued to ask for healing, but still felt the answer was no. Then I realized that it was my will for healing, not God's. So, I prayed that I wanted Katy to be healed, but said "if that's not Your will, then, Jesus just take her and hold her." And I felt peace then. As much as I didn't want to accept it, I felt peace.

About this time the image appeared. I'm a little fuzzy on the exact timing of the prayer and image coming together. It all just flowed together as it was happening.

I continued praying "Jesus, take her and hold her" over and over. And then I saw Katy. With my eyes closed, a bright blue sky filled the background. Imagine the purest, brightest blue sky you've ever seen. I was aware it was sky, but it was used as a backdrop. The blue sky itself was just beautiful. It was really bright too, like the sun was shining. But I never saw the sun or any other light source.

*The background was more beautiful, more intense than anything earthly.*

*Katy was right in front of me. She was gorgeous. Absolutely gorgeous. I hate to over use that word, but it's the only one I could think of to describe her. She had long, beautiful golden blond hair. I could only see her face and shoulders. It was Katy, nothing changed. Just beautiful. Sometimes she would look right at me and other times she would sort of look beyond me, almost over my head. She was sort of smiling and just looked really peaceful. As I continued to pray she sort of floated further and further away, but never out of sight.*

*At some point I stopped praying and opened my eyes. I was overwhelmed with peace and beauty. Although I think a small part of me still wanted to deny that she died, I knew It had happened without really consciously thinking about it.*

*From the moment I prayed for God's will, not mine, I felt so peaceful and relieved. The "vision" was absolutely God's peace and beauty beyond this world.*

*I remember thinking the next day, "How could we have NOT wanted that for Katy?! There's nothing sad or scary about that. I want to go! Why can't we all just be there now?" I felt Heaven as a very real dimension. And it has to be better than we know.*

*Love, Jennifer 10-2-2006*

Amy met Jennifer in the first grade and they became fast friends. Our families routinely spent Friday nights watching movies and eating pizza together. In fact, Amy had been a bridesmaid in her wedding just a few months before this experience. Katy was Jennifer's first babysitter. What is especially significant is that when you take into account the different time zones, Jennifer's "vision" happened exactly when Katy died.

*The city **does not need the sun or the moon or shine on it, for** the glory of God gives it light, and the Lamb is its lamp.*

*— Revelation 21:23*

*They will not need the light of a lamp or the of the sun, for the **Lord God will give them light.***

*—Revelation 22:5*

♦♦♦

*I had a very vivid image of Katy Reel in my sleep. I was sound asleep but the vision that came to me was very real—very true to life. Katy was walking, briskly. She was surrounded by the most beautiful golden light I have ever seen. Her hair, which was pulled back on both sides, was blonde, very blonde and she was more beautiful than she had been here on earth. She looked happy, content, and she was singing.*

*I awoke with a start—it had seemed so real. I truly believe God spoke to me saying dear Katy is at home and happy with the Lord.*

*—Linda Bash*

Linda is another close family friend. Her daughter and Katy were playmates when they were little. Linda used to say that she wanted to be like Katy when she grew up.

***It shone with the glory of God, and its brilliance was like that of a very precious jewel.***

*— Revelation 21:11*

♦♦♦

On January 24, 2007, a little more than a year after Katy passed, I too had a vivid experience that included Katy that felt much more real than a dream. The day before had been difficult and had thrown me back into the deep mourning I had begun to climb out of. I had been walking on a small indoor track, trying to get a little exercise, when I noticed a young woman walking ahead of me. She looked so much like Katy from the back that it took my breath away. Her blond hair, her size, even her gait seemed exactly like Katy. I continued to walk behind her around the track for a few laps, but it got harder and harder. I could hardly breathe. I left before I saw her face. I knew it wasn't her, of course, but I was so shaken by the remarkable resemblance. I drove the short distance to Katy's gravesite to get relief from the oppression that gripped me, but when I got in view of her marker, the lovely Christmas wreath that I had placed there was nowhere to be seen. I was mortified. Who would steal a grave decoration? I drove home feeling even worse and as I walked in the door the phone was ringing. The person on the other end of the line asked for a donation to combat cancer. Didn't I want to help put an end to having parents watch their children suffer and die? I mumbled something and hung up the phone. I was devastated. The burden of the grief I was carrying felt too heavy to bear. That feeling persisted even into the next morning when I fell back asleep after Rick left. I started to dream. The details of the dream before this significant part have faded. I remember moving from place to place, nothing noteworthy or especially emotional, then I was in a kitchen and there was someone seated at the table and shortly (but not instantly), I knew it was Katy. She was there where I was. In the present. I was so amazed and so happy. I was flooded with a feeling that I hadn't known for so long. And I was aware of a joyfulness. I reached out for her.

*"Are you happy?"*

"I'm happy."

*"Are you okay?"*

"I'm okay."

She looked so serene. Just being with her was so wonderful. I instinctively knew this was a visit somehow to assure me. To remind me. To feel this wonder again. It's difficult to find the words that recreate the feeling of happiness that seemed to explode within me and that stayed. Thank you, Lord, for this precious present.

> *Peace I leave with you; my peace I give to you. I do not give as the world gives. Do not let your hearts be troubled and do not be afraid."*
>
> *—John 14:27*

◆◆◆

I believe in the truth recounted in these instances. They are assurances that Katy is at peace, and happy in the presence of the Lord she has loved for so long, who held her in her most difficult days. She had finished the work He had for her; His good work in her, completed.

To know and love Katy is to be patient until we are reunited with her in God's perfect timing.

# Epilogue

A year after Katy died, Kit and Heather organized an Ofrenda for her at Neighborhood Ministries. An Ofrenda is celebrated in the Mexican culture as a memorial held one year after a loved one's passing. Katy's slide show was replayed on the big screen after the church service. Outside, a lovely table was decorated with flowers, candles and pictures of Katy. Kit asked everyone who knew Katy to write down "how your life is better because Katy was part of it, focusing on the gift she was to you." Several people shared what they wrote and told other stories about her. I got a lump in my throat seeing the slide show projected so large, but then I was heartened to hear what was testified about my sweet daughter. Some of those writings are included here.

*I no longer focus on issues that are passing and unimportant; rather I focus on God's direction and blessings. Her sweet attitude even in suffering causes me to examine the "real" issues in life.*

◆

*She just wanted to serve God—even through the end she didn't give up. I admire that and I want to be just like that to love God so much.*

◆

*Looking at you and your life always made me strong and not care about the people doing wrong and going the wrong way. You made me decide to take the right way (God's way) loving and obeying God and having him #1 in my life.*

◆

*You helped me to believe in myself, to see that God was using me even when I was feeling so unsure.*

◆

*You showed me how to pursue kids intensely, to love equally and to have so much fun sharing stories together. Stories are so important to you and now I am now thankful that I got to be part of your story. Even the end.*

◆

*I think your humility helped me to see Jesus. You have brought Jesus' light to our community.*

◆

*Katy taught me how to love in the present. She was always loving those in her presence like you were the only person in the world.*

◆

*Katy help me during a pivotal point in my life. She never gave up on me or anyone. She made any problem feel easy to handle.*

◆ ◆ ◆

**Moms Place,** the Neighborhood Ministries' program serving young moms that Katy helped run, has evolved into, "Parenting Por Vida" (Parenting For Life). There are two main classes: El Major Empiezo, which covers pregnancy, birth, and breast feeding; and Parent College, which concentrates on parenting children from six months of age to five years old. There are fewer teen moms now and they are individually mentored. Most of the girls in the Neighborhood community now see the importance of education and are delaying parenthood until after they finish school. Also, many of the dads are now involved, a huge improvement from when the program started.

◆ ◆ ◆

The **Head Start** classroom at Neighborhood Ministries ended in May of 2010 due to cutbacks in government funding. By then, NM had learned how preschool helps their kids get a running start on life and how vital it is to the whole family. They decided to start their own preschool to serve the low-income families in their community. Many of their children's parents grew up through the holistic programs of Neighborhood Ministries and still live in the neighborhood; some of the children walk to school. It is housed on the Neighborhood campus in a beautiful building of renovated historic grain silos. The sign on the front door states, "Katy's Kids Early Childhood Center." Its education program has been recognized as having high quality standards according to the state of Arizona.

◆ ◆ ◆

Lenny came to Phoenix the day we heard of Katy's illness and stayed. The support pamphlet he wrote tells that part of his story.

*...I knew that I was supposed to stay and take care of her. When she started getting better after the first operation, she went back to the Head Start classroom, and I went with her. I fell in love with all of the children in the class and felt at home. When Katy passed it still felt right to be in the classroom and I am reminded of her and her loving spirit every day when I see the kids. God has brought me to these children to share His love with them.*

*I also mentor Jorge[1]. He is a difficult kid and he gives me a lesson in patience almost every time we are together. There are times when I think it is hopeless and I am never going to get through to him. Then he does some small thing and he gives me a glimpse of*

327

*God in him and I realize that I can't change him. I am not here to change him. I am here to love him.*

*Ephesians 5:1: Be imitators of Christ, therefore as dearly loved children and live a life of love.*

*There are so many other details I could tell you about what I do here, but what really matters is that God has called me to share His love with these children. Even when I am tired. Even when they won't listen. Even when they are causing trouble. Even when they get on my nerves. And even when they don't love back.*

*When I look back on my life so far, I am just amazed at the way in which God has worked. He brought me here. And He told me to love these children of His. Every time I get a smile or a hug from a child, every time I see Jorge and every day I walk into the classroom I know I am where I am supposed to be.*

Lenny became a two-year intern at Neighborhood Ministries working in the Head Start classroom and mentoring students. He also became involved in other parts of Neighborhood programs, led a few hiking and skiing trips, and helped at Kids Club and Kids Camp in the summers. He continued to teach in the preschool when it became "Katy's Kids." He is now on the Neighborhood Ministries staff serving as Director of Katy's Kids. Lenny and his wife Gricelda have blessed us with two wonderful grandchildren who delight us.

◆ ◆ ◆

After graduating from Tyler School of Art in Philadelphia, Katy's sister Amy returned to Indianapolis. She has taught art in two private Christian schools and has a studio where she paints when she gets the opportunity. She has created beautiful images (sculptures and oil paintings) of Katy. In Phoenix, she painted a wonderful, large mural of Katy and the preschool children that overlooks a playground at

NM. Amy and her husband Omar have blessed us with a wonderful grandson who has brought us such joy.

◆ ◆ ◆

A friend of Katy's who was pregnant when Katy died named her baby "Katy." She was the first of five moms to name their children after Katy. I heard the story that at least one of these moms had to insist that her daughter's name be spelled K-A-T-Y on her birth certificate (which is different from the usual Spanish spelling.)

Four of these "Katys" happened to be at Neighborhood Ministries in 2019 and posed holding Katy's photograph. These "Katys" are scattered from Phoenix to New Zealand; Texas to California. What a sweet, loving legacy.

◆ ◆ ◆

Kit Danley handed me this poem she wrote after Katy passed. It offers a path to surviving the desperate grief you experience after the loss of someone dear to you. It is a gentle reminder of the comfort Jesus brings when you seek Him.

## Higher

I wanted to tell you as you climb up from there
About the long journey I had
The paths that I took
And the stumbles that shook
Me and the weather that seemed fairly bad

But my trip to the valley
Was mine all alone
Yours through this country is too
The only way up is to seek for the guide
The man who takes wanderers through

Even though I've been brought up from the valley
All that I seem to have learned
Is not about roads
But concerns what I owed
To that guide who led me to here

I can't climb to you or give you directions
And I'm not too strong anyways
Seek well for that man
Hold tight to his hand
And you're sure to not wander astray

The valley I climbed through was something like this one
So I'm certain that you will be able
To make the long trip
Through the pain and the slips
Should you depend on the one who is able

*Call him by name, I did, and he came*
*Say Jesus, and all will be right*
*It won't make the road safer*
*Or the path cleared of danger*
*Remember it's not about mine but his might*

*You'll notice a hymn has been given to you*
*For this journey, no matter how long*
*The words, they will carry you*
*The words, they will bear you*
*The suffering becoming your song*

◆ ◆ ◆

"Walk in Pure Meadows" is a song that was written the night after Katy's memorial service in Indianapolis by Scott McCelland, who was in Tab's Youth Group with her. "While Katy and I were not particularly close, she touched a lot of people around me in profound ways. The song is about Katy, but it is also about how people deal with loss. Writing it was my way of finding some hope and peace."

### Walk in Pure Meadows

*There once was a girl who said a prayer*
*Dear Lord, I will follow you anywhere*
*Just lead the way*

*The Lord said travel to this far off place*
*And there I will make you full of grace*
*Full of grace*

*She went with a heart so full of love*

*And found that it really was enough*
*To change this world*

*Then the Lord went ahead and called her home*
*And when all her loved ones felt alone*
*They sang these words*

> *We will walk in pure meadows one day*
> *We will sing alleluia along the way*
> *When we meet our Maker*
> *And see her smile again*

*There are so many things I don't understand*
*My home feels like it's a foreign land*
*With no safe port*

*All I can think to do is lift my glass*
*And hold close the ones who hold my past*
*And sing these words*

> *We will walk in pure meadows one day*
> *We will sing alleluia along the way*
> *When we meet our Maker*
> *And see her smile again*

*There's a new angel in heaven now*
*And she's smiling as she's looking down*
*I know that her love is all around*

> *We will walk in pure meadows one day*
> *We will sing alleluia along the way*
> *When we meet our Maker*
> *And see her smile again*

◆ ◆ ◆

**Tab's Youth Group** continues to take mission trips in the summers. For two years, their destination was Neighborhood Ministries' Vacation Bible School, Kids Club. The first time they traveled to Arizona, Tab's youth fell in love with the Neighborhood children and enthusiastically pursued being able to return the next year. They returned the following summer and are also planning to go again. Their leaders are Dan Rexroth and his wife Amy. Dan, who had been Katy's youth director, is again leading Tab's young people.

♦ ♦ ♦

Hanna Miley, the missionary, and her husband, George, still live in Phoenix. They are active in a reconciliation ministry and have spent more than 45 years ministering worldwide. She has written her autobiography, *A Garland for Ashes*, that tells her incredible story.

♦ ♦ ♦

Phoenix has become our second home, our second community. Rick and I try to spend as much time there as possible. I wondered what it would feel like to return there after Katy was gone. How would people relate to us without her? Our identity there had been "Katy's parents." That has evolved to "Lenny's parents" and "Gricelda's in-laws," but, more than that, to just "Rick" and "Patty." We were embraced in 2005 and our relationships with the people there have only grown deeper. There is no pretense among people who dare to come alongside you in times of crisis; nothing is superficial. Their friendships are real and heartfelt, the stuff on which you can build a solid bond. We have been blessed with that sense of belonging as part of the community. Katy drew us there. It was where I had lived with her during her last days, the place where I felt her presence vividly. I can remember conversations we had on the freeway exit, at the bagel shop, on her front porch. But at the same time it is where I feel her absence the most strongly. The first time I returned to Phoenix, her absence hit me hard; it took me several sad days before I could appreciate being there. On subsequent trips through the months and years that followed, the adjustment came more easily, but it was always difficult until I was distracted by Lenny's wedding and the precious grandchildren that came after.

## Notes

1 Name changed.

# Acknowledgements

The idea that grew to become this book was conceived in the midst of Katy's illness in 2005. When we were in Indianapolis for a family reunion that June I went to Tab for the first time since Katy's diagnosis. As I walked into the church I noticed Rod Smith, her former youth director, and shared Katy's initial response when I had first entered her hospital room, "I'm so sorry you're going to have to go through this." He responded, "That's the first sentence of your book. You need to share how you are coping with other hurting parents." I dismissed that notion thinking I couldn't process any book I read right now in my state of mind and I doubt anyone else in similar circumstances could.

But seven months later, after hearing Kit Danley read quotes from Katy's journals during her funerals, several people—especially Jim Babcock and Beth Crozier—asked if they could hear more of what Katy had written. Both Jim and Beth were certain that the world needed to hear her words and through the months, even the years, that followed, they repeatedly asked if I had started to write her story. From its inception, I was aided by people who prayed along with me that above all the book would be accurate and truthful.

At first, I intended to use only Katy's words and what others had written to or about her with brief commentary to connect the different segments. I didn't want to prejudice what anyone would say about Katy by asking them for comments. There was plenty of unsolicited material in her journals, the blog, her emails, condolence notes, cards and letters, and other sources I had gathered without interviewing anyone. However, I discovered I was missing information about a couple of months near the end of her life, so I asked three of Katy's friends, Selina (Alonzo) Helton, Heather (Danley) Ryan, and Ericka (Boltz) Martinez to enlighten me. They graciously agreed, even though it was difficult for them to recount those sad days. I so appreciate their willingness to do that.

As I searched through the accumulated material, I discovered comment after comment praising Katy and saying how she was such a light to them. Those observations urged me to continue as they mitigated my sadness. My husband, Rick, bravely endured this process with me. His support and patience made it possible for me to spend the time I needed to work on it.

I am indebted to Chris Sommers and Kit Danley of Neighborhood Ministries for setting up the blog and writing the entries that kept everyone informed of Katy's condition. Little did they (and the multitude of people who responded) know that it might someday become such an integral part of a book that would share Katy's testimony.

Kit, our dear friend, was so instrumental in helping us all to survive those hard days and picked up the thread when we could not. In addition to writing most of the blog, she wrote Katy's obituary, her eulogy, the poem "Higher," and filled in some gaps about people from the Neighborhood community. Katy was drawn to Kit's passion for serving the lost and the poor; her influence colored the last few years of Katy's life. I so appreciate Kit's encouragement and advice for the creation of this book.

My sister, Judy Baker, who is a pharmacist, provided invaluable help and advice concerning medications, both during my research for this book and during Katy's illness. At least one time Judy saved her from a potentially dangerous drug interaction. It got to the point that Lenny said, "We're not giving Katy any medicine without checking with Aunt Judy first." Words are inadequate to express what her care and expertise meant then and still means.

Early in the writing process, I sought the advice of John Thomas and the recommendations he gave me were invaluable. His suggestions challenged me, but greatly improved what is written on these pages. I am grateful for his help.

I am also thankful for the technical help I got from Jimmy Baker, Ian Thomas, Jane Kukolla, and Ruth Miller who patiently helped me navigate the mysteries of my iPad and computer (which was generously supplied by Lenny Reel and Jose Guatelupe Vazquez).

As I compiled the different parts of Katy's story, I tried to contact each person whose writings I planned to include or whose names were mentioned. Every single one I reached agreed that I could use their name and/or quote them, often saying they would be honored. These people include: Alma Alonzo, Brian Baker, Judy and Boyd Baker, Linda Bash, Kristen Blair, Kathleen and Tom Boltz, Anne Brock, John Bruington, Frank Cooper, Leah Crane, Jennifer Cuzzort, Kit and Wayne Danley, Jody Davis, Amber Drinen, Linda Fisher, Kristen Gable, Kirsten Guidero, Jeffery Hachquet, Selina Helton, Karen Jefferies, Patrick Jenkins, Dianne Johnson, Dr. Michael Johnson, Chuck and Sue Johnston, Julie and Joe Kukolla, Elizabeth Lee, Luis Lemus, Jorge Macias, Leigh and John March, Ericka Martinez, Katie McDaniel, Hanna Miley, Dr. Justin Miller, Holly Moorman, Pete Newlove, Evelyn Oakes, Isaiah Oakes, Lucia Oerter, Gilbert Orban, Sue Pankratz, Betsy and Bryan Paul, Don Pinnick, Mike Plaster, Kyle Ragsdale, Brandon Reel, Scott Reitano, Dan Rexroth, Mary Beth Riner, Nancy Russell, Bob and Helen Ryan, Heather and Dallas Ryan, Jana Smith, Rod Smith, Janet Starkey, David Streit, Maureen Surak, Dr. Julianne Thompson, Billy Thrall, Briahnna Villegas, Dot Ward, Wendy and Sara Wilkerson.

I also want to thank the students, parents and staff of Ocean View Elementary School for their contributions. Likewise, thanks to the Head Start children, parents and staff for their kind words.

Several people helped me by listening patiently when I needed feedback on specific ideas, wording, paragraphs, or entire sections.

Thank you to Wendy Wilkerson, Pam Constable, Kristin Gable, David Streit, and of course, Rick.

I am indebted to the people who supplied information for the Epilogue: Susan Leon (Mom's Place) and Scott McCelland (Walk in Pure Meadows).

One of the all-too-few days we were in Phoenix, Heather Ryan called with an invitation to visit with a friend of Katy's who I hadn't seen in many years, Rachel Lam. She was in town only for a couple of days and I was eager to see her. As we talked about our lives, I mentioned that I was writing Katy's story. Rachel looked at me and said that she was an editor and was looking for a project! What a blessing she has been. It would be almost impossible to enumerate every way she added to this book. I am thankful for her gentle guidance, prayers, encouragement, listening ear and excellent suggestions. At her urging (along with John Thomas') I steeled myself to look closer and examine my own feeling and reactions as I uncovered the details of Katy's life, to go beyond merely quoting the blog and Katy's journals and emails. When I convinced myself to dare to do that, I unearthed another layer to this story. I delved into the details of 2005, that most difficult year, examining each appointment, each prescription, each symptom, each act of kindness and each evidence of God's presence in detail. I hadn't dared to process those things before in such detail and I uncovered several things, including: how difficult Katy's illness and treatments were on her; how she was the glue for her peers and how devastating her loss was for them; how blessed we all were by all the help from so many people; how her love was infectious to everyone—doctors, nurses, kids, friends, strangers; how we didn't comprehend her illness was always terminal, despite current treatments; how her handling of her illness was a testament to her faith; how we thought we'd have much more time with her.

The readers of the first drafts of this book, Scott Carlson, Kit Danley, Judy Fraps, Kristin Gable, Selina Helton, Julie Kukolla, Mary Mills, and John Thomas, contributed much clarity, raised excellent questions, corrected grammar and spelling, and generally affirmed this work. I didn't realize how invaluable their efforts would be, nor how difficult. I can't repay them adequately.

I am so grateful to Dallas Ryan for his outstanding layout and design. His many, many hours of work were a gift to Katy, his dear friend.

I owe many thanks to Bob Ryan for expertly completing the publishing details of this book and getting it printed.

I also thank each and every person who has not been mentioned, who was there for me and my family during Katy's illness, passing, and beyond. You are all part of Katy's story. You have each contributed to this book—I would never have been able to continue in this journey without all the support that came in so many forms.

Finally, I thank God for giving me the inspiration, courage and strength to share Katy's story. This book is a response, a prayer, and a praise to Him. The credit for the making of this work and its impact going forward belongs to Him.

◆ ◆ ◆

# References & Resources

Below is a list of all references and resources mentioned in this book. I believe that Katy would have wanted these passed along. Included:

- Website addresses of any organizations that are still in operation. Organizations that are no longer in operation are included in the notes of the corresponding chapter
- All books/workbooks are listed alphabetically by title
- Medical and other information references
- Resources for grief that were helpful to me, personally

## Organizations & Ministries

Amor, https://amor.org

Biblical Foundation Academy International, www.bfainternational.com

Big Brother, Big Sister, www.bebigforkids.org

Biola University, www.biola.edu

Calvary Chapel Saving Grace, www.calvarychapelsavinggrace.com

Christian Community Development Association (CCDA), www.ccda.org

Compassion International, www.compassion.com

Harvest Crusade, https://harvest.org

Katy's Kids Early Childhood Center, www.nmphx.com

The Lost Boys Center for Leadership Development, https://www.lostboyscenter.org

National Head Start Association, www.nhsa.org

Neighborhood Ministries, https://nmphx.com

Open Door Church, www.odfchurch.org

Operation Mobilization (OM), https://www.omusa.org

Tabernacle Presbyterian Church (Tab), www.tabpres.org

Urbana, https://urbana.org

Virginia G. Piper Cancer Center, http://azhin.org/honorhealth

World Evangelization for Christ, www.wecinternational.org

World Impact, https://worldimpact.org

Young Life, www.younglife.org

## Books & Workbooks

*Beloved* by Henri Nouwen (ch. 5)

*Compassion, A Reflection on the Christian Life* by Henri J.M. Nouwen, Donald P. McNeil, & Douglas A. Morrison (ch. 4)

*The Cost of Discipleship* by Dietrich Bonhoeffer (ch. 5)

*Experiencing God Day-by-Day, The Devotional and Journal* by Henry T. Blackaby and Richard Blackaby (ch. 7)

*Mother Theresa, Meditations from a Simple Path*, compiled by Lucinda Vardey (ch. 10)

*My Dear Children* by Mother Theresa (ch. 5)

*Perspectives on the World Christian Movement: A Study Guide* by Steven C. Hawthorne (ch. 8)

*Redeeming Love* by Francine Rivers (ch. 10)

*The Screwtape Letters* by C.S. Lewis (ch. 10)

## Other References

www.katyreel.blogspot.com (ch. 1)

Blakeley, J. & Grossman, S. (2008). Anaplastic Oligodendroglioma, Current Treatment Options in Neurology, 10(4), 295. (ch. 2)

## Resources for Grief

*\*Beside Still Waters, Words of Comfort for the Soul* by Spurgeon, C.H. (1999)

*For these Tough Times, Reaching Toward Heaven for Hope and Healing* by Lucado, M. (2006)

*\*A Grace Disguised, How the Soul Grows Through Loss* by Sitter, J. (1995)

*A Grief Observed* by Lewis, C. S. (1976)

*\*Grief Therapy, One Caring Place* by Katafiasz, K. (2004)

*Lament for a Son* by Wolterstorff, N. (1987)

*The Lessons of Love, Rediscovering Our Passion for Life When It All Seems Too Hard to Take* by Beattie, M. (1994)

*Life After the Death of My Son, What I'm Learning* by Apple, D.L. (2008)

*The Lively Shadow, Living with the Death of a Child* by Murray, D.M. (2003)

*A Place of Healing* by Tada, J.E. (2010)

*A Severe Mercy, With Eighteen Letters by C. S. Lewis* by Vanauken, S. (1980)

*Stars in the Deepest Night, After the Death of a Child* by Gentry, G.B. (1999)

*Tear Soup* by Schwicbert, P. and DeKlyen, C. (1999)


*"*Held*" (song) written by Christa Wells,
    recorded by Natalie Grant on her album "*Awaken*"

*I found these to be the most helpful.